PHYSICAL EDUCATION

KEY STAGE ONE
SCOTTISH LEVELS A–B

PHYSICAL EDUCATION

GLENN BEAUMONT

Published by Scholastic Ltd,
Villiers House,
Clarendon Avenue,
Leamington Spa,
Warwickshire CV32 5PR

9 456

AUTHOR
GLENN BEAUMONT

EDITOR
SALLY GRAY

SERIES DESIGNER
LYNNE JOESBURY

DESIGNER
BLADE COMMUNICATIONS

ILLUSTRATIONS
CATHY HUGHES

COVER ILLUSTRATION
GAY STURROCK

INFORMATION TECHNOLOGY CONSULTANT
MARTIN BLOWS

SCOTTISH 5–14 LINKS
MARGARET SCOTT AND SUSAN GOW

Designed using Aldus Pagemaker

British Library Cataloguing-in-Publication Data
A catalogue record for this book is available from the British Library.

ISBN 0-590-53412-2

Contents

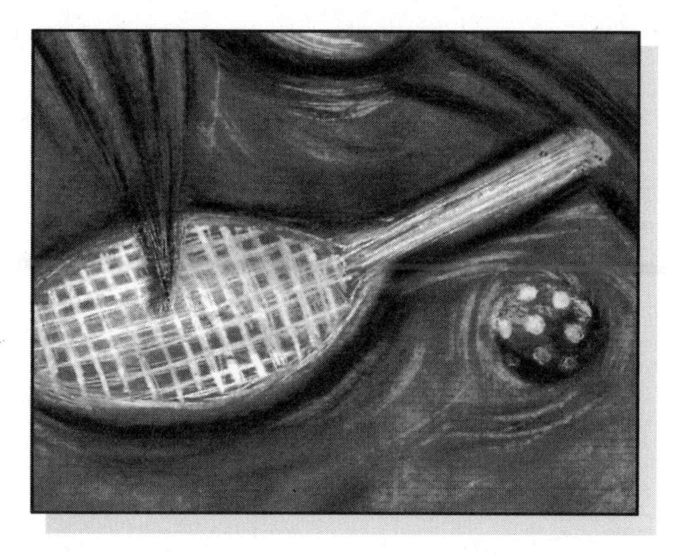

ACKNOWLEDGEMENTS

Glenn Beaumont wishes to acknowledge the invaluable assistance and advice given by Janet Pritchard in compiling this book.

Introduction

Scholastic Curriculum Bank is a series for all primary teachers, providing an essential planning tool for devising comprehensive schemes of work as well as an easily accessible and varied bank of practical, classroom-tested activities with photocopiable resources.

Designed to help planning for and implementation of progression, differentiation and assessment, *Scholastic Curriculum Bank* offers a structured range of stimulating activities with clearly stated learning objectives that reflect the programmes of study, and detailed lesson plans that allow busy teachers to put ideas into practice with the minimum amount of preparation time. The photocopiable sheets that accompany many of the activities provide ways of integrating purposeful application of knowledge and skills, differentiation, assessment and record-keeping.

Opportunities for formative assessment are highlighted within the activities where appropriate, while separate summative assessment activities give guidelines for analysis and subsequent action. Ways of using information technology for different purposes and in different contexts, as a tool for communicating and handling information and as a means of investigating, are provided at the end of the book.

The series covers all the primary curriculum subjects, with separate books for Key Stages 1 and 2 or Scottish Levels A–B and C–E. It can be used as a flexible resource with any scheme, to fulfil National Curriculum and Scottish 5–14 requirements and to provide children with a variety of different learning experiences that will lead to effective acquisition of skills and knowledge.

SCHOLASTIC CURRICULUM BANK PHYSICAL EDUCATION

The Scholastic Curriculum Bank *Physical Education* books help teachers to plan comprehensive and structured coverage of the physical education curriculum, and help pupils to develop the required skills and understanding through activities.

Each book covers one key stage. There is one book for Key Stage 1/Scottish Levels A–B and one book for Key Stage 2/Scottish Levels C–E. These books reflect the programmes of study for PE in the National Curriculum for England and Wales, and in the Scottish National Guidelines, with chapters addressing games, gymnastics, dance, athletics, swimming and outdoor/ adventurous activities in Key Stage 2; and games, gymnastics and dance in Key Stage 1. Additional chapters refer to general considerations when teaching and assessing physical education.

Bank of activities

This book provides a bank of activities that can be used in two ways:

▲ to form a framework for a scheme of work;

▲ to add breadth and variety to an existing scheme.

The activities are designed to encourage children to develop as enthusiastic, responsive and knowledgeable performers in physical education.

Lesson plans

Detailed lesson plans, under clear headings, are given for each activity. They provide material which can be directly implemented in the appropriate space (the hall, playground, field, swimming baths and so on).

Activity title box

The information in the title box at the beginning of each activity outlines the following key aspects:

▲ *Activity title and learning objective.* Each activity has one or more clearly stated learning objectives, given in bold italics. These learning objectives break down aspects of the programmes of study into manageable teaching and learning units, and their purpose is to aid planning for breadth and balance. They can easily be referenced to the National Curriculum and Scottish 5–14 requirements by using the overview grids at the end of this chapter (pages 9 to 12).

▲ *Class organisation/likely duration.* Icons and signpost the suggested group sizes for each activity and the approximate amount of time required to complete it. Timing arrangements are by their nature arbitrary, as many factors are involved (including the children's previous skills and knowledge).

▲ *Health and safety.* Where necessary, health and safety considerations are mentioned in the text. However, it is essential that checks be made as to what LEA regulations are in place.

Previous skills/knowledge needed

The information given here alerts teachers to particular knowledge or skills that the children will need prior to carrying out the activity.

Key background information

The information in this section is intended to set the scene and provide helpful guidance for the teacher. The guidance may relate to children's learning, to teachers' knowledge of physical education or to both.

Preparation

Advice is given for those occasions where it is necessary for the teacher to prepare the children for the activity or to collect and prepare materials ahead of time.

Resources needed

All the equipment, materials and photocopiable sheets needed to carry out the activity are listed here, so that the children or the teacher can gather them together easily before the beginning of the teaching session.

What to do

Easy-to-follow, step-by-step instructions are given for carrying out the activity, including (where appropriate) suggested points for discussion. Issues of playing area management are raised where relevant. In most cases, the activity plan is divided into phases incorporating a warm-up activity, a skill development activity and a conclusion.

Suggestion(s) for extension/support

Where possible, ways of providing for easy differentiation are suggested. Thus the lesson plans can be modified for less able pupils and extended for the more able.

Assessment opportunities

Each lesson plan has clearly-staged assessment opportunities which relate directly to the learning objectives for that activity and provide the framework for ongoing assessment. By taking advantage of these assessment opportunities, teachers can be reassured that the stated learning objectives have been covered.

Opportunities for IT

Where opportunities for IT application arise, these are briefly outlined (on pages 142 to 144) with reference to particularly suitable types of program. The chart on page 144 lists specific areas of IT covered in the activities; the accompanying text provides more detailed guidance on how to apply particular types of program.

Reference to photocopiable sheet(s)

Where activities include the use of photocopiable activity pages, these are referred to in the lesson plans. The photocopiable pages referred to are found in a section towards the end of the book on pages 92–141.

Some sheets may be used for assessment purposes. Other sheets are designed to help the teacher and children with the planning of certain activities, as in gymnastics.

Several of the sheets have been designed to be used for display. They may be enlarged and displayed around the working areas as *aides-mémoire*, both for the children and the teacher. They will help the children to develop the technical aspects of their performance.

Summative assessment

Each lesson plan presents advice on what the teacher should look for during the course of the lesson.

A concluding chapter on assessment in physical education offers advice on how teachers might approach assessment in a summative way towards the end of a particular year or key stage. Because the children's work in physical education will not primarily take the form of written or made products, it is suggested that the child's 'portfolio' for summative assessment purposes be built up in the form of records of achievement (these could include 'merit awards' for performance and effort).

PE AT KEY STAGE 1

The physical education of young children is essentially concerned with building upon and refining basic movement skills. Children start school already equipped with a wide range of maturational behaviours – the majority will be able to walk, run, jump and throw to a greater or lesser degree. The task for the early years teacher is to plan and implement a progressive, challenging and safe programme of physical activity which provides appropriate amounts of time for children to explore their own physical potential while guiding them towards more efficient and technically sound performance.

An effective balance needs to be struck between allowing sufficient opportunity for the children to find out for themselves and more direct teacher intervention. Children will not maximise their physical potential simply by being given ample time to practise on their own. The quality of the advice and direction given by the teacher will ultimately prove critical in the process of motor development and assist greatly in developing the capacity and confidence of children to think analytically about their performance and that of their peers.

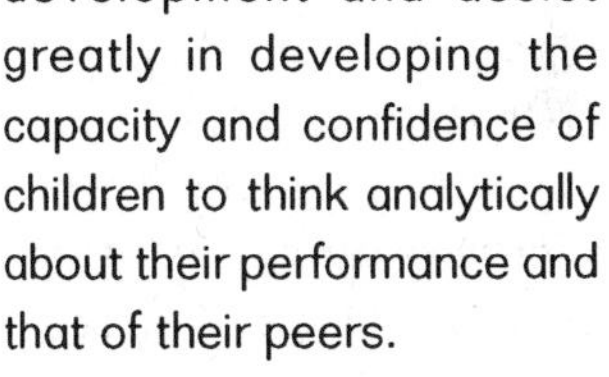

Physical development

The School Curriculum and Assessment Authority in their publication, *Nursery Education – Desirable Outcomes for children's learning on entering compulsory education* have described a series of Desirable Outcomes for pre-school children. The physical development aspect of this document describes the expected stage of development at which the children will be when they begin compulsory schooling. Desirable Outcomes in physical development for children on entry to school include an ability to move confidently and imaginatively with increasing control and co-ordination; and an ability to use a range of small and large equipment and balancing apparatus with a degree of skill.

The physical education curriculum for the early years should seek to provide a broad foundation of basic movement skills upon which the next stage of education can successfully build, with a clear focus upon games, gymnastic and dance

activities. Young children are not equipped to deal with too much complexity. Their perceptual and social development requires that much of the work will be undertaken on an individual basis with an increasing involvement in group activity – co-operative and competitive – towards the end of the key stage. Nor are young children equipped to deal with sustained physical demand. Lessons should be relatively short – no longer than 30 minutes – and enjoyable, yet with a clear sense of purpose and urgency.

Organisation of PE at Key Stage 1

Most schools find it manageable to offer three sessions of physical activity to their children each week. The organisation of this may, of course, vary. For example, some schools may like to provide a lesson in each of the core activities each week. This does not mean that games, gymnastics and dance need to be taught every week throughout the year. At times it may be more suitable to 'block' the work, for example, two lessons of dance per week over a half term may be an effective way of consolidating a topic or theme. The overall balance of the three activities over the three years of this stage of education (5–7 years) should, however, be approximately equal.

Curriculum Bank PE

The chapters ahead seek to assist teachers of 5–7 year-olds in their effective teaching of physical education. They provide progressive lesson material relating to games, gymnastics and dance; consider the health dimension of physical education as highlighted in the General Requirements of the PE National Curriculum and in strands from the Scottish Guidelines concerning 'Investigating and developing fitness' and 'Using the body'; and cover some important principles concerned with good teaching. Suitable material for addressing the health-related aspects of physical education with young children is also included. Advice is also given concerning the importance of encouraging and developing skills of co-operation in these young children. The development of this skill at a young age has long-term benefits that stretch across the curriculum and indeed throughout life in general.

Separate chapters are devoted to games, gymnastics and dance. The final chapter offers some guidance on practical and manageable assessment in physical education.

Each activity chapter begins with an introduction describing its nature and its contribution to the PE curriculum. Safety issues and concerns, where appropriate, are also included. An overview grid which details the content of material addressed over the three years of the key stage is found on pages 9–12. This grid will help the teacher to plan in the longer term and gives the sample lessons a meaningful context. The lessons themselves depict suitable progressions and indicate the kind of work with which a typical class of infant children should be presented at various points in the key stage.

Learning objective	PoS/AO	Content	Type of activity	Page
The essentials of physical education				
To develop an awareness about the effects of exercise on the body.	General requirements: 1a. *Investigating and developing fitness Level A.*	Increasing awareness about the relationship between breathing rate and exercise.	Individual activity and group/whole class discussion.	19
To develop an awareness of personal fitness and to establish the relationship between exercise and health.	General requirements: 1a, 1b. *Investigating and developing fitness Level A.*	Increasing awareness about individual exercise patterns over a typical week.	Individual recording; whole class discussion.	20
To develop a basic understanding about the ways in which the body responds to exercise.	As above. *Investigating and developing fitness Level B.*	Identifying major body organs; how the body changes during exercise.	Working in pairs; whole class discussion.	21
To develop an understanding of how the supply of 'fuel' (oxygen) goes by the bloodstream to working muscles.	As above. *Investigating and developing fitness Level B.*	The body as a 'machine' with its own energy requirements.	Working in groups; whole class discussion.	23
Games				
To develop sending skills and an ability to roll accurately with hands.	Games: 1b, 1c. *Applying skills Level A.*	Rolling and controlling a ball with hands.	Working individually, then in pairs.	28
To develop sending skills and an ability to roll accurately with feet.	As above. *Applying skills Level A.*	Rolling and controlling a ball with feet.	Working individually.	29
To develop sending skills using a bat and ball and to practise skills of sending a ball along the ground using hands and feet.	As above. *Applying skills Level A.*	'Pushing' a ball with control using a bat; investigating sending skills.	As above.	30
To develop sending skills and an ability to strike with accuracy using both hands and feet.	As above. *Applying skills Level A.*	Striking and stopping a ball with hands and feet.	Working individually and with a partner.	32
To develop sending skills using a bat or racquet.	Games: 1a, 1b, 1c. *Applying skills. Co-operating Level A.*	Developing striking skills with a bat.	As above.	33
To consolidate and refine a range of sending skills.	Games: 1a, 1b, 1c. *Applying skills Level A.*	Consolidation of range of taught sending skills using co-operative activity.	Working in pairs.	34
To develop receiving skills and an ability to use hands to stop a ball. To improve catching skills.	Games: 1b, 1c. *Applying skills Level A.*	Throwing and catching a ball from a rebound surface.	Working individually.	35
To develop receiving skills and an ability to use feet to stop a ball.	Games: 1b, 1c. *Applying skills Level A.*	Pushing and controlling a ball using feet.	Working individually as a class group.	37

Learning objective	PoS/AO	Content	Type of activity	Page
To develop the receiving skills of stopping a ball using hands, catching and stopping a ball using feet.	As above. *Applying skills Level B.*	Developing individual catching skills; making up individual catching games.	Working individually.	39
To develop catching skills.	As above. *Applying skills. Co-operating Level B.*	Working with a partner to improve catching skills.	Working individually, in pairs and in small groups.	41
To develop receiving skills using feet.	As above. *Applying skills. Co-operating Level B.*	Controlling a ball with feet and finding space.	As above.	42
To develop and consolidate receiving skills in a stationary position and on the move, using hands and feet. To develop receiving skills using 'hockey' type sticks/bats.	Games: 1a, 1b, 1c. *Applying skills. Co-operating Level B.*	Sending and receiving a ball with a partner and working in a group in a variety of ways including using hockey sticks.	Working in pairs and in small groups.	44
To develop spatial awareness and an ability to move about while controlling a ball.	Games: 1c. *Using the body. Applying skills Level A.*	Moving effectively in space carrying a ball.	Working individually.	46
To learn about and develop close control of a ball using feet.	Games: 1b, 1c. *Applying skills Level A.*	Controlling a ball with feet whilst on the move.	As above.	47
To develop travelling skills using a bat and large light ball.	Games: 1b, 1c. *Applying skills Level A.*	Controlling a ball with a bat whilst on the move.	As above.	48
To further develop travelling skills with hands controlling the ball. To practise a combination of travelling and sending skills in a game situation.	Games: 1a, 1b, 1c. *Using the body. Applying skills. Co-operating and competing Level B.*	Travelling with a ball using hands and feet.	Working individually, then as a small group.	50
To develop ball control using feet and to learn how to change direction. To practise travelling with a ball using feet within a competitive game.	Games: 1a, 1b, 1c. *Using the body. Applying skills. Co-operating and competing Level B.*	Dribbling a ball with feet and changing direction.	Working individually.	51
To consolidate and refine a range of travelling skills with a ball.	Games: 1a, 1b, 1c. *Using the body. Applying skills. Co-operating Level B.*	Consolidation of travelling skills through co-operative and competitive activity.	Working individually and in small groups.	52
Gymnastics				
To explore a variety of actions taking weight on feet and hands and to develop spatial awareness and an ability to work in own space.	Gymnastics: 2a, 2b. *Using the body Level A.*	Basic travelling skills using the floor and small apparatus.	Working individually.	57

Learning objective	PoS/AO	Content	Type of activity	Page
To refine jumping technique using a low platform and to develop awareness of safety and care for others.	As above. *Applying skills Level A.*	Developing sound jumping technique from a low bench onto mats.	Working individually and within a group.	58
To learn how to use more challenging apparatus and to develop the skills associated with working responsibly and safely together.	As above. *Applying skills. Co-operating Level A.*	Exploration of body shape using floor and large apparatus.	Working individually and within a group.	60
To develop and refine jumping skills involving turning actions and to further develop travelling skills with an emphasis upon rolling.	As above. *Applying skills Level A.*	Combinations of turning jumps and rolls using floor and small apparatus.	Working individually and in pairs.	61
To further develop travelling skills on the floor and apparatus and to learn how to contrast speed in movement and to link movements.	As above. *Using the body. Applying skills Level B.*	Combinations of rocking movements and jumps using floor, benches and mats.	Working individually and in groups.	63
To further develop travelling and jumping skills through using large apparatus and to develop the ability to link actions together.	As above. *Using the body. Applying skills Level B.*	Introduction to sequence building using floor and apparatus; devising pathways.	As above.	64
To explore and refine balancing skills using small and large bases.	As above. *Using the body. Applying skills Level B.*	Balancing on different body parts using floor and small apparatus.	Working individually and with a partner.	66
To develop movement quality through an understanding of extension in movement.	As above. *Using the body. Applying skills Level B.*	Combination of rolls and stretched jumps using floor, benches and mats.	Working individually and in groups.	67
To further develop travelling skills linking a variety of actions around large apparatus.	As above *Creating and designing Level B.*	Sequence building on the floor and large apparatus; devising pathways; taking weight on body parts other than feet.	As above.	69
Dance				
To develop a dance based upon the movements of a teddy bear. To develop spatial awareness skills and to appreciate how the body can move with an emphasis on tension.	Dance: 3a, 3b, 3c. *Using the body. Creating and designing Level A.*	Using a familiar object to stimulate dance patterns.	Working individually.	75
To further develop the 'Teddy bear dance' and to gain experience of where the body can move – changing levels.	As above. *Using the body. Creating and designing Level A.*	Incorporating a sense of rhythm into dance form.	Working individually and with partners.	77
To conclude and perform the 'Teddy bear dance' accompanied by music.	As above. *Using the body. Creating and designing Level A.*	Performance of a 'thematic' dance with a beginning, middle and end.	As above.	78

Learning objective	PoS/AO	Content	Type of activity	Page
To develop travelling skills at a low level.	As above. *Using the body. Creating and designing Level A.*	Using the movement of insects and birds to stimulate rhythmic movement in children.	Working individually.	79
To further develop travelling skills showing contrasts in speed and levels of movement.	As above. *Using the body. Creating and designing Level A.*	Using music and 'props' to develop a dance.	As above.	81
To develop and consolidate travelling skills around the theme of caterpillars and butterflies, to work with a partner and to appreciate the work of others.	As above. *Using the body. Creating and designing. Co-operating Level B.*	Performance of a thematic dance; observation and discussion of dance performed by others.	Working individually and with a partner; class discussion.	82
To develop an appreciation of level and shape in dance form. To develop a sense of rhythm in dance.	As above. *Using the body. Creating and designing Level A.*	Using a story to stimulate expressive movement.	Working individually and as part of a large group.	84
To learn circles, turns and twists in a simple dance form and to develop movement patterns to sound.	As above. *Using the body. Creating and designing Level A.*	Using an everyday object – a washing machine – to stimulate dance activity.	Working individually.	85
To combine previous work into a composite dance around the theme of washday and to work as a group and develop combination skills.	As above. *Using the body. Creating and designing. Co-operating Level B.*	To perform a complex dance using a sound stimulus; to evaluate the work of others.	Working individually and in small groups.	86

Entries given in italics relate to the Scottish 5–14 Guidelines on Expressive Arts.

The essentials of physical education

Teachers of young children in primary schools have always recognised the enormous benefits that a well-structured programme of physical activity can bring to the overall development of pupils. The belief that the needs of young children are best served by an integrated curriculum which brings together as often as possible the social, intellectual and physical areas of experience, gives physical education a significant and inter-related role not always apparent in the teaching of older children, where separate subjects make their different demands.

The Scottish Guidelines for Expressive Arts 5–14 emphasise that by taking part in physical activities, pupils develop a range of personal and social skills and an appreciation of the role of exercise in good health. These principles are specifically addressed in this chapter and then re-emphasised where appropriate throughout the activity-specific chapters.

The essentials of Physical education

General Requirements

This chapter examines the General Requirements of the National Curriculum Order for Physical Education in the ways outlined below.

▲ It seeks to explore the implications of the word 'performance', by giving guidance to teachers about how best to develop and evaluate the skills of young children in physical education.

▲ It suggests ways in which the activities themselves – games, gymnastics and dance – can contribute to the personal and social development of children.

▲ It offers a range of practical suggestions, in lesson form, designed to increase children's understanding of the effects of exercise on their bodies and how this promotes good health.

▲ Finally, it makes reference to some of the essentials associated with safe practice and how teachers can encourage a safe working environment in physical education.

Entitlement for all pupils

The 1988 Education Reform Act, together with the Revised Orders from September 1995, require schools to make provision for the physical development of their pupils. In terms of format and structure, the Scottish 5–14 Guidelines are particularly supportive of this developmental view. Within the Scottish Guidelines, PE is placed clearly within the Expressive Arts – alongside Art/Design, Music and Drama. Three common Attainment Outcomes for each activity are identified – Using materials, skills, techniques and media; Expressing feelings, ideas, thoughts and solutions; and Evaluating and appreciating. These Attainment Outcomes indicate a recognition that the learning of young children is often best served through a holistic approach.

The physical education of young children embraces a number of readily identifiable elements unique to physical development. These are reflected in the General Requirements and the activity-specific Programmes of Study for Games, Gymnastics and Dance of the National Curriculum for Physical Education (England and Wales). Over the three year period involving the Reception year, (4–5 year olds), Year 1 (5–6 year olds) and Year 2 (6–7 year olds) in England (P1–P3/ Levels A–B in Scotland) prior to entering Key Stage 2 a successful physical education programme will need to equip children in the ways outlined below.

▲ They should be able to demonstrate a broad range of foundation skills in games, gymnastics and dance.

▲ They should have acquired a basic understanding of what makes effective performance and the ability to think constructively about how to improve.

▲ They should be confident in talking about, planning and evaluating their own actions when responding to a range of movement tasks.

▲ They should be aware that exercise produces a number of predictable bodily changes and be able to describe these, for example, getting hot and sweaty!

▲ They should have developed a number of social skills to enable them to participate to somebody else's rules whilst recognising and valuing the efforts of others.

▲ They should appreciate that physical activity is not risk free and that certain procedures are necessary to ensure safe participation.

Developmental considerations will largely determine teaching style and methodology in meeting these stated objectives. Some of the issues involved, particularly in terms of their relationship with effective teaching, are explored below.

Improving performance

Developing performance and enabling children to become more skilful is a concern that clearly lies at the heart of physical education. It is the teacher's responsibility to help the children towards achieving better performance – irrespective of their ability.

To make a crude analogy, motor performance is to physical education what words and number are to literacy and numeracy. That is, just as the teacher hopes that children will learn, through a range of appropriate teaching and learning experiences, to use language and mathematical skills, effectively equipping them intellectually for life, so PE seeks to further refine the basic movement skills of children so that they may confidently meet life's physical challenges. Skilful performance is relative, of course, and to a young child it may be accomplished and demonstrated by simply throwing a ball into a hoop or jumping down safely from a low bench.

Physical performance has its roots in cognition. Unless children are given the opportunity to think about and reflect upon their actions, the scope for individual improvement becomes very limited.

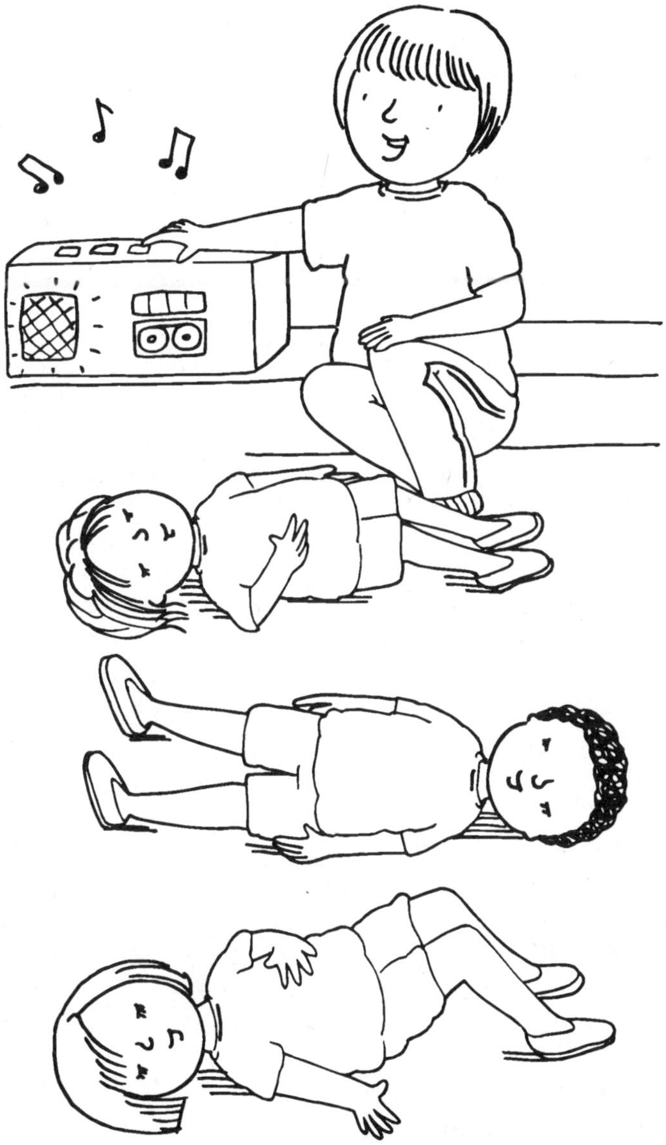

Practice, guidance and appropriateness

The following teaching principles should be considered when providing for the skill enhancement of pupils:

1. *Pupils should be afforded regular practice sessions of sufficient duration*

It is a well-known saying, and critical to the physical development of children, that 'practice makes perfect' or, more realistically, brings about improvement! This saying may not be complete, in that strictly speaking, it is practice accompanied by appropriate guidance that usually 'makes perfect'. Nevertheless, unless the teacher plans and makes provision for frequent and meaningful physical activity then gains in performance and the realisation of desired learning outcomes will not be as hoped for. Throughout the early years schools should attempt to secure at least three periods of physical education per week – allocating one period each to games, gymnastics and dance. Ideally the children should be doing some structured exercise on a daily basis. If it is practical to offer swimming then it should not be at the expense of this 'core' curriculum in terms of time. Actual lessons should approximate to 30 minutes duration (not including changing/organisational time) reflecting the physical, intellectual and emotional characteristics of young children.

Skill levels are seldom progressed when children are tired and concentration is low. Indeed, the possibility of undoing good practice, learning bad habits and compromising safe practice is a significant risk when children are obliged to work in a state of physical and mental weariness.

2. *Pupils need clear guidance*

The performance of any physical action is far more complex than we often assume. Even the simplest of movements involves an enormous amount of neural activity. The actual movement of a limb, or limbs simply represents the final link in an extremely sophisticated chain of events. The nervous system of young children is still very much in the process of maturation and this limits their response in two ways that are particularly relevant to physical performance:

▲ Firstly, the *amount* of information that can enter the young child's central nervous system through vision, sound, touch and, not least, proprioception – consisting of 'internal' specialised nerve endings situated around the body which relay information to the brain about the activity of limbs and muscles and their whereabouts – is relatively low compared to the capability of older children and adults.

▲ Secondly, the *time* taken by young children to 'sift through' all this information is correspondingly slower.

These developmental aspects affect the amount of guidance that the teacher is able to give to the child and also have implications relating to when the guidance is actually given. Keep teaching points short and concise. Don't overload the children. Young children will obtain most benefit from working on only one teaching point at a particular time. In most instances guidance should be given when children have stopped working and are able to give their full attention to it.

3. *Setting appropriate physical challenges*

The reaction time of young children (pre-six years) is approximately twice that of adults – about 0.6 seconds in children compared to 0.3 seconds in a young adult. This means that a five-year-old wishing to catch a ball thrown from 3m at a speed of approximately 5m/sec will need to begin his or her response as soon as the ball leaves the thrower's hand. An adult could afford to ignore the ball until it was halfway between the thrower and the receiver.

This single feature of sensory development in young children accounts for so much in terms of improvement as the child progresses through school. For example, young children will find it very difficult to participate meaningfully in a team game, in which a number of decisions relating to team-mates, opponents, location of the ball and so on are usually made rapidly. Consequently, in games, partner work and situations involving two against two more realistically match the capabilities of young children. Similarly, in gymnastics, avoid too much complexity in tasks on the apparatus and always use floorwork to provide an introduction to new work.

'Playing fairly and trying hard' – the contribution that physical education makes to personal and social development

Physical education provides a wide range of opportunities that seek to encourage personal responsibility in children and their ability to work effectively with others. However it must be emphasised that the activities themselves are not sufficient for these purposes. Simply participating in a team game, for instance, will not automatically improve the co-operation skills of young children. The teacher will need to ensure that positive behaviour is frequently reinforced and rewarded whenever and wherever it occurs. Qualities that may be developed include perseverance, tolerance and thought for others.

A clear understanding by the children about appropriate conduct will need to be established if the activities themselves are to play a part in fostering desirable qualities. The teaching principles below may be useful in this respect.

In games:

▲ Competitive activity is *not* inappropriate for four-to-seven-year olds. When involving young children in a competitive activity, try to ensure that they are well-matched in terms of their ability.

▲ As a general rule ensure that young children only compete in activities with a maximum of 'two against two'. Where skills are less developed, 'one against a small group' (such as in 'tag' type games) is suitable.

▲ Keep the rules very simple – limiting the game to two or three rules and making sure that they are fully understood by all the participants.

▲ Emphasise the importance of praise and encouragement for peers and team-mates, while actively discouraging destructive criticism and blame.

In gymnastics:

▲ Involve all the children in apparatus -handling from reception class onwards. Reception children should be taught to handle their own apparatus beginning with light equipment such as hoops, cones and skittles and progressing to benches, padded platforms and mats. This will require effective co-operation, particularly when manoeuvring and lifting larger pieces of apparatus.

▲ Encourage the children to be aware of others and to respect each other's space when moving freely around the hall or when using apparatus in answering a particular movement task.

▲ Try to use as many individual children as possible for demonstration purposes. All children should feel that their efforts are recognised, irrespective of technical merit, providing that they have tried hard.

In dance:

▲ Encourage the children to value and applaud the contributions made by other children in expressing mood and feeling.

▲ Encourage the children to find ways to refine and improve their performance.

The importance of safety

All schools should ensure that they have in place a written policy for physical education. A framework for drafting a physical education policy for Key Stage 1 is shown on photocopiable pages 92 and 93. The policy should help all the staff to achieve cohesion and uniformity in the teaching of physical education throughout the school. It will need to include a section on safety outlining a range of responsibilities, procedures and routines which will assist the staff in maintaining a safe working environment in physical education including any extra-curricular sessions.

It should be remembered that while any school is in session the teachers are in *loco parentis* and this operates regardless of time, date and place. While in *loco parentis* teachers are required to exercise a duty of care acceptable to a reasonable parent or guardian. It cannot be delegated. Because of increased risk levels in physical education a higher duty of care is placed upon teachers which in turn requires an acceptable level of training and expertise.

A safe teaching environment exists when both teachers and pupils display a good understanding of safe practice. The following guidelines for safety are the responsibility of the teacher and will minimise the risk of accidents. Should an accident occur a teacher would be considered negligent if he or she had not ensured that:

1. All reasonable steps had been taken to ensure the safety of the premises and the equipment.
2. The class had been taught about the need for safety and had been warned against taking risks and behaving inappropriately in a manner suited to the pupils' age, intelligence and experience.
3. The class had been systematically prepared through an appropriate skill progression for the activities being undertaken, and attention had been paid to footwear and clothing.
4. The work and the manner in which it was done, were in keeping with regular and approved practice in other schools in the country.
5. Any local visits or occasional activities away from the school site had proceeded with the prior agreement of parents by means of signed forms of consent and complied, where appropriate, with any local education authority guidelines.
6. Procedures were in place for identifying and making known to all supervising adults those children deemed to be potentially at risk through health problems.

In order for children to be taught effectively about the need for safe and responsible participation (as well as to meet the General Requirements of the National Curriculum in England and Wales) it is important that:

▲ There exists an orderly working environment in which control and concentration are maintained.

▲ Teachers and pupils work to a consistent safety framework throughout the school in which an understanding of safety and responsible participation are regularly reinforced.

▲ Appropriate clothing and footwear are worn, and that the wearing of jewellery is not allowed when children are participating in PE. The issue of jewellery which has religious significance should be approached sensitively. Steps may be taken to minimise the risks of wearing such jewellery, for example, by covering a bangle with a towelling sweatband. When possible, teachers should set a good example by changing into PE clothing or at the very least should change their footwear.

▲ With guidance from the teacher, pupils should be given increasing responsibility for setting out their own equipment and apparatus.

In order to maximise the contribution physical education can make towards the healthy physical development of children the following considerations should be used to inform curriculum planning:

▲ Exercise needs to be taken frequently to assist good health – every day, if possible, with young children.

▲ Sessions should not be prolonged – 20 to 30 minute lessons are usually ample for young children.

▲ It is important to maintain a balance of different types of activity because they contribute in different ways to overall fitness. For example, continuous running, skipping and hopping will develop stamina; climbing, hanging and heaving activities, using the climbing frame and/or ropes, will help to build strength; suppleness will be developed through stretching and extended movement.

The four lessons described on pages 19–24 will help children towards a better understanding about the ways in which their bodies respond to exercise and the relationship between exercise and good health. It is suggested that the first lesson

More specific guidance on safety matters is given later in the book in the appropriate chapters. Finally on safety, it is also strongly recommended that teachers involved in supervising physical education should read *Safe Practice in the Teaching of Physical Education* published by The British Association of Advisers and Lecturers in Physical Education (1995). This comprehensive book provides teachers with safety guidance on all aspects of physical education and is recognised by the DfEE as the definitive work on safety in PE.

Physical education and health

Although there is no conclusive evidence available to us to establish that the children of today are less fit than their counterparts of previous generations, modern lifestyles often lead to a less active existence. For example, fewer children walk to school as a daily routine than previous generations and children's pastimes have become progressively more passive, with watching television and videos and using computers being many children's preferred activities. In a typical week, physical education lessons will provide for many young children their sole experience of reasonably sustained physical activity.

is appropriate for children in the first half of Key Stage 1 (5–6 years; P1 and P2), and that the other three lessons are taught during the second half of Key Stage 1 (6–7 years; P2 and P3) and linked where possible to on-going work in science.

OUT OF BREATH

To develop an awareness about the effects of exercise on the body.

Children working individually.

25 minutes.

Previous skills/knowledge needed

Ability to move safely around a hall.

Key background information

The relationship between exercise and the ways in which the body responds to it will clearly have been felt and experienced by the children through their natural play. This lesson will help them to establish that one of the more obvious changes that takes place in the body when it is active (an increase in breathing), is linked to how demanding the activity is – the harder we work the heavier we breathe!

Preparation

Ensure that the apparatus (hoops) is accessible around the edge of the hall.

Resources needed

Plastic hoops, tambourine.

What to do

Ask the children to find a space to stand in. Warm them up by asking them to stretch and then relax various parts of their body, starting with fingers then hands and progressing through to arms and legs. Finish the warm-up by asking them to shake each part of their body as you call it out. Use a tambourine or shaker to stimulate the activity.

Now invite the children to collect a hoop and lay it down in their space. The whole class must then move slowly around the hall without touching the hoops. At the sound of the tambourine the children must find any hoop to stand inside – only one child to a hoop. Ask the children to bounce with feet close together inside their hoop for a short time (about 20 seconds). Use the tambourine or shaker to encourage the children to work fairly briskly. Then ask the class to move slowly around the hall again. At the sound of the tambourine they must again find a vacant hoop again. This time, ask the children to run on the spot inside their hoops. Again, the class must move around the hall and when the tambourine sounds ask them to find a hoop and practise hopping on their favoured leg. Follow this with slow movement around the hall again.

Invite the children to sit down as a group and discuss which activity they found the hardest. Hopefully the children will answer that one of their hoop activities proved to be the most tiring. Develop the discussion by focusing their attention on the ways in which they found themselves breathing – heavy breathing inside the hoops (lots of puff required) and not so heavy when moving slowly around the hall.

To conclude, repeat one of the hoop activities to reinforce the children's awareness that the harder they work the more breaths they will need to take.

Suggestion(s) for extension
More confident children can explore different ways of moving around the hall in addition to walking.

Suggestion(s) for support
Use demonstration to help less confident children understand what activity to practise in their hoops.

Assessment opportunities
Observe how well the children move about the hall. Do they use the space safely? Are they able to establish the link between breathing rate and level of activity?

MY EXERCISE DIARY

To develop an awareness of personal fitness and to establish the relationship between exercise and health.
Individuals; whole class.
10 minutes per day followed by 30-minute discussion with teacher.

Previous skills/knowledge needed
Basic literacy skills.

Key background information
This activity will help the children to accurately establish how much of the week they spend exercising. As a general rule, at least three sessions per week of moderate/vigorous exercise are required to develop and maintain fitness levels. Lifestyle will inevitably influence this pattern, for example, children who walk to school on a daily basis receive more exercise than children who are transported there. Encourage all children to be as active as possible and to use 'natural' opportunities, such as running and skipping at playtime, wherever it is safe and practical to do so.

Preparation
Ensure that there are sufficient copies of the exercise diary (photocopiable page 94) for each child. You will also need copies of sheet 95 if following the support activity.

Resources needed
Photocopiable page 94 for each child, pencils, crayons, scissors, adhesive. For the support activity: photocopiable page 95 for each child (or a selection of magazine pictures).

What to do
Begin by establishing the concept of exercise. What do the children understand by it? What exactly is it? A useful starting definition and one that the children will have personal experience of could be, 'Any activity which leaves us slightly out of breath'. Ask the children to give some examples of this. These may include: walking the dog; riding a bike; playing tag and so on.

Discuss with the whole class how much exercise the children take in a typical week in and out of school. For instance, how many children attend outside clubs, which offer sport or physical activity, on a regular basis?

If possible, invite someone in to talk to the children to offer a contrasting experience. This could be a senior citizen to talk about their childhood experiences in relation to healthy exercise. Alternatively an athlete, or a member of the local fire service could offer a different perspective.

Over a period of a week, allocate a small part of the day to the completion of the photocopiable page 94, 'My exercise diary'. The children need to draw or stick pictures on the sheet to show the type of exercise they have been doing. During the following week hold class discussions to compare the different amounts and types of physical activity that the children have recorded. Are they doing enough exercise to promote their own fitness and well-being? Is one type of activity pursued more than any other? How many children are able to participate in meaningful physical activity outside school? Try to reach some class decisions and conclusions and record them in a class display.

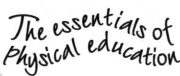

How does exercise keep me fit?

My exercise diary

Name ______________________ Date ______________

▲ Draw or stick down a picture next to each day to show what kind of exercise you did then.

Monday

Tuesday

Wednesday

Thursday

Friday

Saturday

Which activity did you enjoy the most? ______________

Suggestion(s) for extension

The more able children should be encouraged to write in more detail about their physical activity in addition to drawing it. Ask them to record in hours and minutes exactly how much time they spent on a particular activity.

Suggestion(s) for support

Provide access to pictures/photographs from old magazines/ newspapers, or make copies of the simple drawings on photocopiable page 95 for the children to use. Ask them to cut out and stick the pictures into the appropriate day box in order to record their daily physical activity. Provide sufficient copies of photocopiable page 95 for the children to have a free choice of pictures and for them to be able to use the same image more than once if they wish.

Assessment opportunities

Observe how well the children complete their diaries. Are they able to record accurately and make comparisons between their own levels of exercise and those of other children and adults? Do they understand that exercise is a part of healthy living?

Reference to photocopiable sheets

Photocopiable page 94 provides a way for children to record and analyse the type of exercise they have completed over a week-long period. It will encourage them to reflect upon the benefits of exercise to their general health and will provide a basis for discussing and comparing each other's lifestyles. Photocopiable page 95 is to be used with the support activity to help those children who have difficulties with drawing and writing their own ideas.

MY BODY AND EXERCISE

To develop a basic understanding about the ways in which the body responds to exercise.

Individuals; then in pairs; whole class discussion.

30 minutes.

Previous skills/knowledge needed

Basic literacy, numeracy and recording skills to complete written task-sheet.

Key background information

Young children are not always aware, or able to describe, the relationship between exercise and the various changes in body metabolism that occur as a direct consequence of increased, or decreased physical activity. Many children are also unaware about the size and location of important parts of their body. Increases in heart rate, changes in breathing patterns and increased perspiration are the more obvious responses to exercise and can easily be observed by young children. The following activity will help to give some structure to these observations.

Preparation

Make a copy of photocopiable page 96 for each child in the class.

Resources needed

Photocopiable page 96, pencils.

What to do

Begin by asking the children what they think happens to their bodies when they exercise strenuously. Ask them to remember the last time they were out of breath. Were they aware of any other changes that were taking place as they continued to work hard, in addition to heavy breathing? Now focus attention on the heart. Do they know whereabouts in the body it is? What happens to it during exercise?

Give out the photocopiable pages and ask the children to draw in the shape and position of their heart on the figure provided. The correct position is towards the middle of the chest area and about the size of a fist but be prepared to accept some imaginative anatomy! Now ask the children, while they are still sitting down, to place their hand on their chest to see if they can feel their heart beating (this should prove reasonably difficult). They should now complete the next section on the task-sheet.

Take the class to the hall for their normal PE lesson with their task-sheets and pencils. Warm them up with some gentle jogging and stretching. Ask the children if they can feel their hearts beating now. Proceed with your planned lesson, leaving five minutes at the end for some sustained vigorous exercise such as running, hopping and skipping continuously for three or four minutes. Ask the children to describe to a partner how their heart feels now (it should, of course, be thumping away merrily!) then complete the photocopiable page 96.

Hold a class discussion when back in class to consider ways of maintaining a healthy heart through diet and exercise.

Suggestion(s) for extension

Extend the activity by choosing some additional areas to focus on. For example, ask the children to consider their breathing patterns – how many breaths do they take in half a minute before and after exercise? Extend this further by asking the children to locate the lungs on the figure provided. Encourage the children to think about the way their bodies perspire after strenuous activity. Ask them to feel their foreheads to see how hot they are. This may lead to further enquiry.

Suggestion(s) for support

Ensure that those children with less-developed numeracy and literacy skills are given guidance in completing the photocopiable page. Try recording the questions on to audio cassette tape and encourage the children to respond verbally. Working alongside a more able partner will also help.

Assessment opportunities

Observe how well the children complete their task sheets. Are they aware of the changes that occur as a consequence of exercise? Are they able to establish the relationship between exercise and body response? Can they predict the bodily changes that always occur during physical activity?

Reference to photocopiable sheet

Photocopiable page 96 shows a simple human figure outline on which the children are invited to draw where they think the heart is found.

How does exercise keep me fit?

Name ____________________ Date __________

Something happens to your heart when you exercise.

▲ Show where your heart is on the picture.

Can you feel your heart beating? ________

▲ Now do some exercise.

What does your heart feel like now? ____________

MUSCLES NEED FUEL!

To develop an understanding of how the supply of 'fuel' (oxygen) goes by the bloodstream to working muscles.

Children working individually, in pairs and as part of a larger group.

30 minutes

Previous skills/knowledge needed

Ability to work co-operatively with a partner and as part of a large group. Basic movement skills and, in particular, travelling skills.

Key background information

At some stage during Key Stage 1 children will be introduced to concepts relating to machines and energy. This activity will help the children to appreciate that the human body can be likened to a machine or engine and that, like all machines, it needs some kind of fuel to keep working. Muscles do the work of the body in moving it from place to place and lifting a great variety of things. In order to keep going, muscles need a constant supply of fuel (nutrients and oxygen). The fuel is taken to the working muscles by a transportation system (the heart and the blood).

Preparation

You may wish to make some large, very simplified drawings of the heart and the large muscles of the arms and legs. Use these to indicate to the children the different working areas used in this activity.

Resources needed

Bean bags (preferably red), skittles or cones, hoops, cassette with rhythmic machine noises or amplified heart beats recorded on to it, playground working area or hall.

What to do

Explain to the class that they are about to work together as a large 'body' machine which has different parts. Tell them that each part has a different job to do in order to keep it running.

Divide the class into three separate groups. These groups may be further sub-divided to create six groups. One group will represent the heart; another will represent the blood; and a third will act out the working muscles (there may be two groups to each activity, depending on how you have divided up the children). Allocate each group to its working area and with the children's help set out the apparatus (see the diagrams below and on page 24). Warm up the class with some gentle jogging and stretching before returning them to their respective working areas.

Explain the three different activities to all the children, asking them to listen carefully to each one, as they will have a chance to try them all.

Group one – Ask the 'heart' group to work with a partner and to link both hands. They represent the machine that pumps the fuel to the muscles and so must display a continuous rhythmic action, squeezing and releasing their hands (to the recorded sounds, if used) – 'one, two; one, two; one, two' and so on. Remind the children that they must keep going otherwise the blood will not be able to get to the muscles!

Group two – The 'blood' group have the task of transporting the 'fuel' (bean bags) from the heart hoops to the muscle hoops in order to keep the machine running. The bean bags are carried in *one direction only* – from the heart to the muscles. The children may choose how to travel from the heart to the muscles by running, hopping, skipping, rolling and so on. Each time they make a journey from one hoop to the other they must show a different way of travelling. Remind the children that they must keep going otherwise the muscles will have no fuel!

Group three – The 'muscle' group have to perform continuous exercise on the spot – 'star' jumps, for instance are a good activity. Explain to the children that the 'muscle' group can only start to work when bean bags begin arriving in the 'muscle' hoops. To add to the intensity of the activity the teacher may periodically remove the bean bags from the 'muscle' hoops.

Change the groups around at approximately five-minute intervals so that all the children experience the three different roles. Discuss with the children, (when they are suitably tired), the close relationship between the three activities and, in particular, how the 'muscles' need the other functions to keep them going.

Suggestion(s) for extension

This activity can be made more challenging by asking the 'muscles' to vary their rate of work – for example, to faster or slower star jumping. The heart and blood groups must then alter the speed at which they work in order to meet increased or decreased demand.

Suggestion(s) for support

Less confident children may find one way of travelling to be sufficiently challenging when working in the 'blood' group.

Assessment opportunities

Observe how well the children are able to sustain their activities. Do they understand the inter-dependence of the three activities?

Games

The majority of young children find the demands made by small-side competitive games to be beyond their developmental capabilities. The emphasis on teaching games to this age group should be on the foundation skills and concepts essential to games playing. Most of the skills that the children will develop at this age, such as striking with a bat, aspects of ball control or the manipulation of an implement, will be learned individually or, at times, by co-operating with a partner. When competitive elements are introduced to games playing with this age range the competitive activity itself needs to be relatively uncomplicated. Chasing games, for instance, in which children learn to appreciate the effective use of space, are particularly appropriate. Games involving a ball should seek to maximise skill development at all times by minimising any opposition involved.

Games are played at all the key stages of the National Curriculum in England and Wales and are seen in Scotland as a 'core' activity. Games playing with young children focuses on three different types of skill – sending, receiving and travelling. These skills are considered in detail during this chapter and the activities are broken down into sections covering these three areas. Although each lesson may be used in its own right, each skill area follows a progression from the early to the latter part of the key stage, assisting the teacher with long-term planning and showing a development of the three skills. This information is summarised in the section entitled 'Key stage progression' on page 27. Other areas of consideration at Key Stage 1 include decision-making and matters relating to health and safety.

Skills for games

Games playing with young children focuses mainly on three types of skill. They are:

1. sending;
2. receiving;
3. travelling.

1. *Sending*

Sending a ball or an implement such as a bean bag involves throwing or passing it; striking it with hands or a bat; kicking it. Children should be given opportunities to practise this skill by aiming at varied targets which are:

▲ near/far;
▲ high/low;
▲ still/moving.

2. *Receiving*

Receiving a ball or an implement involves catching it; controlling it using different body parts, for example, trapping a football using the foot; and collecting it with an implement, for example, a plastic hockey stick. Practice should include:

▲ self-feed, for example, bouncing a ball and catching it yourself, or kicking it and then chasing it yourself;
▲ receiving from a rebound surface;
▲ receiving when sent by another person.

3. *Travelling*

Travelling involves moving with and without a ball and includes:

▲ starting and stopping;
▲ moving in a straight line;
▲ changing direction;
▲ turning, twisting;
▲ changing pace.

Games playing in the early years involves much more than a series of techniques. As the children develop their basic skills under the careful guidance of their teacher, they are learning a number of other skills. For example, all games or games-related activities, no matter how basic, require the participants to *make decisions.* Young children will be concerned largely in their games activities with making decisions about *when.* When do I move to catch the ball? When should I change direction to outwit a catcher/tagger? When do I pass the ball to my partner? And so on. Games activities, therefore, have the potential to assist developmental processes through decision-making by moving children on from egocentric and associative play to co-operative play. For example, a child will have to consider his or her partner when playing a catching game – are my partner's hands ready to receive a catch from me? Here the response of a partner triggers the action of the sender.

Safety in primary games

Safe practice in teaching games to young children requires careful attention to the following points:

General considerations

▲ Clothing should be appropriate to the activity being played and the area in which the children are working. Care should be taken in the winter months to ensure that children stay warm when working outdoors.

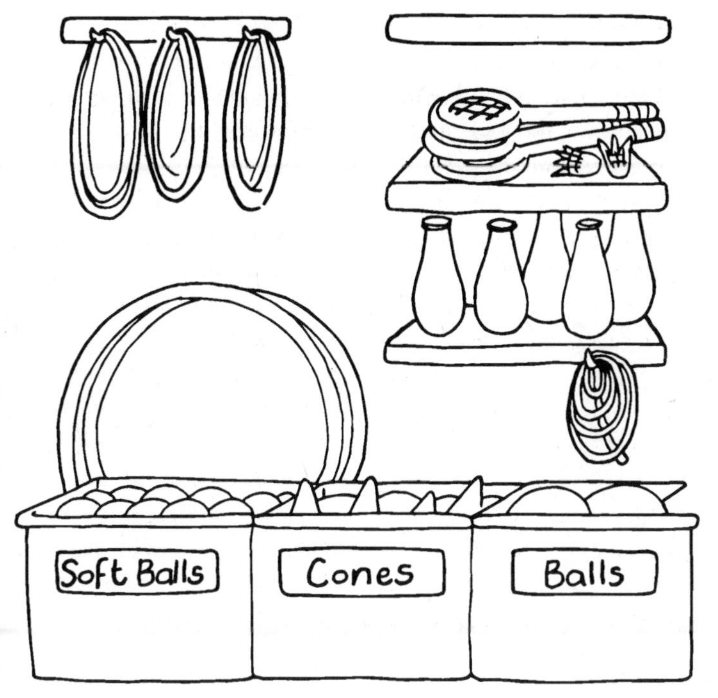

▲ Footwear should be suitable. It is not appropriate for children to play games in bare feet even when indoors.
▲ No jewellery should be worn. (However, see the note on page 18 about religious observance.)
▲ An orderly, working atmosphere should prevail. However, do anticipate some noise in games since pupils may need to communicate with each other. Ensure that this noise is kept to a controlled minimum.
▲ Try to establish a position towards the outside of the working area in order to observe the whole class.

Physical considerations

▲ Games equipment for young children should be compatible with their strength, skill levels and stamina. It should be light, brightly coloured and comfortable to handle.

Venues and working areas

▲ Always make sure that young children have ample space in which to work. Remember that the spatial awareness of young children is not always well-developed.
▲ Always check outdoor playing surface areas for potential hazards. Try to ensure that the working space in the hall is maximised and free from any obstacles that may protrude into the children's working area.
▲ In large spaces, limit and identify the working area with skittles, cones, ropes, chalk and so on.
▲ Equipment should be regularly checked and safely stored.

Key stage progression

Throughout Reception class and Key Stage 1 (England and Wales), Scottish (P1-P3), the children should be given the opportunity to explore, experience and practise different ways of sending a ball or similar object, receiving a ball or similar object and travelling with or without equipment. They should be provided with opportunities to develop spatial awareness and an understanding that rules are necessary. Over the key stage, children will develop and progress in these skill areas and will need to be given structured guidance and encouragement in order to do this. The summary below gives teaching guidelines for each specific year group. These themes will be developed through specific lesson plans later on in this chapter.

RECEPTION (P1)

Sending skills:
▲ rolling balls of different sizes;
▲ bouncing a large ball;
▲ kicking a large ball;
▲ throwing a large ball;
▲ striking a light ball with a bat.

Receiving skills:
▲ stopping a large ball with hands and feet (self-feed);
▲ catching a large ball (self-feed).

Travelling skills (with and without equipment):
▲ running (changing direction, speed and while carrying equipment);
▲ stopping;
▲ chasing;
▲ avoiding;
▲ jumping.

Throughout the Reception year children should be given a range of opportunities to practise individually.

YEAR 1 (P2)

Sending skills:
▲ rolling balls with accuracy at targets and to partners;
▲ bouncing to a partner;
▲ kicking to a partner;
▲ throwing to a partner;
▲ striking towards a target (self-feed).

Receiving skills:
▲ catching with a partner;
▲ stopping and controlling a ball from a partner.

Travelling skills:
▲ running (changing direction, speed and while carrying equipment);
▲ stopping;
▲ chasing;
▲ dodging;
▲ jumping;
▲ dribbling – controlling a ball while on the move.

Throughout Year 1, children should be given increasing opportunities to work with a partner. Competitive activity will be based upon how many, how far, how fast and so on.

YEAR 2 (P3)

Sending skills:

▲ passing to a partner using hands and feet – stationary, to the left and right, on the move;

▲ striking/hitting for accuracy and distance using a partner-feed.

Receiving skills:

▲ running into space to receive a pass;

▲ catching, stopping and retrieving a ball sent by a partner.

Travelling skills:

▲ running (changing directions, speed and while carrying equipment);

▲ chasing and marking;

▲ dodging;

▲ intercepting;

▲ getting free;

▲ dribbling.

Throughout Year 2, children should be given opportunities to make decisions about when, where and how to run and send. Competitive activity will include games involving limited opposition (for example 4 v 1, 3 v 1, 2 v 1).

The lesson plans

The sample lessons described over the next pages are based upon sending, receiving and travelling skills, usually involving a ball. Six lessons are presented on each of these aspects – three appropriate to the first half of Key Stage 1, that is for children aged approximately 4–6 years of age; and three more appropriate for the latter half of the key stage – for children aged approximately 6–7 years of age.

Reference is made at times to 'TOP Play' materials with which teachers are expected to be familiar in the future, as there is an intention to develop this initiative nationally. TOP Play has been designed and developed by the Youth Sport Trust – a national charity with the mission of implementing quality sports programmes for young people. As one in a series of integrated national initiatives TOP Play has three key components – training and ongoing support for teachers; child-friendly equipment; easy to follow resource cards. Training for teachers is initially available via LEA's leading to free equipment and resources. Further information can be obtained from LEA's or the Youth Sport Trust, Rutland Building, Loughborough University of Technology, Loughborough, Leics LE11 3TU (Tel: 01509 228293).

The Games Activity Bank – photocopiable pages 97–106 summarises a wide range of games activities which the teacher may select from when developing particular games skills over the key stage. Reference is made to specific activities from the activity bank throughout the chapter. It is intended also that teachers will use it as an additional resource to extend and practise the specific skills. The ideas may be used as warm-up, skill development and main activities to supplement the lesson plans described in the chapter.

Finally, a lesson review sheet (photocopiable page 107) will help teachers to reflect on the effectiveness of their games lessons in assisting the physical development of the children in their class.

SENDING LESSON 1 (R AND Y1; P1 AND P2)

To develop sending skills and an ability to roll accurately with hands.

Children working individually; then in pairs.

20 minutes.

Previous skills/knowledge needed

Ability to work in designated space safely and to follow instructions.

Key background information

Young children often find difficulty in directing a ball in flight. Although they will be able to throw they will not usually be able to do this accurately. Rolling activities provide opportunities to work with a ball which reflect the existing capabilities of the children. Rolling a ball provides a meaningful foundation activity upon which throwing and catching skills can be built.

Children need time for exploration during part of the lesson. This activity will prove more purposeful when it is directly linked to the particular skills being developed.

Preparation

The teacher should ensure that the games equipment – balls, quoits and hoops are readily accessible around the edge of the working area. Make a copy of photocopiable page 97 for your reference.

Resources needed

A sufficient number of light balls, quoits and hoops – at least one per child, photocopiable page 97.

What to do

Warm-up activity

Warm up the class with a running and stopping activity – make sure that the children demonstrate a controlled stop with feet well spaced.

Skill development

Ask all the children to collect a large ball and practise activity 1 from the Games Activity Bank (photocopiable page 97). Organise the class along a line so that all the children can work safely in the same direction. Demonstrate the task to the children, showing them that the ball needs to be placed close to the feet and rolled slowly ahead into a space. Show them how to walk alongside the ball and stop it with both hands. Invite the children to try, then repeat this activity several times. While the children are practising this activity space out a series of skittles/markers around the edge of the working area.

Organise the children into pairs and allocate a skittle to each pair. Practise activity 4 from the Games Activity Bank (photocopiable page 97). Demonstrate that the starting position is close to the skittle and that two hands are needed for accuracy. Tell the children to take turns in rolling the ball to hit the skittle, and to take a step further away each time the skittle is hit.

After sufficient practice remove the skittles and allow the children a period of time to practise rolling activities with an item of equipment of their own choosing, such as a ball, quoit or hoop.

Games Activity Bank
– sending and receiving

Individually:

1 Put the ball close to your feet. Roll the ball *slowly* in front of you. Can you walk alongside your ball?

2 Roll a ball or quoit forwards. Chase it and capture it.

3 Roll the ball against the wall. Collect the ball when it rebounds.

4 Roll a ball towards a skittle, collect it and repeat. Each time you hit the skittle take a step further away.

5 Bounce the ball gently in front of you. Catch it and repeat.

6 Bounce the ball hard on the ground. Catch it and repeat.

7 Bounce the ball hard on the ground. Can you jump and catch it?

8 Bounce a ball continuously in front of you. Can you bounce it under a leg?

9 Throw the ball in the air. Let it bounce then catch it.

10 Throw a bean bag up in the air. Catch it and repeat.

Conclusion

Conclude the lesson with a game of tag. Calm the children down and ensure that they help you to store the equipment away safely.

Suggestion(s) for extension

Children who find this activity easy should be given a small ball. Encourage them to try rolling the ball using only one hand.

Suggestion(s) for support

Ensure that children who are having difficulty work with a large ball and practise rolling over short distances.

Assessment opportunities

Observe how well the children exercise control over the speed of their ball when rolling. Are they able to achieve accuracy? Are they able to take turns with their partner?

Reference to photocopiable sheet

Photocopiable page 97 acts as a handy reference, providing the section of the Games Activity Bank relevant to the activities suggested in this lesson.

SENDING LESSON 2 (R AND Y1; P1 AND P2)

To develop sending skills and an ability to roll accurately with feet.

Children working individually.

20 minutes.

Previous skills/knowledge needed

Ability to work in designated space safely and to follow instructions. Previous experience of rolling using hands.

Key background information

Controlling a ball with feet can sometimes be a neglected skill. It is an important aspect of the skill development of all children and so needs to feature in the more formalised parts of the lessons.

In the interests of control and accuracy it is important that the ball is still before children attempt to kick it.

Preparation
Ensure that the games equipment (balls) are readily accessible around the edge of the working area. Make a copy of photocopiable page 98 for your reference.

Resources needed
A sufficient number of light balls – at least one per child; a copy of photocopiable page 98.

What to do
Warm-up activity
Warm up the class by using a running and stopping activity. Ask the children to balance on one leg when they stop.
Skill development
Ask the children to collect a large ball each and explain that they will be practising rolling a ball using their feet to control it. Refer to activity 14 from the Games Activity Bank (photocopiable page 98) for specific instructions of what to do.

Organise the class along a line so that all the children can work safely in the same direction. Demonstrate that the ball needs to be placed close to the feet and pushed gently ahead with the foot. Show the children how to follow and collect the ball and stop it by placing the inside of the foot behind it. Encourage the children to try this and repeat the activity several times.

Now organise the children to work against a rebound surface – such as a wall or bench turned on its side – and practise activity 15 from the Games Activity Bank (photocopiable page 98). Emphasise that the ball should be pushed with the foot and not kicked too hard. It will help if low targets are painted or pinned temporarily on to the wall to help accuracy. Make sure that the children begin close to the wall and gradually move away as they achieve success.
Conclusion
Allow the children a period of time to practise sending activities of their choice with a ball (chosen from the Games Activity Bank). Encourage the children to keep the ball close to the ground. Conclude the lesson with a game of tag.

Suggestion(s) for extension
As children become more adept at this skill, challenge them to move further away and aim at more precise targets.

Suggestion(s) for support
Ensure that children who are having difficulty stop the ball using a combination of hands and feet, rather than just feet.

Assessment opportunities
Observe how well the children achieve control and accuracy when kicking the ball. Are they able to stop the ball using their feet? Are they able to work in limited space?

Reference to photocopiable sheet
Photocopiable page 98 can be copied for use by the teacher. It acts as a handy reference, providing the section of the Games Activity Bank relevant to the activities suggested in this lesson.

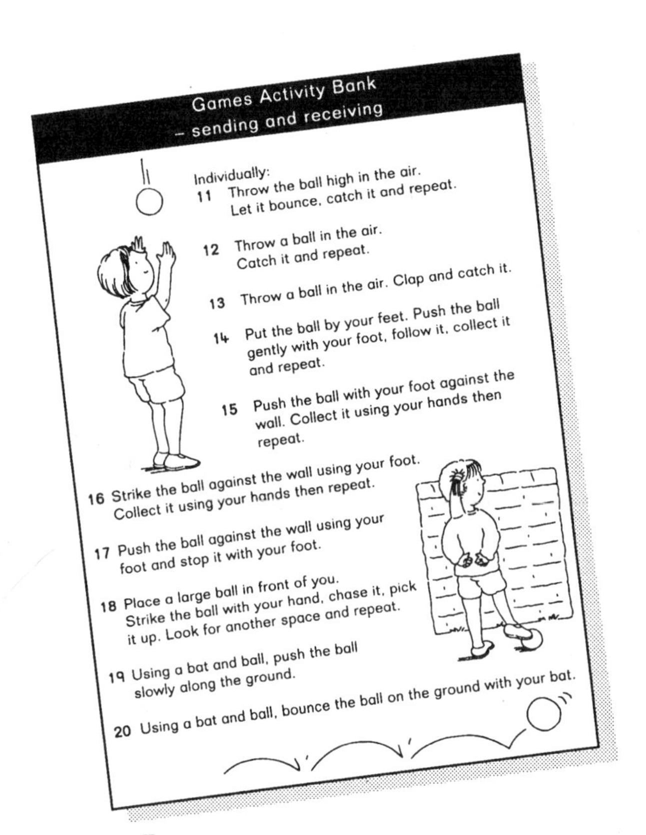

Games Activity Bank
– sending and receiving

Individually:
11 Throw the ball high in the air. Let it bounce, catch it and repeat.
12 Throw a ball in the air. Catch it and repeat.
13 Throw a ball in the air. Clap and catch it.
14 Put the ball by your feet. Push the ball gently with your foot, follow it, collect it and repeat.
15 Push the ball with your foot against the wall. Collect it using your hands then repeat.
16 Strike the ball against the wall using your foot. Collect it using your hands then repeat.
17 Push the ball against the wall using your foot and stop it with your foot.
18 Place a large ball in front of you. Strike the ball with your hand, chase it, pick it up. Look for another space and repeat.
19 Using a bat and ball, push the ball slowly along the ground.
20 Using a bat and ball, bounce the ball on the ground with your bat.

SENDING LESSON 3 (R AND Y1; P1 AND P2)

To develop sending skills using a bat and ball and to practise skills of sending a ball along the ground using hands and feet.

Children working individually.

30 minutes.

Previous skills/knowledge needed
Ability to work in designated space safely and to follow instructions. Previous experience of rolling a ball using hands and of sending a ball using feet.

Key background information
Before children are able to hit a ball accurately with a bat make sure that they have had plenty of opportunities to push a stationary ball along the ground using a bat. Make sure that the children are always spaced well apart when using bats.

Encourage the children to try to hold the bat with one hand as if they were shaking hands with the handle.

Preparation
Ensure that the games equipment – a variety of soft balls and light wooden or plastic bats, quoits and hoops – are readily accessible around the edge of the working area. Make a copy of photocopiable page 106 for your reference.

Resources needed
A variety of bats, balls, hoops and quoits. Photocopiable page 106.

What to do
Warm-up activity
Warm up the class with activity 73 from the Games Activity Bank (photocopiable page 106). Select three children to be 'taggers'. Space the class out in the working area with every child holding a ball with two hands. The taggers must try to tag as many children as possible by *touching* them with their ball. (The ball cannot be thrown to tag a child.) When tagged, the children stand still with feet apart. They can be freed by other children rolling their ball between their feet.

Skill development
Ask the children to collect a bat and organise them along a line so that they can all work safely in the same direction. Ask them to:

▲ place their ball on the ground and push it gently ahead with the bat;
▲ move after the ball and stop it;
▲ stop the ball, pick it up and return to the line;
▲ repeat the activity several times.

Now remind the children of the skills that they have been practising in the previous weeks – rolling using hands and sending using feet. Ask them to try to make up their own individual games sending the ball in a variety of ways but keeping it on the ground. Allow the children plenty of time to practise the activity and choose several children to demonstrate their activity. For example, some children may choose to roll their ball through a partner's legs.

Conclusion
Conclude the lesson with activity 73 from the Games Activity Bank (photocopiable page 106) which was used to commence the lesson.

Suggestion(s) for extension
Encourage more confident children to stop the ball with their bats. Give them markers, such as skittles to use as targets to hit the ball towards.

Suggestion(s) for support
Encourage less confident children to hold their bats with two hands.

Assessment opportunities
Observe how well the children used space in the chasing game. Did they employ a variety of sending skills when asked to make up their own sending games?

Reference to photocopiable sheet
Photocopiable page 106 acts as a handy reference, providing the activity from the Games Activity Bank relevant to this lesson.

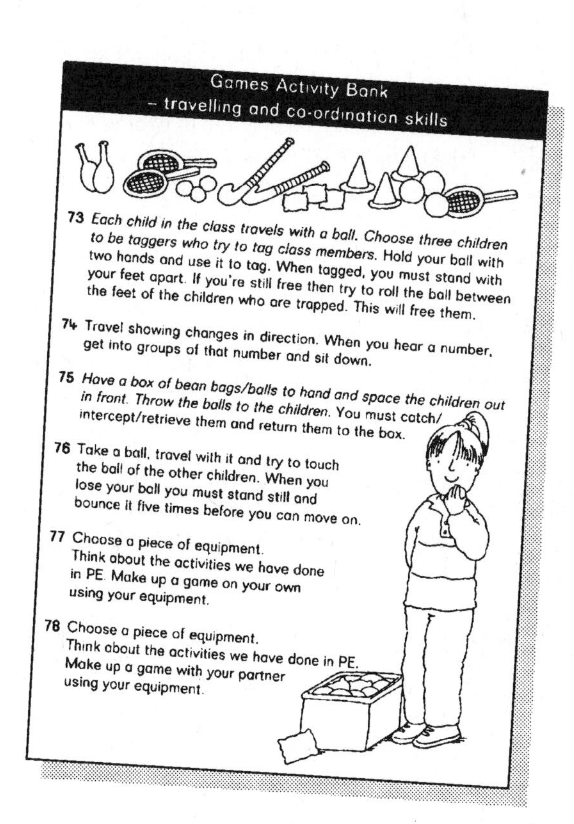

Games Activity Bank
– travelling and co-ordination skills

73 *Each child in the class travels with a ball. Choose three children to be taggers who try to tag class members. Hold your ball with two hands and use it to tag. When tagged, you must stand with your feet apart. If you're still free then try to roll the ball between the feet of the children who are trapped. This will free them.*

74 Travel showing changes in direction. When you hear a number, get into groups of that number and sit down.

75 *Have a box of bean bags/balls to hand and space the children out in front. Throw the balls to the children. You must catch/intercept/retrieve them and return them to the box.*

76 Take a ball, travel with it and try to touch the ball of the other children. When you lose your ball you must stand still and bounce it five times before you can move on.

77 Choose a piece of equipment. Think about the activities we have done in PE. Make up a game on your own using your equipment.

78 Choose a piece of equipment. Think about the activities we have done in PE. Make up a game with your partner using your equipment.

SENDING LESSON 1 (Y1 AND Y2; P2 AND P3)

To develop sending skills and an ability to strike with accuracy using both hands and feet.

Children working individually; then in pairs.

20 minutes.

Previous skills/knowledge needed

Ability to work in designated space safely and to follow instructions. Ability to work co-operatively with a partner.

Key background information

Young children often find difficulty in using a bat or small racquet to direct a ball with control and accuracy. This is primarily because the bat or racquet represents an extension of the arm and this places great demands on hand-eye co-ordination. Although many young children are able to strike a ball with a bat reasonably consistently, their ability to send it in a specified direction is often poorly developed because the striking implement is simply too far away from their body. Part of this lesson will provide the children with some very useful practice with an 'extremely short-handled bat' enabling the children to exercise maximum control over their striking implement. The 'extremely short-handled bats' are, of course, their own hands!

Preparation

The teacher should ensure that the games equipment – balls and skittles – are readily accessible around the edge of the working area. Make one copy each of photocopiable pages 98, 101 and 102 for your reference.

Resources needed

A sufficient number of large light balls (at least one per child), skittles, photocopiable pages 98, 101 and 102.

What to do

Warm-up activity

Warm up the class with the 'Numbers game'. The teacher shouts out various numbers and the children have to respond with the agreed response. For example, '1' means stop; '2' means run forwards; '3' means run sideways and so on.

Skill development

Ask the children to collect a large ball and find a space. Ask them to practise activity 18 from the Games Activity Bank (photocopiable page 98). The children must place the ball on the floor in front of them, strike it at floor level with their hand, chase it and pick it up. They then look for another space and repeat this activity. The children must make sure that they hit their ball into a space – this will involve them in some useful decision-making about when to actually strike the ball.

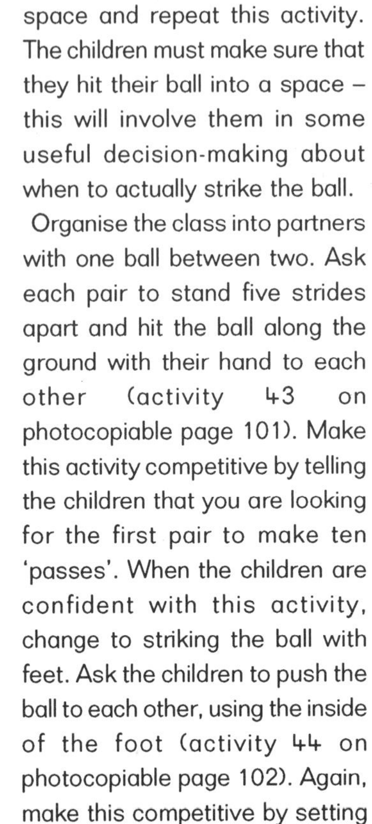

Organise the class into partners with one ball between two. Ask each pair to stand five strides apart and hit the ball along the ground with their hand to each other (activity 43 on photocopiable page 101). Make this activity competitive by telling the children that you are looking for the first pair to make ten 'passes'. When the children are confident with this activity, change to striking the ball with feet. Ask the children to push the ball to each other, using the inside of the foot (activity 44 on photocopiable page 102). Again, make this competitive by setting the challenge: 'Which pair can make ten passes faster than anybody else?'

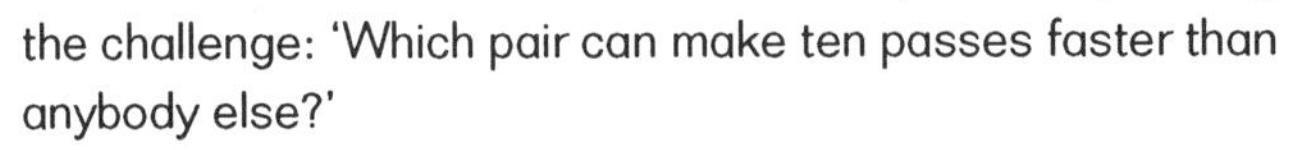

Conclusion

Conclude the lesson with 'stealball'. The children must move about the working space with their ball. They can choose a way of travelling with it – bouncing, kicking, rolling and so on, but are also allowed to knock away anybody's ball as they continue on their way. This game encourages the children to keep their ball close.

Suggestion(s) for extension

Encourage more confident children to strike their ball with their hand after one bounce rather than along the floor. Suggest that they alternate feet when kicking the ball to their partner.

Suggestion(s) for support

Less confident children will need to stand closer together in partner work.

Assessment opportunities

Observe how accurate the children are when passing to a partner. Are they able to keep control of their ball in the concluding game?

Reference to photocopiable sheets

Photocopiable pages 98, 101 and 102 form part of the Games Activity Bank and provide a list of ideas to develop the children's skills in the areas of sending and receiving. The activities relevant to this lesson plan are included on these sheets.

Games Activity Bank
– sending and receiving

With a partner:
44 Place a large ball in front of you. Strike the ball using the inside part of your foot. Your partner stops the ball and returns it.
45 Kick the ball to yo...

Games Activity Bank
– sending and receiving

With a partner
38 Dribble the ... '8'. Have t...
39 Dribble th... figure of '...
40 Roll a bal... ball with ... to you.
41 Each pa... Stop the...

Games Activity Bank
– sending and receiving

Individually:
11 Throw the ball high in the air. Let it bounce, catch it and repeat.
12 Throw a ball in the air. Catch it and repeat.
13 Throw a ball in the air. Clap and catch it.
14 Put the ball by your feet. Push the ball gently with your foot, follow it, collect it and repeat.
15 Push the ball with your foot against the wall. Collect it using your hands then repeat.
16 Strike the ball against the wall using your foot. Collect it using your hands then repeat.
17 Push the ball against the wall using your foot and stop it with your foot.
18 Place a large ball in front of you. Strike the ball with your hand, chase it, pick it up. Look for another space and repeat.
19 Using a bat and ball, push the ball slowly along the ground.
20 Using a bat and ball, bounce the ball on the ground with your bat.

SENDING LESSON 2 (Y1 AND Y2; P2 AND P3)

To develop sending skills using a bat or racquet.
Children working individually; then in pairs.
20 minutes.

Previous skills/knowledge needed

Ability to work in designated space safely and to follow instructions. Previous experience of striking a ball with hand and bat. Ability to work co-operatively with a partner.

Key background information

The development of hand-eye co-ordination, together with increasing strength, enables young children to strike a ball with a bat or racquet with a measure of consistency. At this stage, young children should be introduced to the challenges involved in anticipating the flight of a ball and in moving towards it. Help them to understand that in order to strike a ball effectively, they need to position themselves sideways on to the ball and be in a well-balanced position. Explain to them that getting their feet in the correct position – widely spaced and to one side of the ball – will make all the difference when seeking to make effective contact with it.

Preparation

The teacher should ensure that the games equipment – balls, bats or racquets, skittles and hoops are readily accessible around the edge of the working area. Make a copy of the Games Activity Bank on photocopiable page 103 for your reference.

Resources needed

A sufficient number of light plastic or foam balls, round wooden or plastic bats or racquets, cones and hoops, photocopiable page 103.

What to do

Warm-up activity

Warm up the children with a game of 'forwards and sideways'. Ask the children to run freely about the working area. When the teacher calls 'sideways!' the class have to move sideways with a skipping action. They continue this way of travelling until the teacher calls 'forwards!' when they resume a normal running action again. The teacher then proceeds to alternate the calls.

Skill development

Organise the children into pairs. Ask each pair to collect a ball, a bat each and a hoop. Each pair then practises activity 52 (photocopiable page 103) in their own space. A hoop is placed in the middle. One partner throws the ball gently into the hoop so that it bounces and the other hits it back for the partner to catch. Each partner has five hits and then they must change over.

When the children are sufficiently confident with this activity try activity 51 (photocopiable page 103). Replace the hoop with two cones placed three strides apart. Ask each set of partners to stand either side of the cones. One of the pair must drop the ball and then strike it through the cones. The other has to field it and bring it back.

Each partner has five hits and then changes over. Let the children decide how far from the cones they wish to stand but emphasise that the ball has to be struck through the cones. After a period of practice make it competitive by looking for the first pair to complete ten successful hits (five each).

Conclusion

Finish the lesson by repeating the game of 'forwards and sideways' before winding down gradually. Ensure that the children help you to store the equipment away safely and carefully.

Suggestion(s) for extension

Extend the activity for more able children by providing them with a smaller tennis-sized ball and reduce the space between the cones.

Suggestion(s) for support

Ensure that children who are having difficulty work with a large ball. In the hoop activity they should be asked to hit the ball without necessarily returning a catch to their partner.

Assessment opportunities

Observe how well the children hit the ball – is their striking accurate and controlled? Are they able to self-feed the ball reliably in the cones activity?

Reference to photocopiable sheet

The Games Activity Bank on photocopiable page 103 provides many ideas for sending and receiving activities. The sheet outlines the activities used in this lesson plan and acts as handy reference material.

Games Activity Bank
– sending and receiving

With a partner:

50 Using a bat and ball, drop the ball in front of you. Hit the ball into a space. Your partner fields the ball and brings it back to you. Have five turns each.

51 Using a bat and ball drop the ball in front of you. Hit the ball between two cones. Your partner fields the ball and brings it backto you. Have five turns each.

52 Place a hoop between you and your partner. Throw the ball gently into the hoop. Your partner gently hits the ball back with a bat for you to catch.

53 Place a rope between you and your partner. Bounce the ball over the rope. Your partner catches it after one bounce then bounces the ball back to you over the rope.

54 Each partner has a bat. Bounce the ball (self-feed) to hit it to your partner. Your partner hits it to return it to you. Can you each hit the ball after just one bounce?

55 In threes, using a large ball, play 'piggy in the middle'.

SENDING LESSON 3 (Y1 AND Y2; P2 AND P3)

To consolidate and refine a range of sending skills.

Children working in pairs.

30 minutes.

Previous skills/knowledge needed

Experience of sending a ball with bats, feet and hands. Ability to control a moving ball with a bat and with feet. Ability to catch a large ball in flight.

Key background information

In order to develop the children's skills in games, it is important to give them frequent opportunities for practice. Lack of practice will ultimately lead to a lowering of performance. Lessons similar to the one described below should feature at regular intervals – at least every three weeks – throughout the games programme, as a useful means of 'embedding' basic games skills.

Preparation

Ensure that the equipment is easily accessible around the edge of the working area.

Resources needed

Bats, large and small balls, skipping ropes and skittles.

What to do

Warm-up activity

Commence the lesson with a game of 'four towns' as a suitable 'warm-up activity'. Ask the children to spread out around a working 'grid'. Give each corner of the grid the name of a town. When the teacher shouts the name of a particular town the children have to run as quickly as possible to the appropriate corner.

Activity A	Activity B	Activity C
Send your ball to your partner by striking it with your bat.	Send your ball to your partner by kicking it through the skittles.	Send your ball to your partner with your hands.

Skill development

Organise the class into three activity groups and direct them them to work in the way shown in the diagram above.

The children should practise each activity for approximately seven to eight minutes and then rotate – moving to the next activity and leaving their equipment ready for the following group.

Conclusion

Conclude the lesson by asking the children to return their equipment to its appropriate box. Ask them to reflect on the skills that they have been practising. Did they notice any improvements?

Suggestion(s) for extension

Encourage the more confident children to space out widely and challenge themselves with performance 'targets'. For example, 'Can I make ten successful passes?'.

Suggestion(s) for support

Less confident children will need to stand fairly close to their respective partners.

Assessment opportunities

Observe how well the children are able to maintain their own activity. Do they co-operate well with their partner? How accurate and consistent are they in sending their ball to their partner?

RECEIVING LESSON 1 (R AND Y1; P1 AND P2)

To develop receiving skills and an ability to use hands to stop a ball. To improve catching skills.

Children working individually and as part of a larger group.

20 minutes.

Previous skills/knowledge needed

Ability to work safely in an organised space and to follow instructions. Previous work on basic sending skills.

Key background information

Young children find sending skills easier to master than receiving skills. The skill of 'receiving' requires the children to be able to track a ball and to respond quickly by processing information into actions via their senses . Start by practising how to retrieve a ball from a rebound surface or by catching from a bounce. This will provide more time for the children to anticipate the position of the ball and will therefore allow them to gain confidence in their ability to stop, control and catch a ball, reflecting the existing capabilities of the children. Receiving a ball from a rebound surface or from a bounce provides a meaningful foundation activity upon which catching skills can be built.

When asking the children to invent their own individual games, guide them to apply the skills that they have been developing in this or recent lessons. For example, the activities involved in this lesson will include:

▲ receiving a ball from a rebound surface with hands;
▲ throwing ball in air, bounce, catch;
▲ throwing ball in air, catch.

For organisational purposes it is a good idea to place the children in regular groups, labelled by colour. In addition it can be most helpful to organise each 'colour group' by

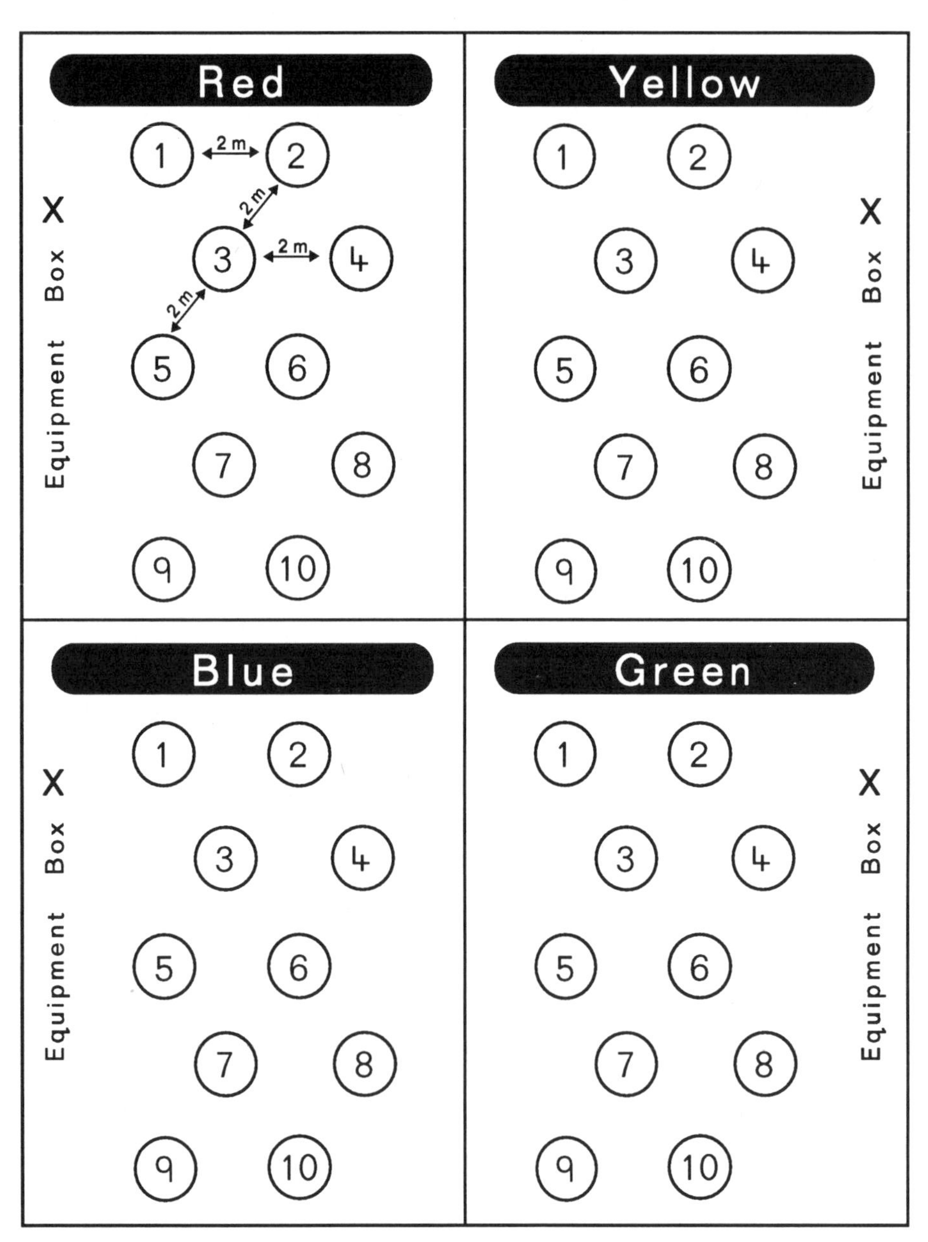

What to do

Warm-up activity

Warm up the class with activity 75 from the Games Activity Bank (photocopiable page 106). The teacher will need a box of balls. Space the children out in front of you. The teacher rolls the balls in different directions among the class. The children intercept, retrieve and return them to the box. Ask them to jog to return the ball themselves (later in Key Stage 1 they can be asked to roll them to receivers who will be waiting near the box).

Skill development

Next, ask every child to collect a large ball and tell them that you want them to practise activity 3 (on photocopiable page 97) from the Games Activity Bank. Explain the activity to the children – they must roll the ball towards the wall and retrieve it when it rebounds. Initially, the children should be encouraged to roll the ball towards the wall using both hands. Ensure that they move their feet to the position that they anticipate to receive the ball. They should use two hands with their fingers pointed downwards to collect the ball.

Then ask the children to go to their colour groups (on the grid) and stand on a number. This is their working area for the next activity. Demonstrate activity 9 (from the Games Activity Bank on photocopiable page 97) – throw the ball above head height, let it bounce and then catch it. Ask the children to try this, repeating the activity several times. Introduce and demonstrate activity 11 (photocopiable page 98) – throw the ball in the air, catch, repeat. Allow time for the children to practise. Select a number of children to demonstrate this skill.

When they have gained some confidence in these skills, set them the task of making up their own individual games which involve one or a combination of the following:

▲ rolling a ball;
▲ throw, bounce, catch;
▲ throw, catch.

Conclusion

Conclude the lesson with activity 75 (photocopiable page 106) as used for the 'warm-up activity'. As before, space out the children in front of you and roll or throw the balls in

painting the numbers 1–10 on the playground within the four 'coloured working grids' (see the diagram above). This allows the teacher to allocate changes to equipment without congestion. It is also particularly helpful when you wish to organise the children into small groups.

Preparation

Ensure that there is a selection of balls of various sizes readily accessible in boxes around the edge of the working area.

Some children will feel more comfortable with a larger ball, while other more confident children will choose a smaller ball.

Make a copy of each of the photocopiable pages 97, 98, and 106 for your reference.

Resources needed

A selection of balls – at least one per child, photocopiable pages 97, 98 and 106.

different directions among the class. The children intercept, retrieve and return them to the box. Vary the activity by asking the children to jog, skip or hop to return the ball themselves.

Suggestion(s) for extension

For activity 3 (photocopiable page 97) encourage more able children to use a small tennis-sized ball and send it with one hand. For activities 9 and 11 (photocopiable pages 97 and 98) ensure that the more capable children use a smaller ball.

Suggestion(s) for support

For activity 3 (photocopiable page 97) children who are experiencing difficulty should be encouraged to move their feet and whole bodies to where they anticipate the ball is going to arrive. For activities 9 and 11 (photocopiable pages 97 and 98) ensure that less capable children use a larger ball and allow them to catch the ball after two bounces. For the 'warm-up' and 'conclusion' sessions make sure that when the balls are distributed they reach the less competitive children too.

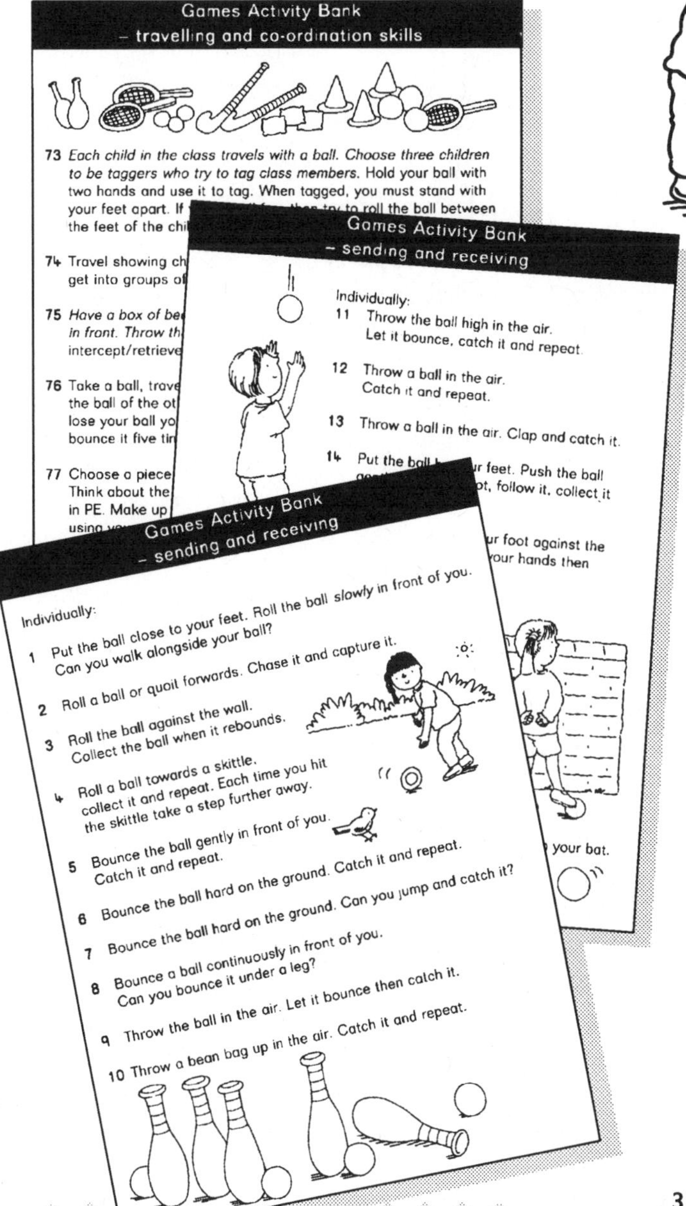

Games Activity Bank – sending and receiving

Individually:

1 Put the ball close to your feet. Roll the ball slowly in front of you. Can you walk alongside your ball?

2 Roll a ball or quoit forwards. Chase it and capture it.

3 Roll the ball against the wall. Collect the ball when it rebounds.

4 Roll a ball towards a skittle. Each time you hit collect it and repeat. Each time you hit the skittle take a step further away.

5 Bounce the ball gently in front of you. Catch it and repeat.

6 Bounce the ball hard on the ground. Catch it and repeat.

7 Bounce the ball hard on the ground. Can you jump and catch it?

8 Bounce a ball continuously in front of you. Can you bounce it under a leg?

9 Throw the ball in the air. Let it bounce then catch it.

10 Throw a bean bag up in the air. Catch it and repeat.

Games Activity Bank – sending and receiving

Individually:

11 Throw the ball high in the air. Let it bounce, catch it and repeat.

12 Throw a ball in the air. Catch it and repeat.

13 Throw a ball in the air. Clap and catch it.

14 Put the ball ... feet. Push the ball ... follow it, collect it

Games Activity Bank – travelling and co-ordination skills

73 *Each child in the class travels with a ball. Choose three children to be taggers who try to tag class members.* Hold your ball with two hands and use it to tag. When tagged, you must stand with your feet apart. ...

Assessment opportunities

Observe how well the children are able to anticipate the direction of the ball after it has hit the wall. Do they move their feet to receive the ball as it rebounds off the wall? Can the children catch consistently?

Reference to photocopiable sheets

The photocopiable pages 97, 98 and 106 include outline descriptions of the activities referred to in this lesson plan and a number of other relevant suggestions for linked skill-building exercises.

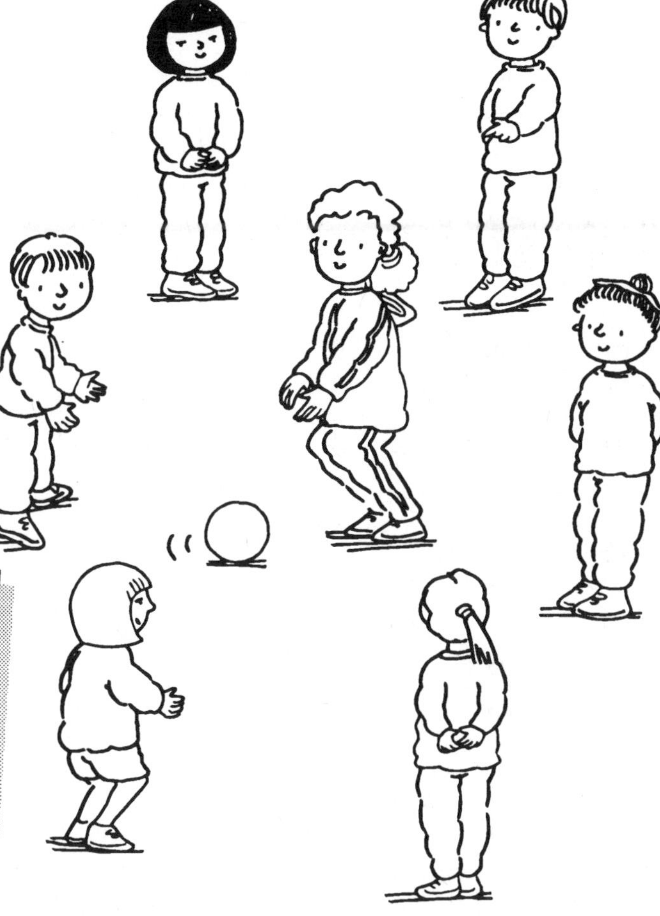

RECEIVING LESSON 2 (R AND Y1; P1 AND P2)

To develop receiving skills and an ability to use feet to stop a ball.

Children working individually and as part of a larger group.

20 minutes.

Previous skills/knowledge needed

Ability to work safely in an organised space and to follow instructions. Previous work on basic sending skills using feet. Previous experience of activity 73 from the Games Activity Bank (photocopiable page 106).

Key background information
Young children can be tempted to kick a ball hard with little control or accuracy when carrying out activities which involve sending with feet. From the outset of the lesson ensure that you praise those children who are pushing the ball gently with control.

Encourage the children to use the inside part of the foot when making contact with the ball to send and receive it. The ball should be kept on the ground at all times. In the interest of control and accuracy it is important that the ball is stationary before children attempt to push it.

Preparation
Ensure that there is a selection of balls readily accessible in boxes around the edge of the working area. Make one copy of each of the photocopiable pages 98 and 106.

Resources needed
A selection of balls – at least one per child, photocopiable pages 98 and 106.

What to do
Warm-up activity

Warm up the class with activity 73 from the Games Activity Bank (photocopiable page 106). Select three children to be taggers. Space the class out in the working area with every child holding a ball with both hands. The taggers must try to tag as many children as possible by touching them with their ball. When tagged, the children stand still with feet apart. They can be freed by other children rolling their ball between their legs. The children should send the ball slowly using both hands to roll and to retrieve. Emphasise that the children need not roll the ball too hard.

Skill development

Organise the children along a line so that all of them can work safely in the same direction. Introduce activity 14 from the Games Activity Bank (photocopiable page 98). Ask them to:

▲ place their ball on the ground and push the ball gently ahead with their foot;

▲ move after the ball and stop the ball initially using their hands;

▲ return to the line and then repeat the activity several times.

Once the children have mastered this, ask them to try to stop the ball using their feet. Allow some children to demonstrate good control to the rest of the class.

Then introduce activity 17 from the Games Activity Bank (photocopiable page 98). Organise the children to work against a wall or rebound surface. Ask them to start off close to the wall and gradually move away as they achieve success. Encourage the children to keep the ball close to the ground and make sure that they understand that the ball must be stopped with their feet before they push it against the wall again. After they have had time to practise this activity ask them to count how many times they can push and stop the ball using their feet without losing control. Ask the children to put the balls away safely.

Conclusion

Conclude the lesson with activity 75 in the Games Activity Bank (photocopiable page 106). You will need a box of balls. Space the children out in front of you. Roll the balls in different directions among the class, asking the children to try to stop a ball using their feet. If they stop one, they must pick it up and return it to the box placed at the side of the working area.

Suggestion(s) for extension
The more capable children could use a small ball to make the activity more challenging.

Suggestion(s) for support
Encourage those children who are having difficulty stopping the ball with their feet to stop the ball using a combination of hands and feet. Feed the ball gently by hand to individuals who are struggling. In activity 75 (photocopiable page 106) make sure that when the balls are distributed they reach the less competitive children.

Assessment opportunities
Observe whether or not the children can take up a balanced position to stop the ball with their feet. Could the children push and stop the ball against the wall a number of times?

Reference to photocopiable sheets
Photocopiable pages 98 and 106 contain the activities from the Games Activity Bank that are used in this lesson plan.

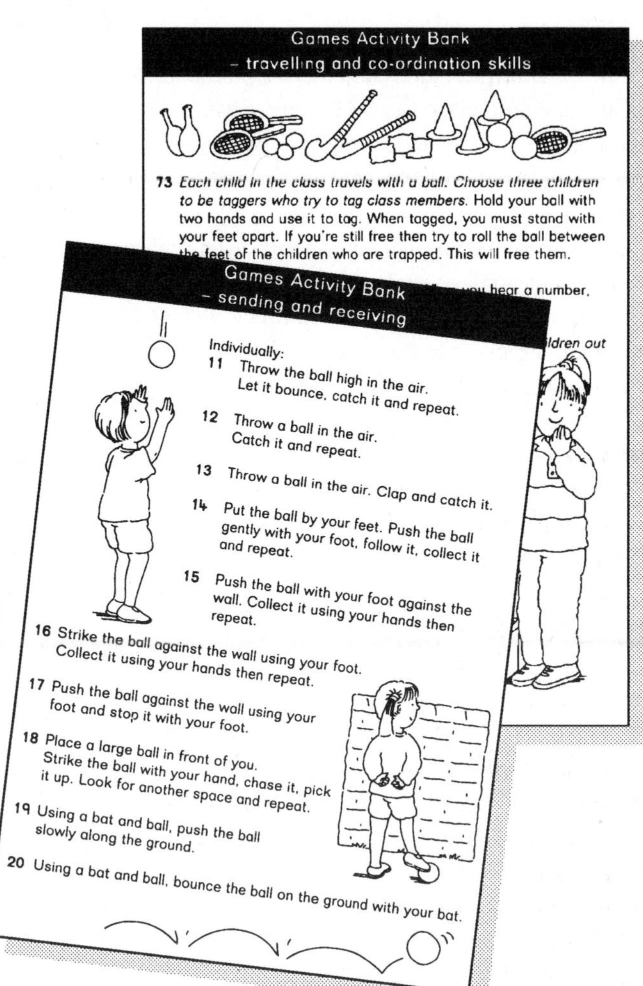

Games Activity Bank
– travelling and co-ordination skills

73 *Each child in the class travels with a ball. Choose three children to be taggers who try to tag class members.* Hold your ball with two hands and use it to tag. When tagged, you must stand with your feet apart. If you're still free then try to roll the ball between the feet of the children who are trapped. This will free them.

Games Activity Bank
– sending and receiving

Individually:

11 Throw the ball high in the air. Let it bounce, catch it and repeat.

12 Throw a ball in the air. Catch it and repeat.

13 Throw a ball in the air. Clap and catch it.

14 Put the ball by your feet. Push the ball gently with your foot, follow it, collect it and repeat.

15 Push the ball with your foot against the wall. Collect it using your hands then repeat.

16 Strike the ball against the wall using your foot. Collect it using your hands then repeat.

17 Push the ball against the wall using your foot and stop it with your foot.

18 Place a large ball in front of you. Strike the ball with your hand, chase it, pick it up. Look for another space and repeat.

19 Using a bat and ball, push the ball slowly along the ground.

20 Using a bat and ball, bounce the ball on the ground with your bat.

RECEIVING LESSON 3 (R AND Y1; P1 AND P2)

To develop the receiving skills of stopping a ball using hands; catching and stopping a ball using feet.

Children working individually and as part of a larger group.

20 minutes.

Previous skills/knowledge needed
Ability to work safely in an organised space and to follow instructions.

Previous experience of the following activities from the Games Activity Bank (photocopiable pages 97 and 98):

- ▲ activity 9: throw, bounce, catch;
- ▲ activity 11: throw, catch;
- ▲ activity 14: push ball with feet, follow, stop, collect.

Key background information
When aiming to develop the children's receiving skills there are four main teaching points that must be considered. The children must be encouraged to: watch the ball all of the time; use two hands to catch with fingers spread; be in a ready position on balls of feet; bring the ball into the body when caught. It is essential that you do not overload the children by teaching all four points simultaneously – it is better to highlight one thing at a time.

During this lesson the children will be asked to recap the activities from the previous two lessons. They will then be encouraged to make up their own individual games which involve stopping and catching items of small equipment. They should be invited to experiment with a variety of balls. You will need to organise opportunities for the children to change their piece of apparatus efficiently.

Preparation
The teacher should ensure that there is a selection of balls of various sizes readily accessible in boxes around the edge of the working area. Make a copy of each of the photocopiable pages 97, 98, and 106.

Resources needed
A selection of balls, hoops (if there are no circles included in the line markings of the working area), a whistle, photocopiable pages 97, 98 and 106.

What to do
Warm-up activity

If the children have been assigned to a colour group as discussed on pages 35–36, then assemble them into their groups. Using the idea for organising the working area into a colour grid (see page 36, 'Receiving lesson 1'), ask the children to stand on a number in their colour grid.

Invite them to show you how they can jump into and out of their circle (use hoops if no markings are available). Ask the children to show you different ways of travelling around the working area. When you blow your whistle they should go to any circle and perform five springy jumps in and out of that circle. Demonstrate jumping from two feet to two feet and encourage them to copy you. Repeat this 'game' a few more times.

Skill development

Tell the children to stand on a number in their colour group again. Ask all number 2's and 9's to collect a large ball from their equipment box. Repeat this with other pairs of numbers until all the children have collected a ball and returned to their place.

The children are going to be working in their own area around their number circle. Explain that they must look for space and that they must not send their ball very far away from their starting position. Ask them to:

▲ place their ball on the ground and push the ball gently ahead with their hands;
▲ move after the ball and stop the ball using hands;
▲ return to their starting position to repeat.

Demonstrate the same activity, only this time using feet (activity 14, Games Activity Bank, photocopiable page 98).

Ask the children to throw the ball in the air, let it bounce and then catch it. (Activity 9, Games Activity Bank, photocopiable page 97). Ask them to try to catch the ball after just one bounce.

Once again, working in their own number circles, ask them to throw the ball in the air and catch it without a bounce. Can they make five catches without dropping the ball? How many can they do? Select some children to demonstrate good catching skills:

▲ watching the ball closely;
▲ fingers spread and hands ready to receive the ball;
▲ ready to catch, poised on the balls of their feet;
▲ bringing the ball into the body when caught.

Explain to the children that you would now like them to make up their own individual game. They must work in, and immediately around, their number circle. Can they show you good ways of stopping or catching their ball?

At an appropriate point stop the class and allow the children to change their ball using the same method of organisation as earlier in the lesson (calling out two numbers at a time). Walk around the groups and offer individual teaching points based upon your observations.

Conclusion

To conclude the lesson, use activity 75 in the Games Activity Bank on photocopiable page 106. You will need a box of balls. Space the children out in front of you. Vary the activity by sending the balls in a variety of different ways – some along the ground; some for the children to catch. They should stop or catch the balls and return them to a box at the side of the working area.

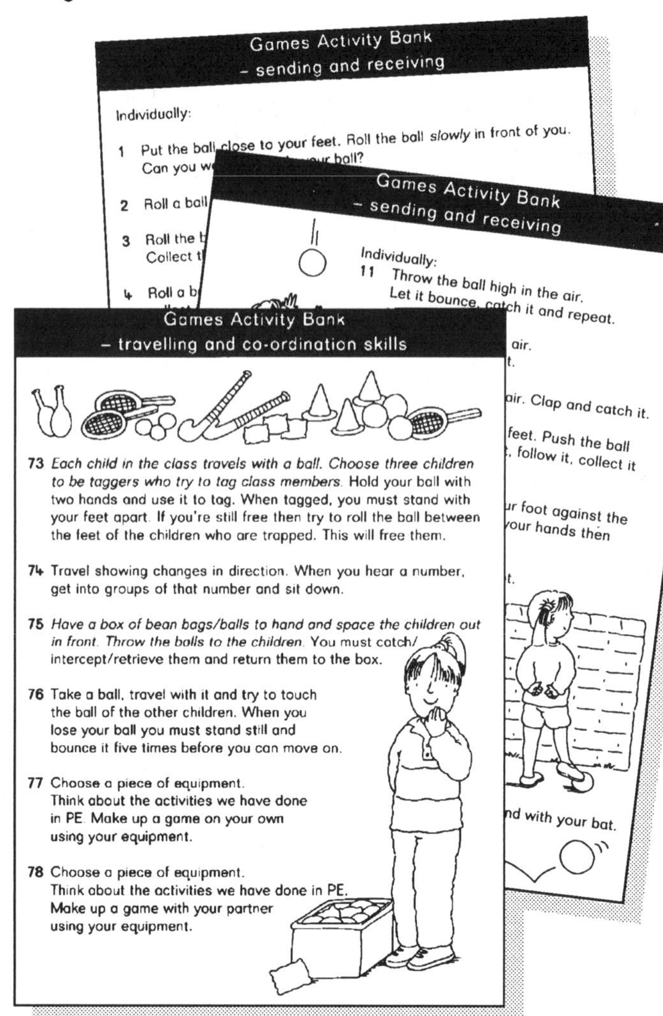

Games Activity Bank
– sending and receiving

Individually:

1 Put the ball close to your feet. Roll the ball *slowly* in front of you.

Games Activity Bank
– sending and receiving

Individually:

11 Throw the ball high in the air. Let it bounce, catch it and repeat.

Games Activity Bank
– travelling and co-ordination skills

73 *Each child in the class travels with a ball. Choose three children to be taggers who try to tag class members.* Hold your ball with two hands and use it to tag. When tagged, you must stand with your feet apart. If you're still free then try to roll the ball between the feet of the children who are trapped. This will free them.

74 Travel showing changes in direction. When you hear a number, get into groups of that number and sit down.

75 *Have a box of bean bags/balls to hand and space the children out in front. Throw the balls to the children.* You must catch/intercept/retrieve them and return them to the box.

76 Take a ball, travel with it and try to touch the ball of the other children. When you lose your ball you must stand still and bounce it five times before you can move on.

77 Choose a piece of equipment. Think about the activities we have done in PE. Make up a game on your own using your equipment.

78 Choose a piece of equipment. Think about the activities we have done in PE. Make up a game with your partner using your equipment.

Suggestion(s) for extension

To make these activities more challenging for the more capable children, the teacher should ask them to send the ball higher in the air. Confident children should be guided to select harder, heavier and smaller balls.

Suggestion(s) for support

Feed the ball to those children who are having difficulty with self-feeding the ball accurately when doing the 'throw, bounce, catch' and 'throw, catch' activities. If necessary these children should be given a bean bag for throwing and catching.

Assessment opportunities

Observe how well the children position their bodies to receive a catch. Can they catch consistently? When asked to make up their own game do they stay on task? Do they work sensibly within their designated space?

Reference to photocopiable sheets

Photocopiable pages 97, 98 and 106 form part of the Games Activity Bank, containing outlines of the activities that are practised in this lesson.

RECEIVING LESSON 1 (Y1 AND Y2; P2 AND P3)

To develop catching skills.

Children working individually, in pairs and in small groups.

30 minutes.

Previous skills/knowledge needed

Ability to follow instructions and work safely in an organised space. Experience of throwing and catching individually. Experience of moving to receive a ball. The ability to understand and remember the sequence of numbers 1–4.

Key background information

When the children are involved with pair-work activities they need to be encouraged to send the ball 'sympathetically' for their partners to catch. Ensure that you reward accurate and gentle throwing. The position for receiving should include a balanced base with feet apart – one in front of the other with hands and fingers facing the ball. When developing the game called '1-2-3-4' allow plenty of time for the children to identify who is number 1, 2 and so on in a stationary position before attempting the activity on the move.

Preparation

Ensure that there is a selection of balls readily accessible in boxes around the edge of the working area. Make a copy of each of the photocopiable pages 100 and 104 for your reference.

Resources needed

A selection of balls, photocopiable pages 100 and 104.

What to do

Warm-up activity

Begin the lesson by playing the following version of 'What time is it Mr Wolf?'

▲ The children stand along a line. 'Mr Wolf' (the teacher) stands opposite the children.

▲ The children call out, 'What time is it Mr Wolf?' and take five big steps forward, standing still to listen to the 'Wolf's' reply.

▲ The 'Wolf' answers by saying, 'It's 1 o'clock', or, 10 o'clock and so on.

▲ Every time the children ask the time they take five steps forward and stand still until the wolf replies 'It's dinner time'.

▲ Then the children run back to their home line before the wolf catches them! Those children who are caught stand with the 'Wolf' and when the 'Wolf ' calls out that it's 'dinner time', the captured children run and chase the other children.

Skill development

Invite the children to stand in their colour groups on a number (see the suggestion for a playground layout on page 36, 'Receiving lesson 1'. Ask all the children who are standing on even numbers to collect a ball from their equipment box (if they need help, ask the children to call out the even numbers as a class first). Number 1 will partner number 2, number 3 will partner number 4 and so on.

Ask each child to face his or her partner where they will bounce the ball on the ground between them. Tell the children to try to catch the ball after just one bounce (activity 32, Games Activity Bank, photocopiable page 100). Challenge the children to count how many bounce passes and catches they can do in a row without losing control. After they have practised this skill, ask them to throw the ball to their partner, aiming for their hands (activity 34, Games Activity Bank, photocopiable page 100). Explain that you will be selecting those children who are throwing carefully and gently to demonstrate. When you have selected some children to demonstrate, ask the children to watch for the position of the receiver's hands and feet rather than just focusing upon the sympathetic pass.

Can the children throw the ball to their partner, move into a space, stop, catch the ball sent from their partner?

Ask the children to put their ball away and organise the class into groups of four to introduce the 'TOP Play' activity '1-2-3-4'. Demonstrate the activity for the children. The

players are numbered 1–4 and start off by standing in a square. The ball is passed from 1 to 2, 2 to 3, 3 to 4 and 4 back to 1. After you have explained this to them ask each group to try to set this up for themselves. Repeat the demonstration for those who are unsure and send the groups off to a designated space with a ball to practise the activity.

Conclusion

Conclude the lesson with activity 61, from the Games Activity Bank (photocopiable page 104). Ask the children to stand in their colour grids on a number. Each child will need a ball. Ask them to roll the ball using their hands across their tummies and, if they can, around their waists. The ball should be kept in contact with the body all the time. Can they roll their ball across or along other body parts? Return the equipment to the boxes.

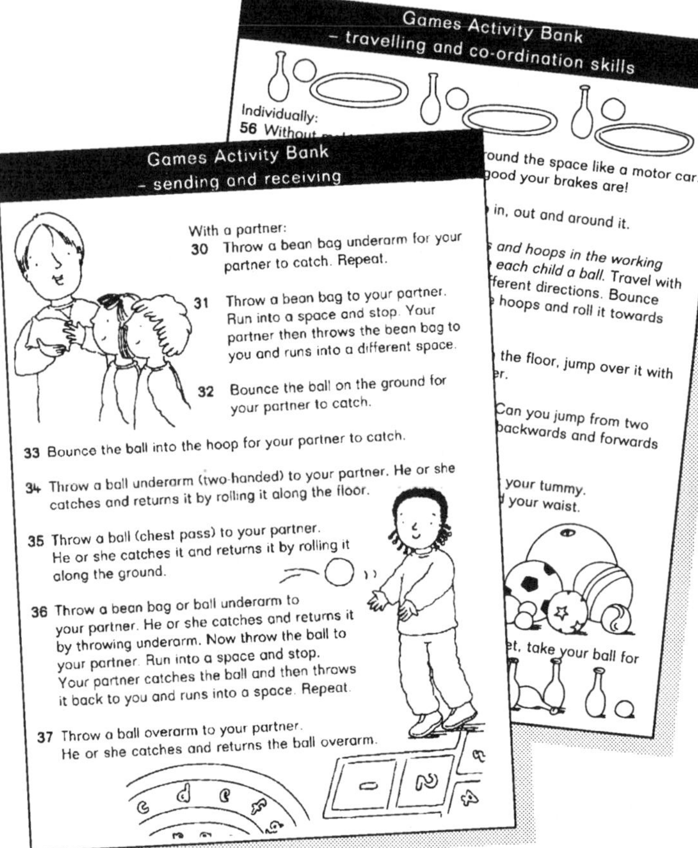

Games Activity Bank
– travelling and co-ordination skills

Individually:
56 Without ...
...ound the space like a motor car. ...ood your brakes are!
... in, out and around it.
... and hoops in the working ... each child a ball. Travel with ...ferent directions. Bounce ... hoops and roll it towards
... the floor, jump over it with ...r.
...Can you jump from two ...backwards and forwards
... your tummy. ... your waist.
...t, take your ball for

Games Activity Bank
– sending and receiving

With a partner:
30 Throw a bean bag underarm for your partner to catch. Repeat.
31 Throw a bean bag to your partner. Run into a space and stop. Your partner then throws the bean bag to you and runs into a different space.
32 Bounce the ball on the ground for your partner to catch.
33 Bounce the ball into the hoop for your partner to catch.
34 Throw a ball underarm (two-handed) to your partner. He or she catches and returns it by rolling it along the floor.
35 Throw a ball (chest pass) to your partner. He or she catches it and returns it by rolling it along the ground.
36 Throw a bean bag or ball underarm to your partner. He or she catches and returns it by throwing underarm. Now throw the ball to your partner. Run into a space and stop. Your partner catches the ball and then throws it back to you and runs into a space. Repeat.
37 Throw a ball overarm to your partner. He or she catches and returns the ball overarm.

Suggestion(s) for extension

Children who are confident in throwing and catching with a partner should be encouraged to throw over a longer distance and use a smaller ball. When moving into a space to receive the ball, encourage the more confident children to throw the ball for the receiver to catch whilst they are still on the move. In this case the ball should be sent ahead of the receiver. Groups that quickly master '1-2-3-4' with success should be asked to move about as they throw the ball in the same order 1-2-3-4.

Suggestion(s) for support

Children who are experiencing difficulty with throwing and catching with a partner should be moved closer together.

Assessment opportunities

Observe how well the children catch the ball. Are they remembering to have their hands ready to catch without being reminded? Could they understand the format of the '1-2-3-4' game when in a stationary position? Did they co-operate when working in fours?

Reference to photocopiable sheets

The photocopiable pages 100 and 104 form part of the Games Activity Bank and provide outlines of some of the activities that the children are performing within this lesson.

RECEIVING LESSON 2 (Y1 AND Y2; P2 AND P3)

To develop receiving skills using feet.

Children working individually, in pairs and in small groups.

30 minutes.

Previous skills/knowledge needed

Ability to work safely in an organised space and to follow instructions.

Previous experience of pushing and stopping a ball using feet. Experience of the 'TOP Play' game '1-2-3-4' introduced in 'Receiving lesson 1', on page 41. Experience of the game 'What time is it Mr Wolf?', outlined in the previous activity on page 41.

Key background information

Children find receiving a ball with feet more difficult than with hands. Encourage the children to stand spaced well apart. They will need to do this, as they may well be lacking in control and accuracy. The ball should be kept on the ground during this activity and sent and received using the inside part of the foot. The sending leg should follow through after the ball

is pushed. The children must be taught to look up when moving into a space to receive a ball. Carefully explain to the children, when they are working in small groups, that if they are experiencing difficulty, then they may use their hands to help them control the ball so that they can participate in the activity successfully.

Preparation

Ensure that there is a selection of balls readily accessible in boxes around the edge of the working area. Make one copy of each of the photocopiable pages 102 and 104.

Resources needed

A selection of balls, photocopiable pages 102 and 104.

What to do

Warm-up activity

Commence the lesson by playing 'What time is it Mr Wolf?' which was introduced in the previous lesson (on page 41). In this lesson the children must return to their home line by hopping. When children are caught they return with the teacher as chasers. They must also hop to catch the others when the 'wolf' calls, 'It's dinner time!'.

Skill development

Divide the children into groups and label each group with a colour name (they may already be in groups of your own choosing). Using the guidelines for a playground layout as shown on page 36 ('Receiving lesson 1'), direct the children to stand in their colour groups on a number. Ask all the children who are standing on even numbers to collect a ball from their equipment box.

Ask the children to face their partners (number 1 with number 2 and so on). Explain that they must push the ball with their feet to their partner, who must stop the ball with his or her feet and return it (activity 44, Games Activity Bank, photocopiable page 102). Ask the children to count how many passes they can do in a row without losing control.

Then challenge the children to pass the ball to their partner with their feet, then move into a space. The partner stops the ball with his or her feet and then passes the ball back to his or her partner. Continue with this activity for a few minutes, or until the children have gained some confidence in this.

Ask the children to put their ball away and organise the class into groups of four. Remind them of the 'TOP Play' activity '1-2-3-4' that was introduced last lesson (page 41).

Demonstrate the activity. The players are numbered 1–4 and start off by standing in a square. The ball is passed from 1 to 2, 2 to 3, 3 to 4 and 4 back to 1. In this lesson the ball is passed and stopped by using feet. Send the groups of four into designated spaces with a ball. After spending some time on this activity, encourage the children to move about and continue to pass the ball from 1 to 2 to 3 and to 4.

Conclusion

To conclude the lesson, ask the children to stand in their colour grids on a number. Each child will need a ball. Ask them to roll the ball using their hands across their tummies and, if they can, around their waists. The ball should be kept in contact with the body all of the time (activity 61, Games Activity Bank, photocopiable page 104). Can they roll their ball across or along other body parts? Return the equipment to the boxes.

Suggestion(s) for extension

Children who are very confident performers may be grouped together as a four, when practising their passing and receiving skills. Add some extra challenges – counting numbers of consecutive passes or seeing how many passes they can do in a set amount of time.

Suggestion(s) for support

Children who are experiencing difficulty in sending the ball accurately to their partners using their feet should be asked to roll the ball using their hands.

Assessment opportunities

Observe how well the children stop the ball with their feet. Did they co-operate when working in fours? Did they look up to see if it was safe to move into a space?

Reference to photocopiable sheets

The photocopiable pages 102 and 104 contain an outline description of some of the skills included in this lesson plan.

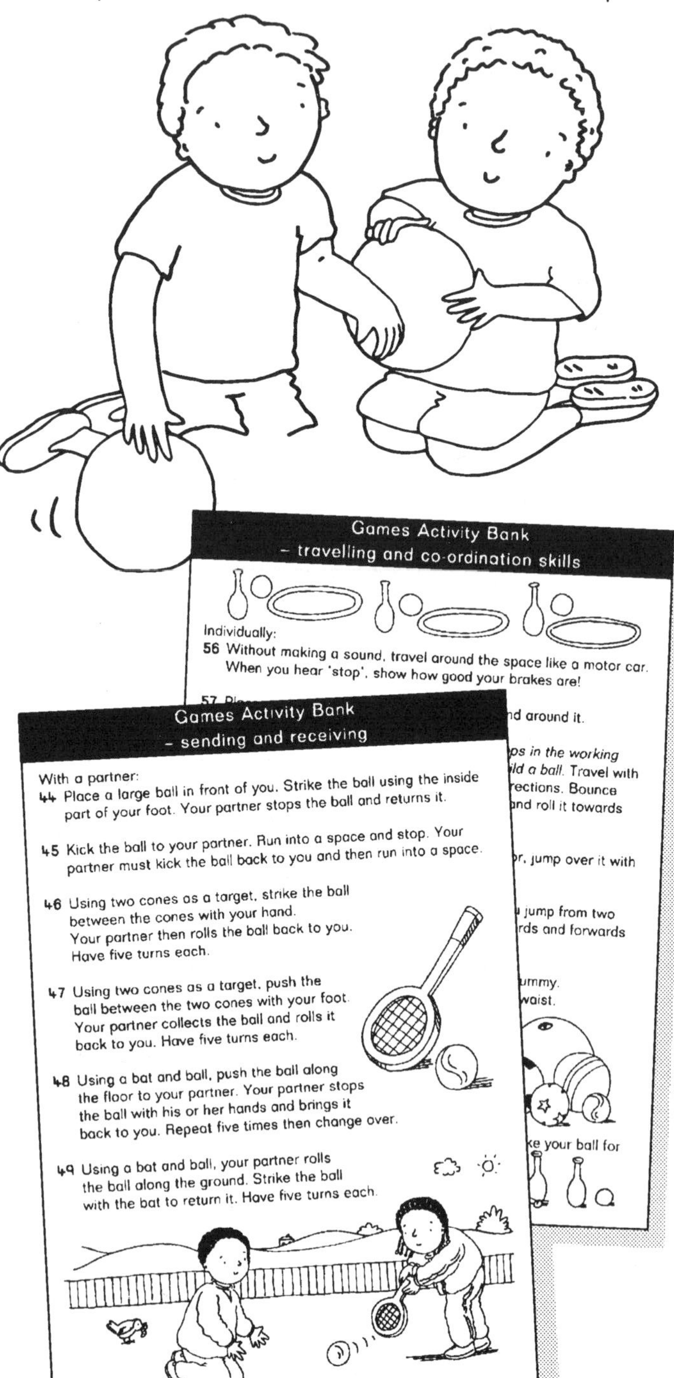

Games Activity Bank
– travelling and co-ordination skills

Individually:
56 Without making a sound, travel around the space like a motor car. When you hear 'stop', show how good your brakes are!

Games Activity Bank
– sending and receiving

With a partner:
44 Place a large ball in front of you. Strike the ball using the inside part of your foot. Your partner stops the ball and returns it.
45 Kick the ball to your partner. Run into a space and stop. Your partner must kick the ball back to you and then run into a space.
46 Using two cones as a target, strike the ball between the cones with your hand. Your partner then rolls the ball back to you. Have five turns each.
47 Using two cones as a target, push the ball between the two cones with your foot. Your partner collects the ball and rolls it back to you. Have five turns each.
48 Using a bat and ball, push the ball along the floor to your partner. Your partner stops the ball with his or her hands and brings it back to you. Repeat five times then change over.
49 Using a bat and ball, your partner rolls the ball along the ground. Strike the ball with the bat to return it. Have five turns each.

RECEIVING LESSON 3 (Y1 AND Y2; P2 AND P3)

To develop and consolidate receiving skills in a stationary position and on the move, using hands and feet. To develop receiving skills using 'hockey' type sticks/bats.

Children working in pairs and in small groups.

30 minutes.

Previous skills/knowledge needed

Previous experience of:

▲ pushing and stopping a ball in twos using feet;
▲ throwing and catching in twos;
▲ applying these skills in a game of '1-2-3-4' in fours (see 'Receiving lesson 1' on page 41).

Key background information

When using a 'hockey' type stick, always encourage the children to stop the ball before hitting it back. To stop the ball effectively, the body should be behind the stick and hands should be apart. The ball should be pushed gently and be kept on the floor.

Preparation

While the children are changing, it may be helpful to remind them of the activities and games played in previous lessons. For example:

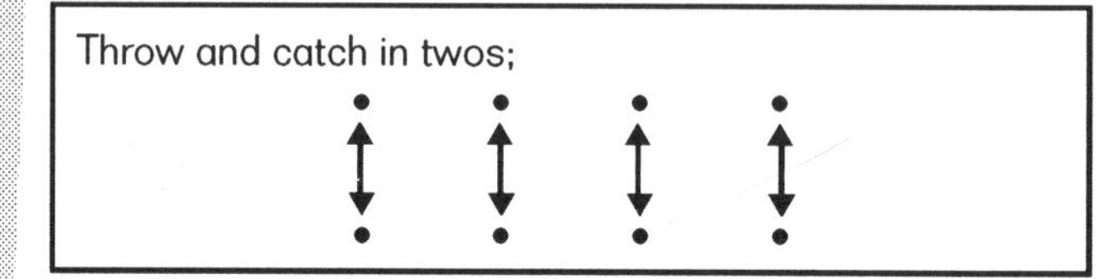
Throw and catch in twos;

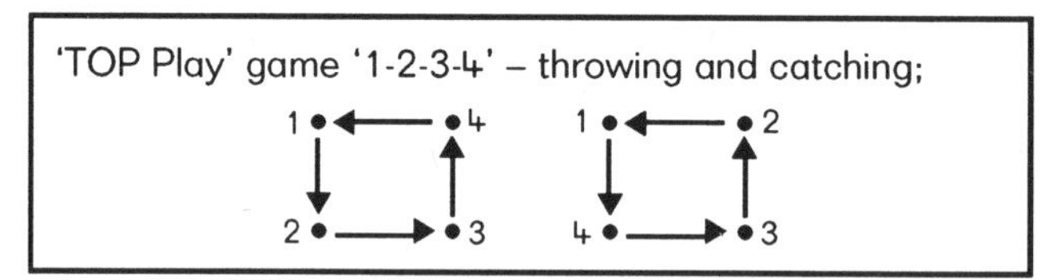
'TOP Play' game '1-2-3-4' – throwing and catching;
1 4 2 3
1 2 4 3

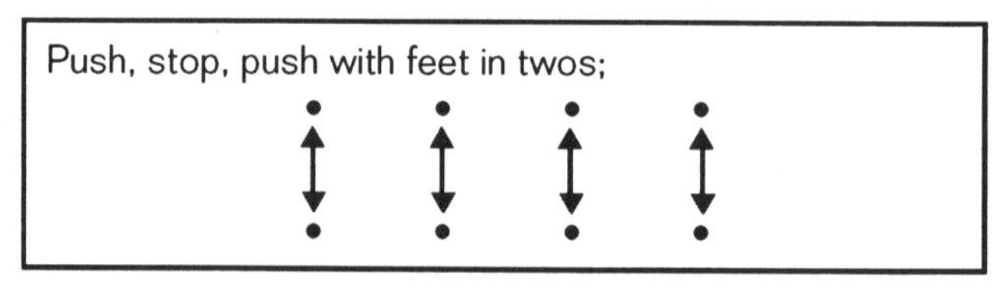
Push, stop, push with feet in twos;

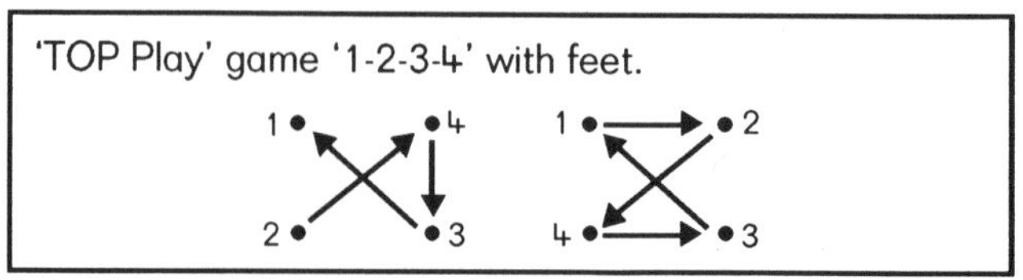
'TOP Play' game '1-2-3-4' with feet.
1 4 2 3
1 2 4 3

Ensure that the equipment is readily accessible. Set out markers and cones to indicate working areas. Make a copy of each of the photocopiable pages 100 and 101.

Resources needed

A selection of balls, marker cones, 'hockey' type sticks/small wooden bats, photocopiable pages 100, 101 and 102, watch with seconds hand or stopwatch.

What to do

Warm-up activity

Begin the lesson by playing 'What time is it Mr Wolf?' (see page 41, 'Receiving lesson 1' for a description of the game). This time the children must return to their home line by jumping two feet – two feet. When the children are caught they return with the teacher as chasers. They too must jump to catch the others when the 'Wolf' calls 'It's dinner time!'.

Skill development

Divide the class into three groups: A, B and C. All of the groups will be working in twos for the first part of the lesson. Organise the class as shown in the diagram below.

Using the photocopiable pages 100, 101 and 102 as a reference, explain the activities for groups B and C to the children and send them off to start. While these two groups start work introduce activity 40 (photocopiable page 101) to group A. The children will need to work with a partner.

▲ One child rolls the ball gently along the ground to his/her partner who has to stop it with the stick/bat.

▲ The ball is then pushed back to the sender with the stick/bat.

▲ Repeat the activity several times before swapping the roles of sender and receiver.

Once this activity is underway, spend some time observing groups B and C. After a couple of minutes, stop these two groups and ask them to see how many passes they can make with their partners in one minute (time this for them with a watch or stopwatch).

Conclusion

Now combine the pairs within each activity into fours and conclude the lesson with 'TOP Play', '1-2-3-4'. See the diagram on page 46 for how to organise this activity:

▲ TOP Play, '1-2-3-4' – with hockey sticks/bats;

▲ TOP Play, '1-2-3-4' – with feet;

▲ TOP Play, '1-2-3-4' – throwing and catching.

Repeat the lesson at other times, rotating the groups, so that the children will try the other activities.

Suggestion(s) for extension

Include the more confident children in one group to enable them to play '1-2-3-4' on the move. The introduction of an interceptor (or 'piggy-in-the-middle') will bring further challenge to their game.

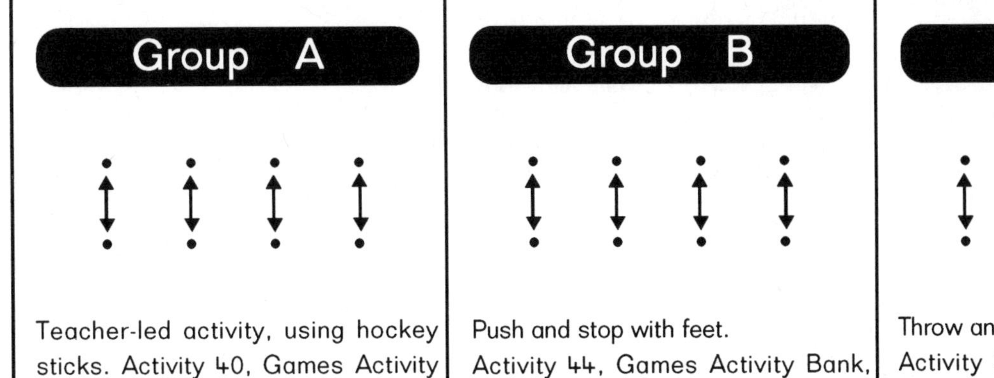
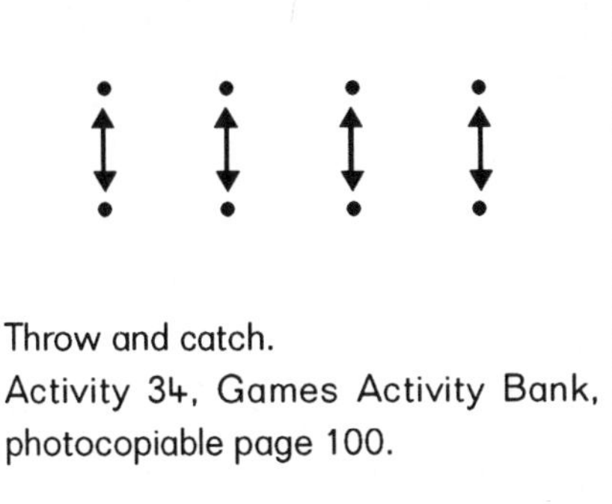

Group A	Group B	Group C
Teacher-led activity, using hockey sticks. Activity 40, Games Activity Bank, photocopiable page 101.	Push and stop with feet. Activity 44, Games Activity Bank, photocopiable page 102.	Throw and catch. Activity 34, Games Activity Bank, photocopiable page 100.

Suggestion(s) for support

Less confident children may find the game '1-2-3-4' easier to master, working in groups of three.

TOP Play 1• 2 • 3 • 4 with hockey sticks	TOP Play 1• 2 • 3 • 4 with feet	TOP Play 1• 2 • 3 • 4 throwing and catching
1• 4• 1• 4•	1• 2• 1• 2•	1• 4• 1• 4•
2• 3• 2• 3•	4• 3• 4• 3•	3• 2• 3• 2•

Assessment opportunities

Observe how well the children work independently without immediate direct intervention.

Reference to photocopiable sheets

Photocopiable pages 100, 101 and 102 provide outline descriptions of some of the activities used in the lesson plan.

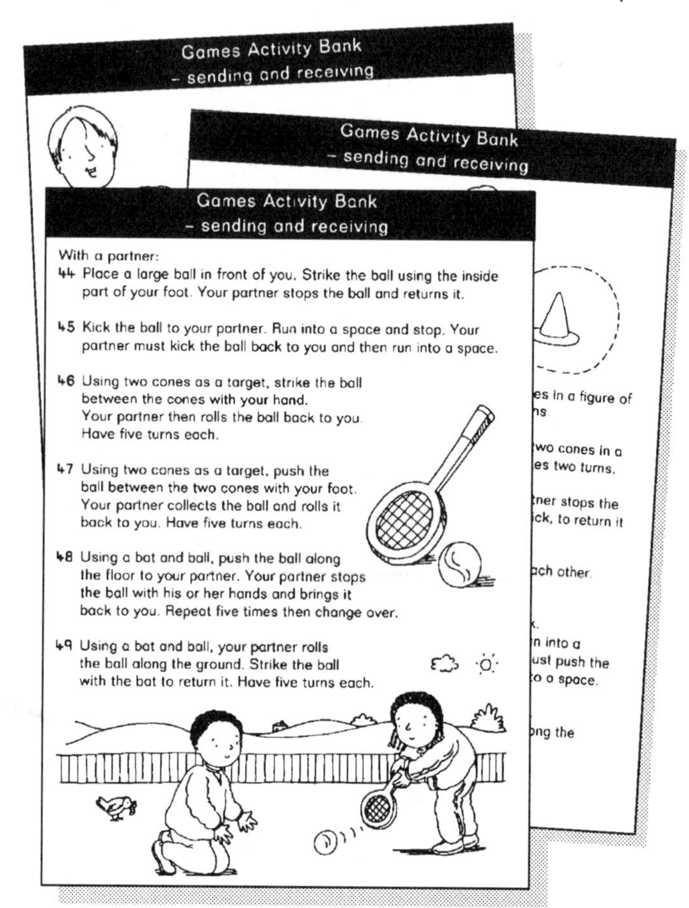

Games Activity Bank
– sending and receiving

With a partner:

44 Place a large ball in front of you. Strike the ball using the inside part of your foot. Your partner stops the ball and returns it.

45 Kick the ball to your partner. Run into a space and stop. Your partner must kick the ball back to you and then run into a space.

46 Using two cones as a target, strike the ball between the cones with your hand. Your partner then rolls the ball back to you. Have five turns each.

47 Using two cones as a target, push the ball between the two cones with your foot. Your partner collects the ball and rolls it back to you. Have five turns each.

48 Using a bat and ball, push the ball along the floor to your partner. Your partner stops the ball with his or her hands and brings it back to you. Repeat five times then change over.

49 Using a bat and ball, your partner rolls the ball along the ground. Strike the ball with the bat to return it. Have five turns each.

TRAVELLING LESSON 1 (R AND Y1; P1 AND P2)

To develop spatial awareness and an ability to move about while controlling a ball.

Children working individually.

20 minutes

Previous skills/knowledge needed

Ability to respond to instructions and to carry, bounce and roll a ball.

Key background information

Young children need a considerable amount of time and practice to develop their spatial awareness. This ability is fundamental to games playing. Until children are able to safely manage their movement among their peers in limited space, little progress can be made towards co-operative and ultimately, competitive play. The majority of lessons with young children should allocate time for the development and consolidation of this important quality. Children should be reminded to constantly look around while moving in a space with others.

Preparation

Ensure that the equipment – balls, hoops and skittles – is safely positioned to the outside of the working area. Make a copy of photocopiable page 104 for your reference.

Resources needed

Large, light, plastic balls (one for each child), skittles, hoops, photocopiable page 104.

What to do

Warm-up activity

Space the children out around the working area and practise activity 56 from the Games Activity Bank (photocopiable page 104). Ask the children to move about the working space, slowly at first, stopping as soon as possible on command. Practise this skill several times.

Skill development

Next, ask the children to collect a hoop and return to their own space. Ask them to jump into it and around it (activity 57 from the Games Activity Bank, photocopiable page 104). Encourage the children to move about the working area slowly. This time, as they move, they should jump into any hoop that is free. Stress the importance of being aware of each other and not bumping into anyone.

Now place a series of hoops and skittles around the edge of the playing area and allocate a ball to each child. Ask the children to move freely around the playing area carrying their ball with two hands. Explain that you are going to play a game, where the children have to do one of the following things when you give a command (demonstrate the skills to the children):

▲ bounce the ball in the hoop;
▲ roll the ball against the skittles from two or three paces away in order to knock them over (explain that the children must stand the skittles up again when they have been knocked over).

Ask the children to move freely about the working area carrying their ball, they must listen carefully for your command. When they hear it, they should run to a hoop or skittle to practise these skills (see activity 58 on photocopiable page 104).

Conclusion
Ask the children to put their balls away carefully and conclude by asking them to move slowly around the area without bumping into any obstacles or each other.

Suggestion(s) for extension
More confident children should be challenged by dispersing the hoops and skittles across the working area, requiring the children to move in different directions.

Suggestion(s) for support
To help children with poorly developed spatial awareness, restrict the final activity to bouncing in the hoops only.

Assessment opportunities
Observe how well the children are able to move about the working space. Can they still move as well when working with a ball?

Reference to photocopiable sheet
Photocopiable page 104 provides a selection of ac suitable for developing travelling skills. Some of the activitie are used within the lesson plan.

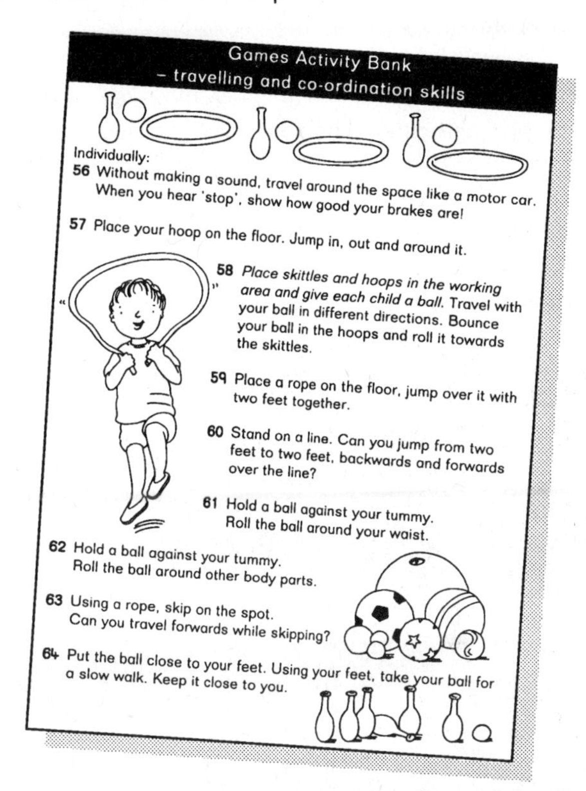

Games Activity Bank
– travelling and co-ordination skills

Individually:
56 Without making a sound, travel around the space like a motor car. When you hear 'stop', show how good your brakes are!
57 Place your hoop on the floor. Jump in, out and around it.
58 *Place skittles and hoops in the working area and give each child a ball.* Travel with your ball in different directions. Bounce your ball in the hoops and roll it towards the skittles.
59 Place a rope on the floor, jump over it with two feet together.
60 Stand on a line. Can you jump from two feet to two feet, backwards and forwards over the line?
61 Hold a ball against your tummy. Roll the ball around your waist.
62 Hold a ball against your tummy. Roll the ball around other body parts.
63 Using a rope, skip on the spot. Can you travel forwards while skipping?
64 Put the ball close to your feet. Using your feet, take your ball for a slow walk. Keep it close to you.

TRAVELLING LESSON 2 (R AND Y1; P1 AND P2)

To learn about and develop close control of a ball using feet.

Children working individually.
20 minutes.

Previous skills/knowledge needed
Ability to respond to instructions.

Key background information
Young children need to observe their own actions in the early stages of skill development. In order to maintain control of a ball with feet they will need to watch it carefully, virtually all of the time. It is thus very important that the children are given ample space in which to work, or are given clear instructions about the direction in which to work, since less of their attention is available to look around them. When children are practising control of a ball with feet, encourage them to form the habit of frequently stopping the ball in order to take a good look at their surroundings.

Preparation
Ensure that a large, light ball is available for each child. Make a copy of each of the photocopiable pages 104 and 105.

Resources needed
Large, light, plastic or foam balls, lines on the playground, photocopiable pages 104 and 105.

What to do
Warm-up activity
Warm up the children with a game of 'run, skip, hop'. Play this by assembling the class along a line and placing a set of markers about 20 metres away. The children will make three journeys. On command they must first run to the markers, turn and run back; then skip there and back; and finally, hop there and back.
Skill development
Ask the children to collect a large ball each, find a space and place the ball at their feet. When it is still they must use their feet to push it gently ahead and follow it. The ball should be kept as close to their feet as possible and stopped at regular intervals with hands or feet. (See activity 64, photocopiable page 104.)

Games Activity Bank
– travelling and co-ordination skills

Individually:
56 Without making a sou…
When you hear 'stop'…

57 Place your hoop on t…

62 Hold a ball agai…
Roll the ball aro…

63 Using a rope, s…
Can you travel…

64 Put the ball cl…
a slow walk. K…

Games Activity Bank
– travelling and co-ordination skills

Individually:
65 Find a line on the playground.
Dribble the ball along the line using your feet.

66 Using your feet, dribble the ball between two cones in a figure of '8'.

67 Using a hockey stick, dribble the ball between the two cones in a figure of '8'.

68 Using a bat, push the ball across the playground.
Stop the ball with the bat.

69 Using a hockey stick and ball, take your ball for a slow walk. Keep the ball close to the stick (slightly in front of your body).

70 Find a line on the playground. Using a stick and ball, dribble the ball along the line.

71 Balance a ball on your bat. Let the ball move around.
Can you go for a slow walk?

72 Balance a ball on your bat. Let it fall off and bounce.
Can you collect it on your bat again?

Ask the children to find a line on the playground. After making sure they can move safely ahead, ask the children to practise dribbling the ball along the line with their feet (activity 65, photocopiable page 105). Remind the children to keep the ball close to them and use the inside of their feet for better control.
Conclusion
Conclude the lesson with 'football tag'. Choose three or four children to be taggers. All the children carry a ball with two hands. The taggers must touch the others with their ball.

When tagged, the children must stand stationary and place the ball between their feet to keep it still. The children who have been caught have to remain frozen until the end of the game when all the children have been tagged.

Suggestion(s) for extension
Ask the more confident children to use both feet to dribble the ball forward.

Suggestion(s) for support
Encourage less confident children to use their hands, if necessary, to stop the ball and keep it close.

Assessment opportunities
Observe how closely the children are able to keep their ball to their feet. Can they keep the ball on the line? Do they keep the ball still in the tagging game when caught?

Reference to photocopiable sheets
Photocopiable pages 104 and 105 contain a bank of activities useful for developing the children's travelling and co-ordination skills. Some of the activities used in the lesson plan are outlined on these sheets.

TRAVELLING LESSON 3 (R AND Y1; P1 AND P2)

To develop travelling skills using a bat and large light ball.
Children working individually.
20 minutes.

Previous skills/knowledge needed
Ability to hold and manipulate a small bat with one or both hands. Ability to respond to instructions.

Key background information
Young children will find controlling a ball with an implement while on the move very difficult, and will have to concentrate hard in order to achieve some success. In the early stages, a large ball together with a large bat face will ensure that contact with the ball is made.

Preparation

Ensure that sufficient bats and balls are available to equip the whole class. Make a copy of photocopiable page 105 to refer to.

Resources needed

Light wooden or plastic bats, large plastic or foam balls, photocopiable page 105.

What to do

Warm-up activity

Warm up the children with the 'sideways shuffle'. Assemble them along a line and ask them to turn sideways on. On command they have to move sideways across the playing area with a 'step-close-step' action. Try it slowly at first and then quicken up a little.

Skill development

Organise the children to collect a bat and ball. Show them how to push the ball across the playground with the bat (activity 68, photocopiable page 105). Explain to the children that the ball should remain on the ground and the bat should remain close to it. The children may grip the bat with one or two hands. Encourage them to stop the rolling ball with the bat at frequent intervals. Remind them to keep their feet out of the way and to stay to the side of the ball. Allow the children ample time to practise.

When the children have gained some confidence in this skill, invite them to push the ball with the bat a little harder. This time they should run after it and stop it with the bat. Practise this several times. Let the children explore different ways of pushing and stopping the ball with their bats.

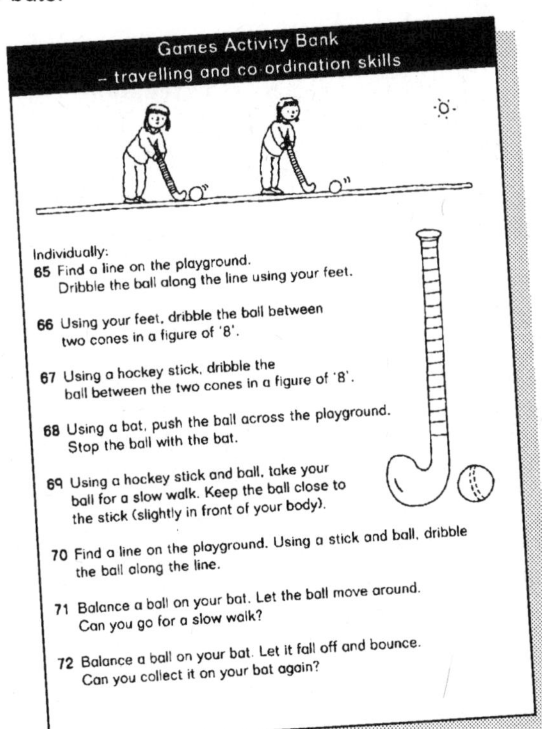

Games Activity Bank
– travelling and co-ordination skills

Individually:

65 Find a line on the playground. Dribble the ball along the line using your feet.

66 Using your feet, dribble the ball between two cones in a figure of '8'.

67 Using a hockey stick, dribble the ball between the two cones in a figure of '8'.

68 Using a bat, push the ball across the playground. Stop the ball with the bat.

69 Using a hockey stick and ball, take your ball for a slow walk. Keep the ball close to the stick (slightly in front of your body).

70 Find a line on the playground. Using a stick and ball, dribble the ball along the line.

71 Balance a ball on your bat. Let the ball move around. Can you go for a slow walk?

72 Balance a ball on your bat. Let it fall off and bounce. Can you collect it on your bat again?

Conclusion

Ensure that the children put the equipment away safely and then conclude the lesson with 'run, hop, skip' (see the Warm-up activity on page 48).

Suggestion(s) for extension

Make the activity more challenging for more able children by inviting them to use small plastic hockey sticks (they should continue to work with a large ball).

Suggestion(s) for support

Those children who find handling a bat difficult should practise using their hands as the bat.

Assessment opportunities

Observe how closely the children manage to keep the ball to their bat. Are they able to stop the ball effectively with their bats? Can they keep their feet out of the way of the ball when dribbling it forward with their bats?

Reference to photocopiable sheets

Photocopiable page 105 provides useful reference material including many activities covering the skills of co-ordination and travelling.

TRAVELLING LESSON 1 (Y1 AND Y2; P2 AND P3)

To further develop travelling skills with hands controlling the ball. To practise a combination of travelling and sending skills in a game situation.

Children working individually and as a small group.

20 minutes.

Previous skills/knowledge needed
Confidence in handling a large ball. Ability to move safely and quickly around the working space.

Key background information
In the latter half of the key stage, young children are able to respond to more complex challenges. They begin increasingly to interact with their peers in meaningful ways and are able to put together combinations of their own actions with consistency. Skill practice can now include directional change and variability, with turning movements, as the children should be less constrained by an ability to work in one direction only.

Preparation
Ensure that sufficient balls, hoops and ropes are available for each child in the class. Make a copy of photocopiable page 104 for your reference.

Resources needed
Large, light balls, hoops and ropes, photocopiable page 104.

What to do
Warm-up activity

Warm up the class up with the 'numbers game'. The children play by moving freely about the working area. They must start the game at walking pace and under your guidance, speed up. At intervals, call out a number and explain that the children must organise themselves as quickly as possible into groups of that number. For example, '2!' means pairs, '3!' means groups of three and so on.

Skill development

Invite the children to collect a ball and explore as many ways as possible to move about the space with their ball using hands and feet. Whichever way the children choose, encourage them to keep their ball as close to their bodies as they can.

Use the 'numbers game' to organise the children into groups of three. Choose one group to act as taggers for 'tunnel tag'. Every child carries a ball and the taggers try to touch the others with their ball or alternatively, if using foam balls, hit them below the waist with their ball. The balls may be thrown but *not* kicked. The children who are tagged must then stand still with their legs apart. They can be freed if somebody else rolls their ball between their legs. Don't forget to regularly change the taggers.

Conclusion

Conclude the lesson by asking the children to work individually on activities 61 and 62 (photocopiable page 104), in which the children have to roll their ball in a controlled manner around their bodies.

Suggestion(s) for extension
More confident children should be encouraged to change their speed and direction of travel as often as possible.

Suggestion(s) for support
Less confident children should practise only one way of travelling with their ball rather than seeking to practise a variety of methods.

Assessment opportunities
Observe how well the children retain control of their ball when moving with it. Do they keep it close? Are they able to use either hand when bouncing the ball and either foot when dribbling along the ground? How well do they use space in the tagging game?

Reference to photocopiable sheets

Photocopiable page 104 contains a bank of ideas suitable for developing and using in this activity.

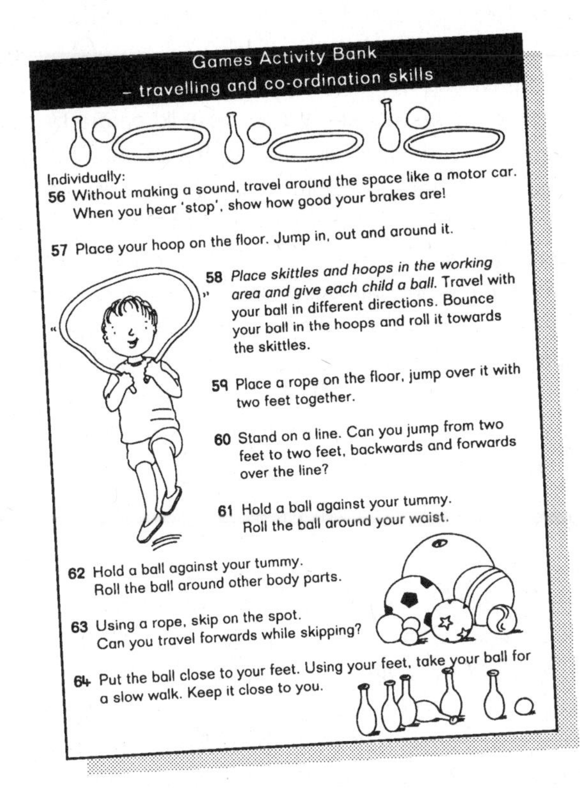

Games Activity Bank
– travelling and co-ordination skills

Individually:

56 Without making a sound, travel around the space like a motor car. When you hear 'stop', show how good your brakes are!

57 Place your hoop on the floor. Jump in, out and around it.

58 *Place skittles and hoops in the working area and give each child a ball.* Travel with your ball in different directions. Bounce your ball in the hoops and roll it towards the skittles.

59 Place a rope on the floor, jump over it with two feet together.

60 Stand on a line. Can you jump from two feet to two feet, backwards and forwards over the line?

61 Hold a ball against your tummy. Roll the ball around your waist.

62 Hold a ball against your tummy. Roll the ball around other body parts.

63 Using a rope, skip on the spot. Can you travel forwards while skipping?

64 Put the ball close to your feet. Using your feet, take your ball for a slow walk. Keep it close to you.

TRAVELLING LESSON 2 (Y1 AND Y2; P2 AND P3)

To develop ball control using feet and to learn how to change direction. To practise travelling with a ball using feet within a competitive game.

Children working individually.

20 minutes.

Previous skills/knowledge needed

Ability to control a ball with feet when working in a straight line. Ability to move confidently in the working area.

Key background information

This activity places greater demands on the children by asking them to co-ordinate a change of direction while still retaining control of the ball. In effect, they are required to do two things at once – manage their own bodies in space as well as directing the ball. Mastery of this skill represents a significant step forward in the growing ability of young children to play a competitive game in a meaningful way.

Preparation

Ensure that sufficient balls, cones and hoops are available for each child. Sub-divide the working area into three equal areas using lines or cones.

Resources needed

Large, light balls, hoops and cones.

What to do

Warm-up activity

Warm up the class with 'closing in' – an activity which gradually reduces the working space of the children. Ask them to move freely about the working area. Start slowly at first and then quicken up. Then restrict the space by a third. After practice, restrict the working area by another third, so that the children are then having to move around in a much smaller space. Encourage them to be vigilant. They will have to stop, turn and change their direction much more frequently.

Skill development

Ask the children to collect a ball and hoop each. Ask them to practise dribbling the ball with their feet around the hoop in one direction and then the other. After a few minutes practice, encourage them to stop the ball with their foot when they are half-way around, pause and then carry on dribbling it. Remind the children to use the insides of their feet for better control, making sure that they keep the ball close to their feet.

Conclusion

Conclude the lesson with 'name ball'. Ask the class to return all the balls to their storage baskets. Retain a basket of balls in the centre of the working area. The teacher then calls out five or six names and rolls the same number of balls in several directions away from the centre. The children whose names have been called must chase a ball, stop it with their foot and then dribble it back to the centre as fast as possible. The rest of the class must remain still, acting as obstacles for the dribblers. Work through the whole class so that every child has an opportunity to retrieve a ball.

Suggestion(s) for extension
Encourage the more confident children to use both feet for dribbling the ball – not just their preferred one.

Suggestion(s) for support
Less confident children may need further practice dribbling the ball ahead in a straight line. Ask them to lay out a skipping rope and practise dribbling around it, following the line closely.

Assessment opportunities
Observe how well the children keep control of the ball when they are being required to constantly change direction as they circle their hoops. How quickly and accurately are they able to return the ball to the centre in 'name ball'?

TRAVELLING LESSON 3 (Y1 AND Y2; P2 AND P3)

To consolidate and refine a range of travelling skills with a ball.

Children working individually and with a partner.

30 minutes.

Previous skills/knowledge needed
Experience of a range of travelling skills with a ball using hands and feet. Ability to practise independently.

Key background information
This type of lesson should be included in the games programme at regular intervals. As well as introducing new skills to children it enables them to practise and refine existing ones.

Preparation
Ensure that sufficient equipment is available – balls, hoops, skittles. Divide the working space into six equal areas (see the diagram below).

Resources needed
Large, light balls, hoops, skittles.

What to do
Warm-up activity

Warm up the class with a game of 'scarecrow tag'. Choose three children to be taggers. When the children are tagged they must stand still with their arms stretched out. They can be 'freed' if another runner ducks under their outstretched arms.

Skill development

Organise the children into six groups and allocate them to one of the six activities described below (see diagram). Position yourself close to games 5 and 6 where the activity is new and most guidance will be required. Allow four or five minutes' practice on each activity and rotate the groups.

▲ Game 1 – bounce the ball around the skittle and back.
▲ Game 2 – dribble the ball with your feet around the skittle and back.
▲ Game 3 – carry your ball around the skittle and back.
▲ Game 4 – dribble the ball around the skittle and back using a hockey stick.
▲ Game 5 – 'tunnel tag' as described in 'Travelling lesson 1' on page 50.
▲ Game 6 – 'tunnel tag' (as for Game 5, above).

Conclusion

Ensure that the children help you put back all the equipment. Make time to talk about the work they have done. Do they feel that their techniques have improved during this practice?

Suggestion(s) for extension/support
This lesson represents consolidation and there should be no need to differentiate. It enables all the children to improve and concentrate on the basic travelling skills.

Assessment opportunities
Observe how well the children remain on task and persevere with their practice. Are they able to evaluate their work?

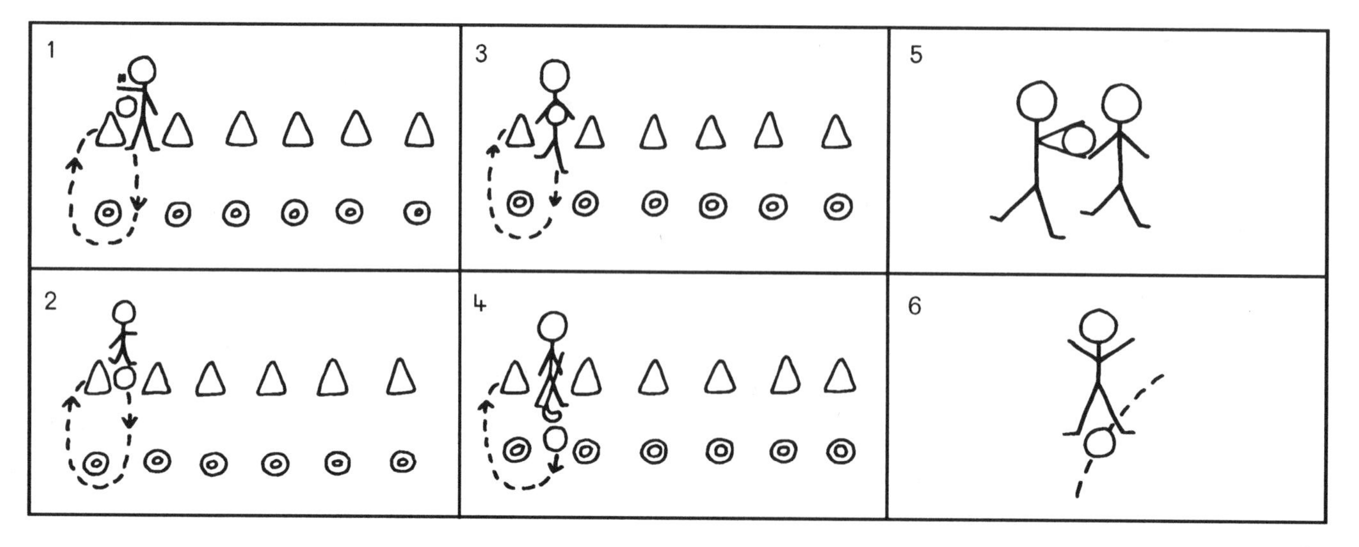

Gymnastics

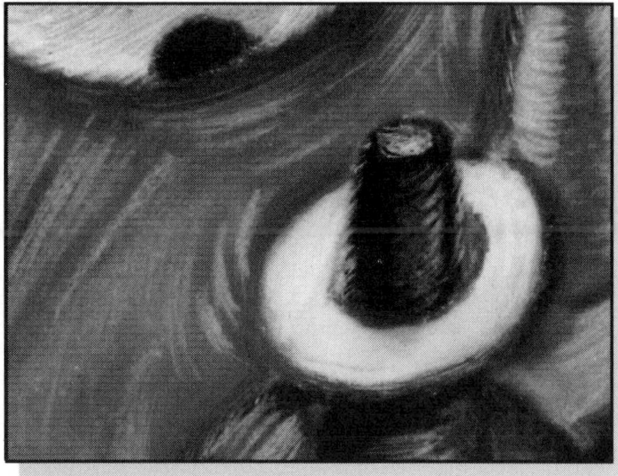

An effectively taught gymnastics curriculum will enable young children to learn much about the possibilities and limitations of their bodies in movement. They will come to appreciate that, in answering a series of movement tasks, their bodies are capable of responding with a wide variety of actions and combinations of actions.

The gymnastics programme for young children additionally seeks to enhance maturational physical development by extending the basic skills, such as walking, running, climbing and jumping through a series of progressive physical challenges. Floorwork will present opportunities for the children to explore, refine and extend basic movement patterns. Work on apparatus will bring excitement and further challenge as children experience jumping off and over, hanging, heaving (lifting body weight when hanging by arms), climbing, and balancing upon.

Children will spend most of their time in gymnastics in active exploration of movement themes and tasks. This necessitates a good deal of appropriate guidance and encouragement from the teacher. The children should be presented with open-ended tasks which they seek to answer in their own way and at their own level, always within prescribed safety limits. There are times, however, when the teacher should adopt a more direct approach and introduce whole class activities in order to encourage the movement qualities associated with control and sound technique, such as good landings when jumping, safe rolling and so on.

The gymnastics lesson

The sample lessons described in this chapter are examples of gymnastic activities that are appropriate for young children of five to seven years. Three lessons are offered for each year group at Key Stage 1 (P1 to P3 in Scotland), making a total of nine lessons over the key stage. The lessons are progressive within each year and over the three year period. They can be added to and adapted to provide further lessons. This may be done using the activity ideas outlined in the Gymnastics Activity Bank (photocopiable pages 108 to 116). Alternatively, you may decide to focus on a particular skill, depending on the needs and stage of development of your children.

Gymnastics in these early years is essentially concerned with helping children to refine their running and jumping skills while equipping them with the confidence and skill to manage and manoeuvre their body weight using body parts other than feet. Travelling in a variety of ways across the floor, and over apparatus, provides a unifying focus for the work and the lessons described suggest ways in which a wide range of travelling skills can be developed using appropriate movement themes and tasks.

A series of 'prompt sheets' (photocopiable pages 117 to 124) are provided which can be enlarged and displayed at strategic points around the working area. The sheets serve two purposes. Firstly, you may choose to use them as an *aide-mémoire*, particularly when encouraging the children to bring more variety into their work. Secondly, as the children become older and effective readers themselves, you may ask them to refer to the sheets directly in seeking their own responses and ideas to a particular movement theme.

Two technical sheets (photocopiable pages 125 and 126) are provided which refer to the forward and backward roll. It is inevitable that some children will offer these rolls as a response to a movement task. From a health and safety perspective it is critical that children are taught to perform these rolls in a technically sound manner. These sheets highlight the important teaching points in achieving safe rolling actions.

The Gymnastic Activity Bank (photocopiable pages 108 to 116) suggests a wide range of appropriate activities associated with the main gymnastic actions – jumping, rolling, travelling and balancing – which can be used to further develop the work suggested in the sample lessons.

Safety in gymnastics

Gymnastics in physical education, in particular the use of apparatus, requires stringent safety procedures. Teachers are, in general, very aware of the potential hazards that these lessons represent and the guidelines below answer some of the main concerns that teachers hold.

Young children are very interested in finding out about their physical capabilities but are not always able to make sound judgements about what constitutes an appropriate response to a movement task. You must be prepared to give clear guidance at all times to ensure that progression always builds upon known skill levels.

The following guidelines address some of the commonly asked questions regarding the creation of a safe working environment in gymnastics.

How do we ensure that the equipment is safe to use?

Gymnnastics equipment should be frequently checked by all teachers using it. Any equipment deemed unsafe for use should be clearly labelled and removed from the working area until it has been repaired. All large, fixed and portable apparatus should be subject to an annual inspection and maintenance programme by a qualified maintenance firm. Apparatus should conform to standards recognised by the British Standards Institute or meet the European CEN Standard.

Teachers *should not* under any circumstances attempt to fix broken apparatus themselves.

Questions regarding the safety of gymnastics equipment might include the following:

How should we store and maintain our mats?

▲ Where possible mats should be stored flat.

▲ They should be free of holes and tears.

▲ Mats should be covered with a material that is easy to clean, and have a base which is stable when in contact with the floor (this necessitates cleaning the underside from time to time).

▲ They should meet existing fire regulations.

Where should we place mats in the apparatus part of the lesson?

The use of mats to absorb landings is a feature of the gymnastics programme. Matting should be placed to indicate a suitable landing area when dismounting from apparatus. They should not be placed indiscriminately around the working area. Where possible, work away from walls towards the centre of the hall.

In addition to using mats to indicate a landing area, it is wise to place mats beneath pieces of apparatus such as the climbing frame and ropes, where children are encouraged to work from a height – particularly in the early stages of skill development. You may like to use coloured tape to indicate to the children the height to which they are allowed to go, depending on their stage of development. General purpose gymnastic mats ought to offer protection against serious head injury, should a fall occur. Make sure that the children are aware, from the outset, of the difference between mats placed for landing purposes and those used in a precautionary way.

Should the teacher help to move equipment?

Yes. The teacher will clearly need be involved in helping the children to move the largest and most awkward items of apparatus in the initial stages of learning. The care with which the teacher lifts, carries and places equipment will act as a positive role model for the children to copy.

Teach the children to lift apparatus in a technically safe manner by keeping their backs straight and using their legs. As a general rule, apparatus should be lifted by the minimum number of children required to do so. It helps to organise the apparatus around the edge of the hall where practicable so that children do not have to carry the apparatus very far.

Ensuring suitability of work and providing appropriate challenges

It is important that the school establishes a whole-school scheme of work for gymnastics, and that teachers pass on accurate records of the work they have covered. Any child with co-ordination or medical problems should be known to the whole staff, so that appropriate provision can be made and extra precautions taken if necessary.

What is a safe working noise level?

Young children will naturally wish to express their enjoyment and delight of physical activity and this should be expected. However, it is essential that you set clear rules for noise levels, explaining when you expect the children to be silent and helping them to understand the dangers of a noisy working environment. For example, the children must be silent when you are giving instructions to the whole class. Encourage them to perform movement as sensitively and quietly as possible, as quiet movement is usually controlled movement. The teacher's voice should always be able to be heard and it should never be necessary to use a whistle.

A checklist of good practice

The following checklist provides a set of guidelines for you to observe at regular intervals in order to monitor and review the effectiveness of your lessons.

Teaching objectives:

▲ to provide a clear purpose to all lessons with specific reference to skill progression, underpinned with health and fitness;

▲ to create a positive classroom atmosphere, conveying that gymnastics is something that all children can take part in, irrespective of their ability;

▲ to value all positive contributions to the lesson, encouraging individual and collective efforts;

▲ to give technical advice in addition to encouragement;

▲ to encourage children to build upon previous work in progressing levels of skill and creativity;

▲ to set tasks that reflect the capabilities and needs of the children;

▲ to use a variety of appropriate teaching and learning styles;

▲ to provide opportunities for the children to evaluate and plan their work and the work of others.

Good lessons are characterised by:

▲ effective class organisation;

▲ high levels of activity and involvement;

▲ a safe, yet challenging environment;

▲ a brisk pace, but with opportunities for consolidation, refinement and reflection;

▲ well-motivated children who are concentrating well, extending themselves physically and working hard.

Key stage progression

Throughout Key Stage 1, the children should adapt, refine and practise, both on the floor and on apparatus, the basic actions of:

▲ travelling using hands and feet;

▲ turning;

▲ rolling;

▲ jumping;

▲ balancing;

▲ swinging and climbing.

They should also be given opportunities to link and repeat a series of actions, both on the floor and using apparatus. Over the key stage, children will develop and progress and will need to be given structured guidance and encouragement in order to do this. The summary below gives guidelines for the content appropriate to each specific year group.

Reception (P1)

▲ Exploring a variety of actions taking weight, and travelling, on hands and feet;

▲ jumping – using the floor, and from low platforms, with an emphasis upon safe landings;

▲ developing effective use of space;

▲ lifting, carrying and placing mats.

Main focus – shape in movement, changing direction and movement pathways.

Year 1 (P2)

▲ Jumping quarter and half turns using floor and low apparatus, with an emphasis upon lift at take-off and controlled landings;

▲ rocking and rolling actions;

▲ linking actions together;

▲ lifting, carrying and placing mats and benches.

Main focus – changes and contrasts in speed of movement.

Year 2 (P3)

▲ Holding balances on small and large bases;

▲ extension in movement;

▲ sequence-making, linking similar types of movement for example, two different rolling actions;

▲ refinement and repetition of movement patterns;

▲ lifting, carrying and placing of mats, benches and portable apparatus.

Main focus – working at different levels and creating different shapes in movement.

GYMNASTICS – RECEPTION /P1 (LESSON 1)

To explore a variety of actions taking weight on feet and hands and to develop spatial awareness and an ability to work in own space.

Children working individually.

30 minutes.

Previous skills/knowledge needed

Ability to follow simple instructions and an understanding of basic action words such as stretch, high, low and small.

Key background information

Much time will need to be given to developing the spatial awareness of young children so that they are able to work safely in the relatively crowded and small working space afforded by the typical infant school hall. It is equally important, in the interests of safety, that young children learn to respond rapidly to instructions. The movement skills of young children will be at an early stage of development. Movement tasks and themes should therefore involve actions using large stable body parts, or a combination of small body parts, with the emphasis upon control.

Preparation

Ensure that the apparatus (hoops) is accessible and safely stored around the edge of the hall. Make a copy of each of the photocopiable pages 109, 110, 113 and 114 (to develop the main activity, if required).

Resources needed

Plastic hoops, one per child; photocopiable pages 109, 110, 113 and 114.

What to do

Warm-up activity

Invite the children to find a space and sit down. In their own space ask them to stand and stretch up high ('thin as a pin'). Now ask them to curl up small ('small as a ball') on the floor. Repeat this task several times. Then ask them to walk *slowly* making different pathways around the hall, reminding the children to be careful of others. Explain that when you say 'Stop!' the children should sit down immediately. Practise this several times.

Gymnastic activity

Ask the children to collect a hoop, bring it back to their own space and sit in it. Make sure that the hoops are spaced out as much as possible. Explain that you would like the children to walk around the hall *without* stepping into a hoop and then return to their own hoop again.

Encourage the children to practise the following skills:

▲ jumping in and out of their own hoop;

▲ jumping around their hoop, first in one direction then the other;

▲ moving on all fours around their hoop, first in one direction and then the other – encourage the children to move slowly and with good control.

When the children have had sufficient time to practise these new skills, ask them to return their hoops carefully and go back to their spaces.

Conclusion

Conclude the lesson with running or bouncing very lightly on the spot. Develop the work in future lessons with selected activities from the Gymnastic Activity Bank – 'Jumping' (photocopiable pages 109 and 110), and 'Travelling' (photocopiable pages 113 and 114).

Suggestion(s) for extension

More confident children should be encouraged to work *across* their hoops on all fours making sure that they do not touch them with either hands or feet.

Suggestion(s) for support

It will help less confident children if the hoops are spaced around the hall prior to the class entering, in order to immediately define individual working spaces.

Assessment opportunities

Observe how well the children respond to instructions. Do they stop immediately on command? Can they work effectively in their own space and answer the task?

Reference to photocopiable sheets

Photocopiable pages 109, 110, 113 and 114 suggest a range of ideas that may be used to support and develop the main activity. They may be used within the lesson or as the basis for subsequent gymnastic lessons.

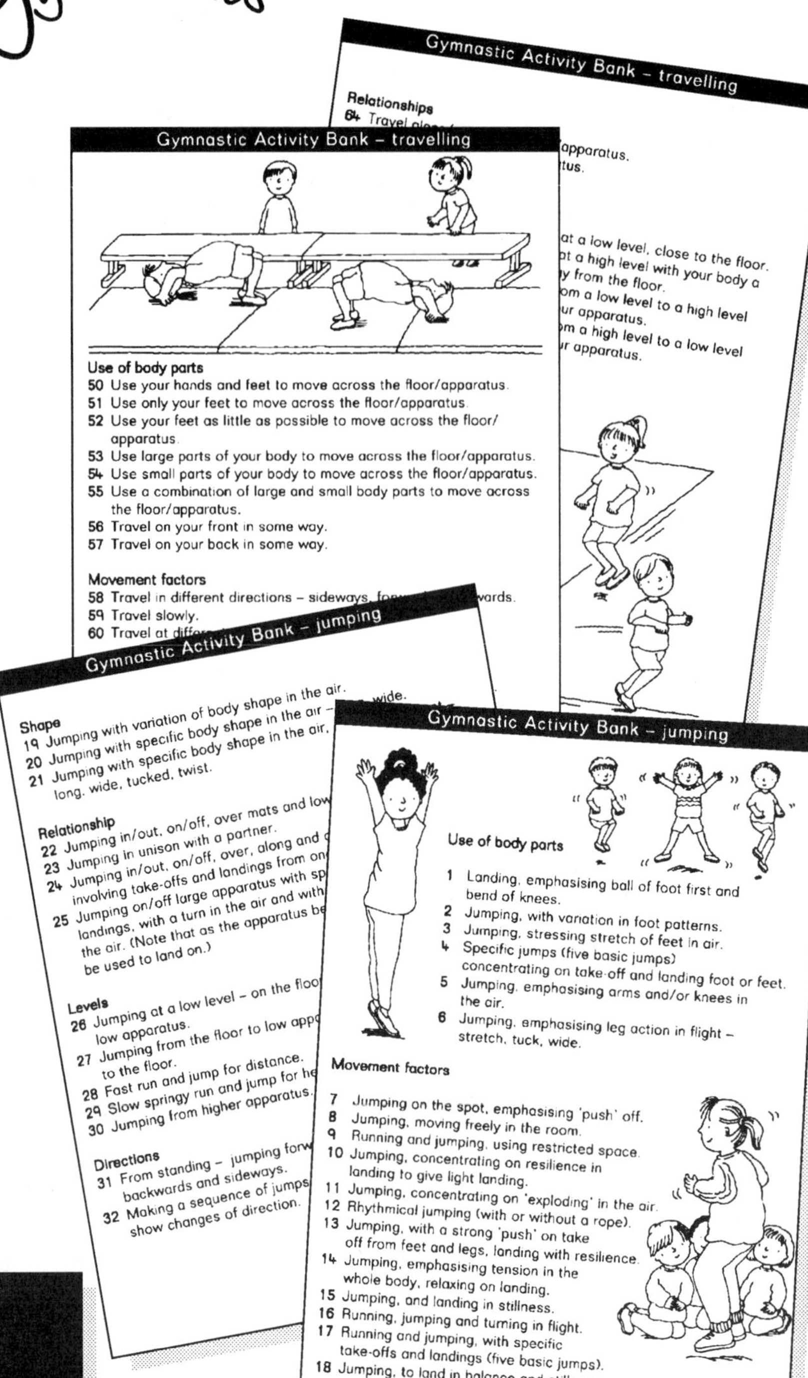

Gymnastic Activity Bank – travelling

Relationships
64 Travel ...
...apparatus.
...tus.
...at a low level, close to the floor.
...t a high level with your body a...
...y from the floor.
...om a low level to a high level
...ur apparatus.
...m a high level to a low level
...r apparatus.

Gymnastic Activity Bank – travelling

Use of body parts
50 Use your hands and feet to move across the floor/apparatus.
51 Use only your feet to move across the floor/apparatus.
52 Use your feet as little as possible to move across the floor/apparatus.
53 Use large parts of your body to move across the floor/apparatus.
54 Use small parts of your body to move across the floor/apparatus.
55 Use a combination of large and small body parts to move across the floor/apparatus.
56 Travel on your front in some way.
57 Travel on your back in some way.

Movement factors
58 Travel in different directions – sideways, ...wards.
59 Travel slowly.
60 Travel at ...

Gymnastic Activity Bank – jumping

Shape
19 Jumping with variation of body shape in the air.
20 Jumping with specific body shape in the air – ... wide.
21 Jumping with specific body shape in the air, long, wide, tucked, twist.

Relationship
22 Jumping in/out, on/off, over mats and low...
23 Jumping in unison with a partner.
24 Jumping in/out, on/off, over, along and ... involving take-offs and landings from on...
25 Jumping on/off large apparatus with sp... landings, with a turn in the air and with... the air. (Note that as the apparatus be... be used to land on.)

Levels
26 Jumping at a low level – on the floo... low apparatus.
27 Jumping from the floor to low app... to the floor.
28 Fast run and jump for distance.
29 Slow springy run and jump for he...
30 Jumping from higher apparatus.

Directions
31 From standing – jumping forw... backwards and sideways.
32 Making a sequence of jumps... show changes of direction.

Gymnastic Activity Bank – jumping

Use of body parts
1 Landing, emphasising ball of foot first and bend of knees.
2 Jumping, with variation in foot patterns.
3 Jumping, stressing stretch of feet in air.
4 Specific jumps (five basic jumps) concentrating on take-off and landing foot or feet.
5 Jumping, emphasising arms and/or knees in the air.
6 Jumping, emphasising leg action in flight – stretch, tuck, wide.

Movement factors
7 Jumping on the spot, emphasising 'push' off.
8 Jumping, moving freely in the room.
9 Running and jumping, using restricted space.
10 Jumping, concentrating on resilience in landing to give light landing.
11 Jumping, concentrating on 'exploding' in the air.
12 Rhythmical jumping (with or without a rope).
13 Jumping, with a strong 'push' on take off from feet and legs, landing with resilience.
14 Jumping, emphasising tension in the whole body, relaxing on landing.
15 Jumping, and landing in stillness.
16 Running, jumping and turning in flight.
17 Running and jumping, with specific take-offs and landings (five basic jumps).
18 Jumping, to land in balance and stillness.

GYMNASTICS – RECEPTION/P1 (LESSON 2)

To refine jumping technique using a low platform and to develop awareness of safety and care for others.

Children working individually and within a group.

30 minutes.

Previous skills/knowledge needed

Ability to respond rapidly to instructions and to work collectively.

Key background information

The ability to jump and land with good control is an essential skill in gymnastics and it is important that children are taught sound jumping technique from the very outset. The main teaching points are:

▲ bend your legs to spring up high;
▲ keep your head up;
▲ land on your toes with your feet apart and knees bent;
▲ try to be still when you land, taking care not to topple forward.

Preparation

Ensure that the apparatus (benches and mats) is readily accessible around the hall. Make a copy of each of the photocopiable pages 109, 110, 113 and 114, if required, (to develop the main activity).

Resources needed

Benches and mats, photocopiable pages 109, 110, 113 and 114 (optional).

What to do

Warm-up activity

Encourage the children to find their own space. Ask them to run lightly around the hall making different pathways. Change to skipping around the hall and then hopping.

Gymnastic activity

After they have practised these skills, ask them to lie down on their backs on the floor. Set the task of making their bodies as wide as possible in this position, then as thin and as narrow as possible. Can they change from one shape to the other as smoothly as possible? Next, turn over onto fronts and repeat this activity – first a wide shape and then a narrow one. Ask the children to move from a wide shape on their back to a narrow shape on their front and vice versa.

Organise the class into groups of six children. Ask each group to set out a bench and two mats as illustrated in the diagram below.

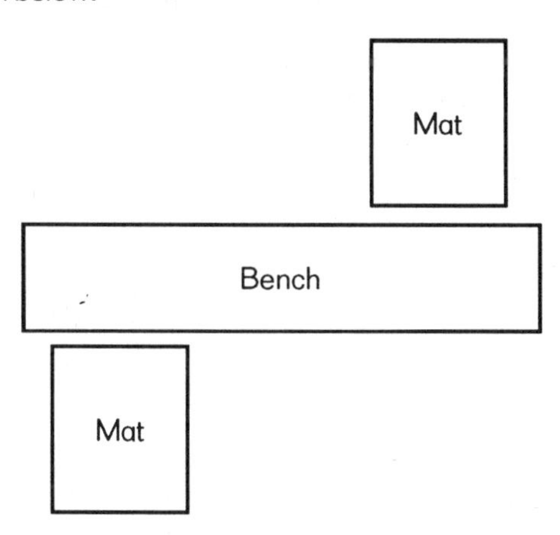

(Ensure that the children are carefully supervised: four children to lift a bench and four to lift a mat – one child to each mat corner. Encourage the children to keep their backs straight and bend their knees when lifting and all lift together.)

Divide each group into two sets of three on either side of their bench facing a mat. Working continuously in a clockwise direction, the task is for each child in turn to *step* onto the bench and show a long, stretched jump from the bench onto the mat. Remind the children that they must not start their jump until they have looked to see that their landing mat is clear. Encourage the children to jump *up* rather than *off* the bench, letting them decide whether to take-off using one foot or two. Ask them: how long can you stay in the air? Remind them to land safely on two feet.

Conclusion

Conclude the lesson by asking each group in turn to put away the apparatus carefully and tidily.

Develop the work with selected activities from the Gymnastic Activity Bank, such as those on photocopiable pages 109, 110, 113 and 114.

Suggestion(s) for extension

Encourage more confident children to make different body shapes on their sides as well as on their fronts and backs.

Suggestion(s) for support

Give less confident children the opportunity to step on and off the bench in the early stages of the activity.

Assessment opportunities

Observe how well the children demonstrate shape in movement. Are they able to jump with confidence and remain still when landing?

Reference to photocopiable sheets

Photocopiable pages 109, 110, 113 and 114 provide a range of ideas that may be used to supplement the main activity, or as the basis for subsequent gymnastic lessons. In addition you may like to use them to focus on a particular skill.

Gymnastic Activity Bank – travelling

Relationships
64 Travel along/across the floor/apparatus.
65 Travel over/under your apparatus.
66 Travel around your apparatus.

Levels
67 Travel at a low level, close to the floor.
68 Travel at a high level with your body a long way from the floor.
69 Move from a low level to a high level using your apparatus.
70 Move from a high level to a low level using your apparatus.

Directions
71 Travel in a straight line.
72 Travel in a curved line.
73 Travel in a circle.
74 Travel in a square.
75 Travel making a zig-zag pathway.

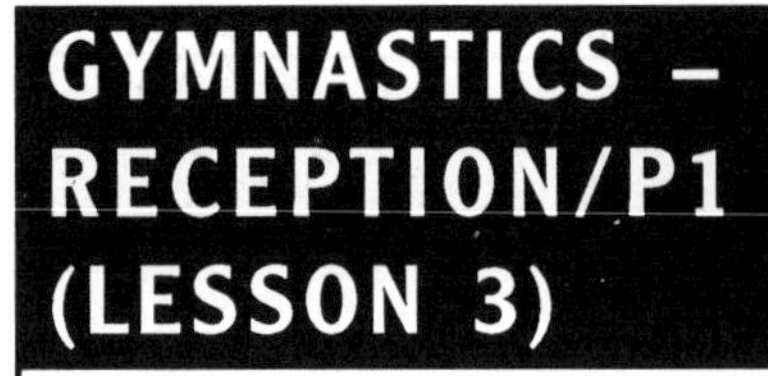

GYMNASTICS – RECEPTION/P1 (LESSON 3)

To learn how to use more challenging apparatus and to develop the skills associated with working responsibly and safely together.

Children working individually and within a group.

30 minutes.

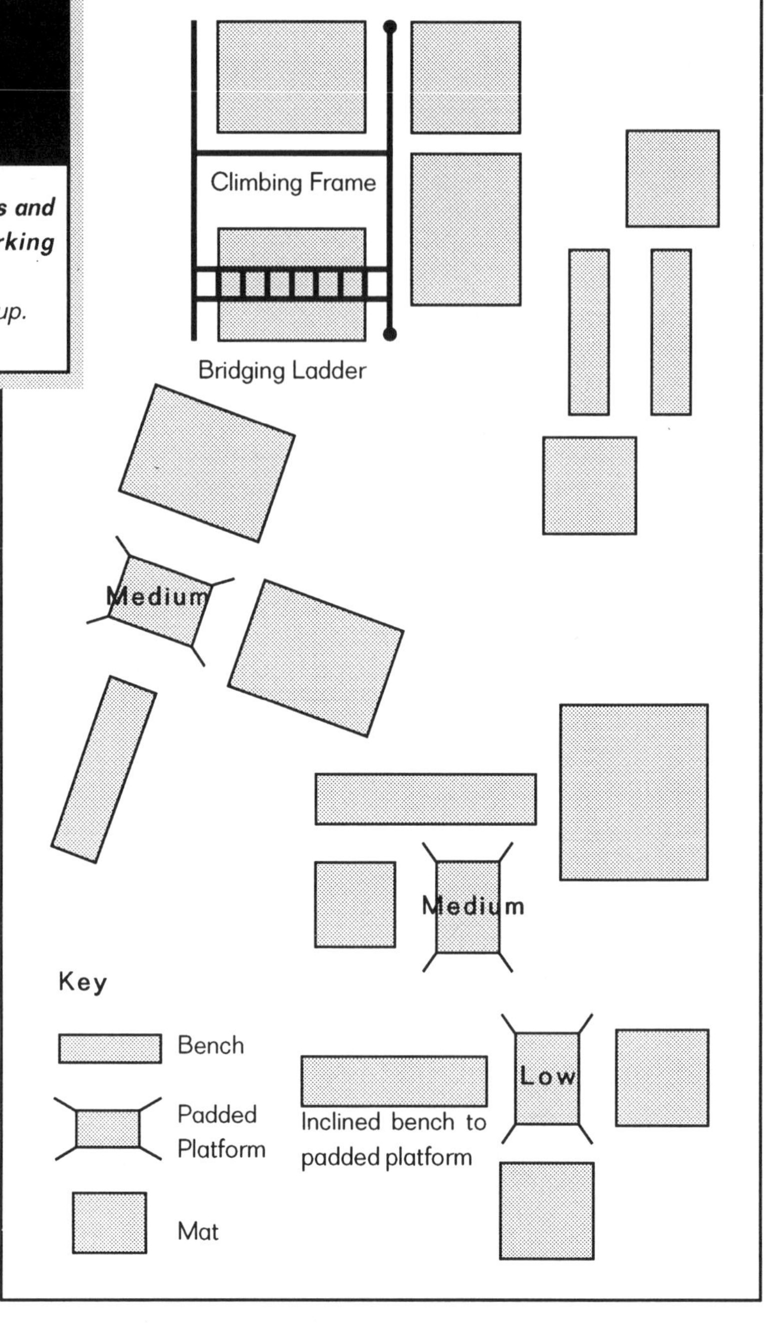

Previous skills/knowledge needed

Confidence in lifting and carrying apparatus and a sound jumping technique.

Key background information

The progression on to large apparatus represents a significant development in the gymnastics programme. Reception children develop rapidly in this year, and it is appropriate that they should experience large apparatus so that they can take part in climbing, hanging and heaving activities. The teacher will need to be confident that the class is ready to respond to, as well as benefit from, more complex and challenging apparatus layouts, particularly in terms of ability to dismount from apparatus.

It is wise to restrict children to a particular height on larger apparatus so that you can readily and easily offer assistance should this prove necessary. Height limitations can be indicated easily by red or brightly coloured tape.

Preparation

Ensure that for easy access the apparatus is located safely around the edge of the hall. Copy each of the photocopiable pages 109, 110, 113 and 114 (to develop the activity if required).

Resources needed

Benches, mats, climbing frame, padded platforms, planks, photocopiable pages 109, 110, 113 and 114 (optional).

What to do

Warm-up activity

Ask the children to find a space. Begin by asking the class to run lightly making different pathways around the hall. On the command 'Jump!', the children must show a high, stretched jump with a controlled, still landing – 'freezing' in their landing position until instructed to move again.

Gymnastic activity

Invite the children to move around the hall into spaces, with a wide body shape; then a thin body shape. Can they move using both their feet and hands to travel across the floor, firstly with their tummies to the ground and then with their tummies facing up? After a suitable period of practice, ask them to travel in this way in a wide shape or in a narrow shape.

Organise the children into groups of five or six. Ask each group to set out its apparatus in turn, giving assistance where necessary. A suitable apparatus layout is shown in the diagram above (individual schools will of course modify this according to their existing provision).

All the children should follow the same 'route' around their own apparatus. Ensure that you allow sufficient time for investigation and exploration of each item of equipment as the children establish the direction of their apparatus pathway. Encourage the children to show at least one wide shape –

still, or on the move – as they work their way around their apparatus. Can they include a narrow shape as well?

Conclusion

Conclude the lesson by carefully putting away the apparatus, one group at a time.

Develop the work in future lessons with selected activities from the Gymnastic Activity Bank, 'Jumping' and 'Travelling' (photocopiable pages 109, 110, 113 and 114).

Suggestion(s) for extension

Ask more confident children to change frequently from 'tummy up' to 'tummy down' whilst working on the floor. Can they show 'tummy up' on their apparatus?

GYMNASTICS – YEAR 1 P2 (LESSON 1)

To develop and refine jumping skills involving turning actions and to further develop travelling skills with an emphasis upon rolling.

Children working individually and with a partner.

30 minutes.

Previous skills/knowledge needed

Sound jumping technique and ability to work co-operatively with a partner.

Suggestion(s) for support

Less confident children will be more comfortable with 'tummy down' actions.

Assessment opportunities

Observe how much control the children bring to their movement. Are they confident on large apparatus? Are they able to translate activity involving shape and body position from the floor to apparatus?

Reference to photocopiable sheets

The photocopiable pages 109, 110, 113 and 114 offer ideas from the Gymnastic Activity Bank that will develop and consolidate the sample lesson described above.

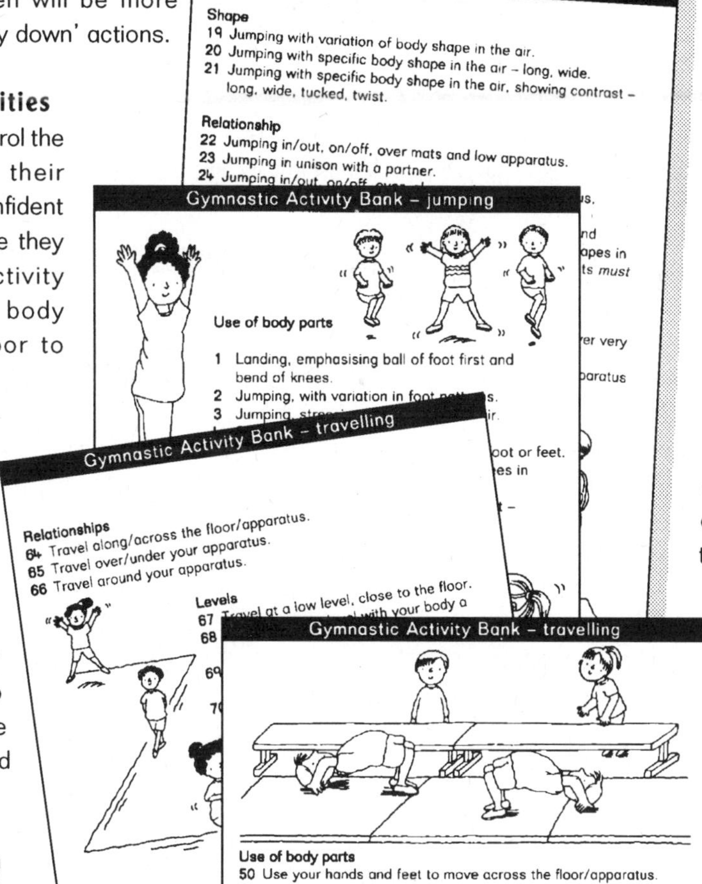

Gymnastic Activity Bank – jumping

Shape
19 Jumping with variation of body shape in the air.
20 Jumping with specific body shape in the air – long, wide.
21 Jumping with specific body shape in the air, showing contrast – long, wide, tucked, twist.

Relationship
22 Jumping in/out, on/off, over mats and low apparatus.
23 Jumping in unison with a partner.

Gymnastic Activity Bank – jumping

Use of body parts
1 Landing, emphasising ball of foot first and bend of knees.
2 Jumping, with variation in foot patterns.

Gymnastic Activity Bank – travelling

Relationships
64 Travel along/across the floor/apparatus.
65 Travel over/under your apparatus.
66 Travel around your apparatus.

Levels

Directions
71 Travel in a straight
72 Travel in a curved
73 Travel in a circle.
74 Travel in a square
75 Travel making a z

Gymnastic Activity Bank – travelling

Use of body parts
50 Use your hands and feet to move across the floor/apparatus.
51 Use only your feet to move across the floor/apparatus.
52 Use your feet as little as possible to move across the floor/apparatus.
53 Use large parts of your body to move across the floor/apparatus.
54 Use small parts of your body to move across the floor/apparatus.
55 Use a combination of large and small body parts to move across the floor/apparatus.
56 Travel on your front in some way.
57 Travel on your back in some way.

Movement factors
58 Travel in different directions – sideways, forwards, backwards.
59 Travel slowly.
60 Travel at different speeds – quickly, slowly.

Body shape
61 Travel using different body shapes – long, round, wide, thin.
62 Travel with your body as small as possible.
63 Travel with your body as big as possible.

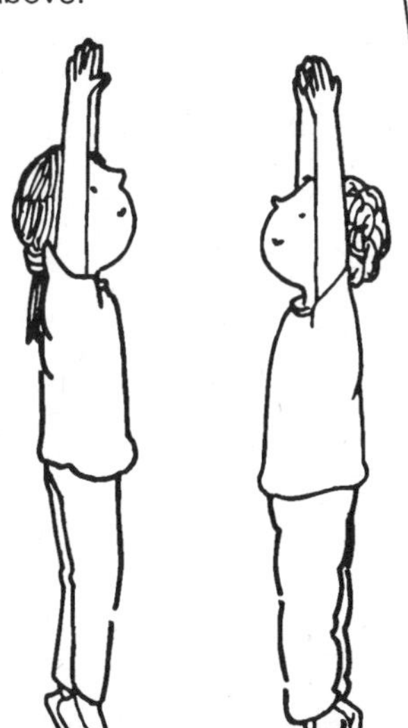

Key background information

Once children have acquired the ability to jump and land confidently, more challenging tasks should be introduced. These may involve turning and body shape in flight. Turning in the air is easier with the body in a long, stretched shape.

As spatial awareness develops, children are more able to work safely within a free-flowing gymnastic environment. They begin to be able to make their own decisions about when it is safe to initiate their own activity relative to others in close proximity. A useful progression towards this involves working simultaneously with a partner around simple, shared apparatus remaining alert to each other's movements. It is important to note that within the progression there is an expectation of better *quality* in movement.

Preparation

Ensure that sufficient apparatus is available around the edge of the hall. Make a copy of each of the photocopiable pages 109, 110 ('Jumping'), 111 and 112 ('Rolling') if required, to develop the main activity.

Resources needed

Hoops and mats, photocopiable pages 109, 110, 111 and 112 (optional).

What to do

Warm-up activity

Begin the lesson with some basic jumping. Ask the children to make a short approach – no more than three strides – and jump high in the air into a space. Encourage the children to stretch out and land in a still position. Practise this continuously for a few minutes.

Gymnastic activity

Ask the children to find their own space and stand still, all facing the same way. Set them the following task:

▲ start with your feet slightly apart;

▲ bend your knees and spring up high into a long, stretched shape;

▲ turn in the air so that you land facing a different direction.

Restrict the children to a quarter turn (a turn through 90 degrees). Ask them to start their jump facing a certain way, such as 'the hall stage' and land facing a side wall. Let the children decide which direction they want to turn. Repeat this several times.

Now ask the children to lie on their backs. Can they roll in a stretched shape on to their front, first in one direction and then the other? Add to this task by starting in a standing, stretched position and moving slowly on to the back before rolling in a long shape across the floor.

Organise the children into pairs. Ask one child in each pair to collect a hoop. Group the children into fours while they set out enough mats for each pair. Show them how to set out their apparatus with the mat close to the hoop (see the diagram below).

Set the following task: one partner starts by the hoop and the other starts on the mat. The children must stay in their pairs and work on their own apparatus. They must jump into and out of their hoop and then roll slowly across their mat. Finishing by standing and showing a turning jump. Ensure that each child has a turn to lead the activity with their partner following. Remind the children that, for safety reasons, they must not enter the hoop until their partner has moved on and they must not begin their rolling until their partner has cleared the mat.

Conclusion

Develop the work in future lessons with selected activities from the Gymnastic Activity Bank on photocopiable pages 109, 110, 111 and 112.

Suggestion(s) for extension

Encourage more confident children to practise their turning jumps in both directions progressing to half and full turns.

Suggestion(s) for support

When jumping into and out of the hoop, less confident children should initially begin by *stepping* into and out of their hoop.

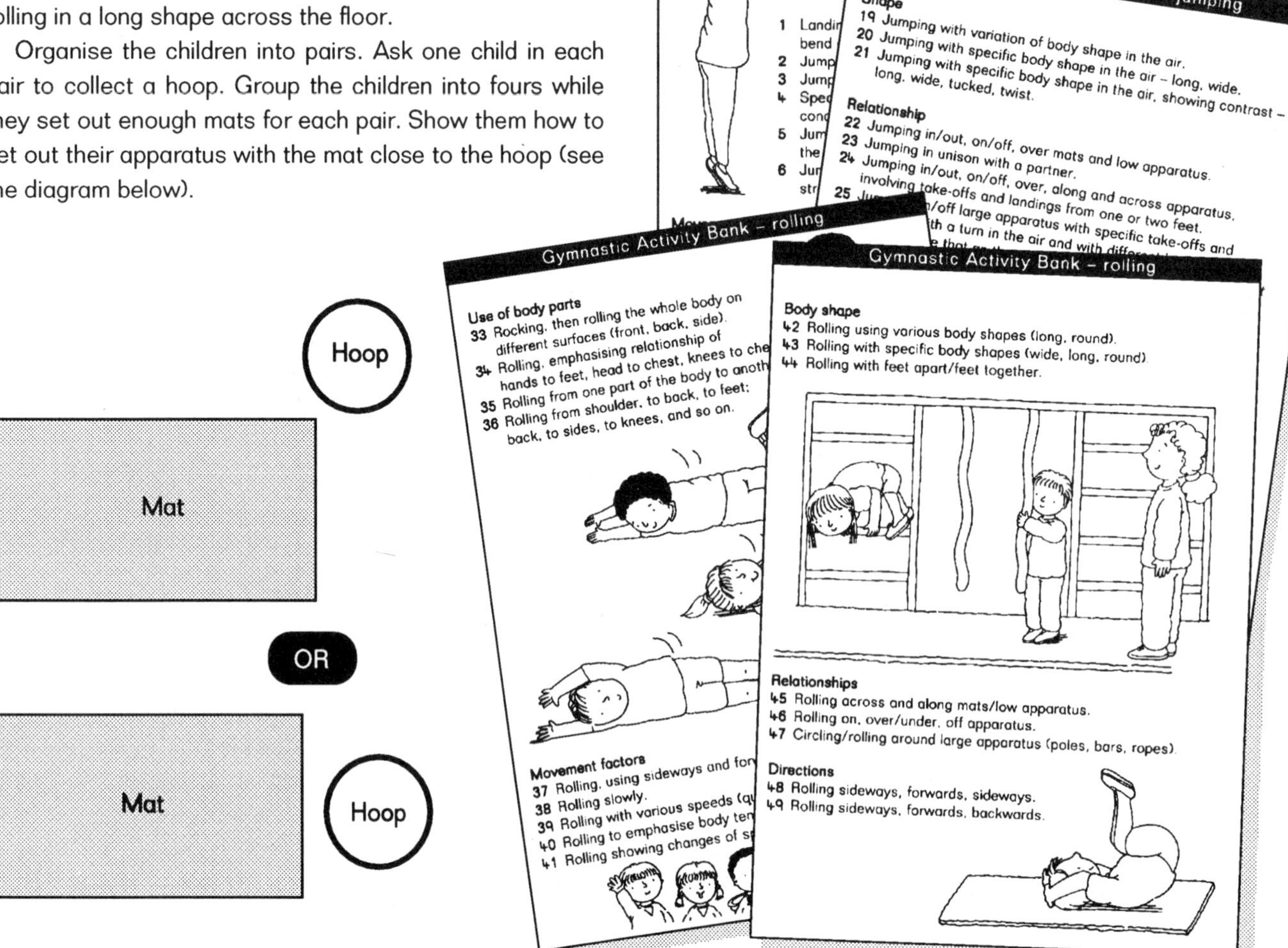

Assessment opportunities

Observe how much control the children bring to their turning jumps and rolling movements. Are they still on landing and do they roll slowly? Do they work co-operatively with their partner and wait until the apparatus is clear for them to use?

Reference to photocopiable sheets

Photocopiable pages 109, 110, 111 and 112 are from the Gymnastic Activity Bank and offer ways to support the main activity. They may equally be used to develop or focus on a particular skill.

GYMNASTICS – YEAR 1/ P2 (LESSON 2)

To further develop travelling skills on the floor and apparatus and to learn how to contrast speed in movement and to link movements.

Children working individually and within a group.

30 minutes.

Previous skills/knowledge needed

An ability to transfer weight from feet to other body parts and to jump and land with confidence. Ability to work co-operatively within a group.

Key background information

It is not necessary or desirable that large apparatus is used in every gymnastics lesson. When introducing new themes or tasks, limiting the complexity of the apparatus will lead to more effective learning. Use of the floor alone will help the children to establish an understanding about the movement requirements of a new theme. This understanding can be further developed in situations using limited apparatus such as benches and mats. Limiting the amount of apparatus used will also help children to plan their actions more easily within the context of a group with others working around them.

Preparation

Arrange the apparatus safely around the edge of the hall. Make a copy of each of the photocopiable pages 113 and 114 (if required, to develop the main activity).

Resources needed

Benches and mats. Photocopiable pages 113 and 114 (optional).

What to do

Warm-up activity

Begin the lesson by asking the children to find a space. Invite them to curl up tightly in a ball on the floor and then begin to stretch out slowly to a standing position. When standing, the children must show a high, stretched jump on the spot. Repeat this several times. This activity serves as a useful warm-up but also establishes the concept that some movements are slow and very controlled (stretching out) whereas others are fast and explosive (jumping).

Gymnastic activity

Have a brief discussion with the children about what a rocking action is. For example: it stays in the same place; it's like a see-saw with one part of the body high and another low, which change over; it has its own rhythm like a pendulum or ticking clock.

Ask the children to lie on their backs and curl up again. Can they show a rocking movement on their back in this curled position? Can they show one on their front? Set the following task:

▲ start on your feet and move smoothly on to your back and show a rocking movement;

▲ turn over on to your front and show another rocking movement;

▲ return slowly to your feet and finish with a high, stretched jump.

Repeat this several times encouraging the children not to rush their actions.

Organise the class into apparatus groups of five or six children and ask them to set out their benches and mats in their apparatus space (see diagram below).

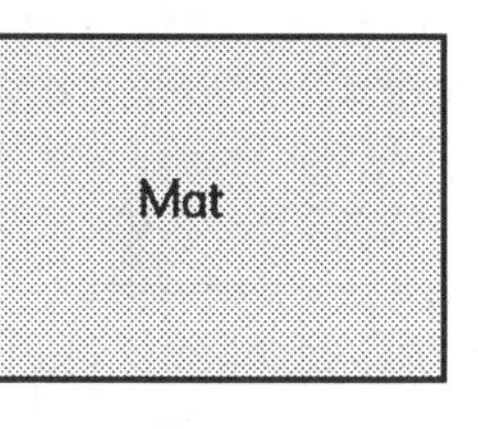

Set the following task:

▲ start at one end of your bench and choose a way of moving *along* it;

▲ when you get to the end, show a high, stretched jump on to your mat.

Ask the children to try to think of different ways of returning to the starting position. Can they think of ways which do not use their feet very much? Repeat this activity several times. Invite the children to include at least one rocking movement somewhere in their 'journey' around their apparatus.

Conclusion

Conclude the lesson by asking the children to put their apparatus away carefully.

Develop the work in future lessons with selected activities from the Gymnastic Activity Bank, 'Travelling' on photocopiable pages 113 and 114.

Suggestion(s) for extension

More confident children can try to show their rocking action while on the bench.

GYMNASTICS – YEAR 1/ P2 (LESSON 3)

To further develop travelling and jumping skills through using large apparatus and to develop the ability to link actions together.

Children working individually and within a group.

30 minutes.

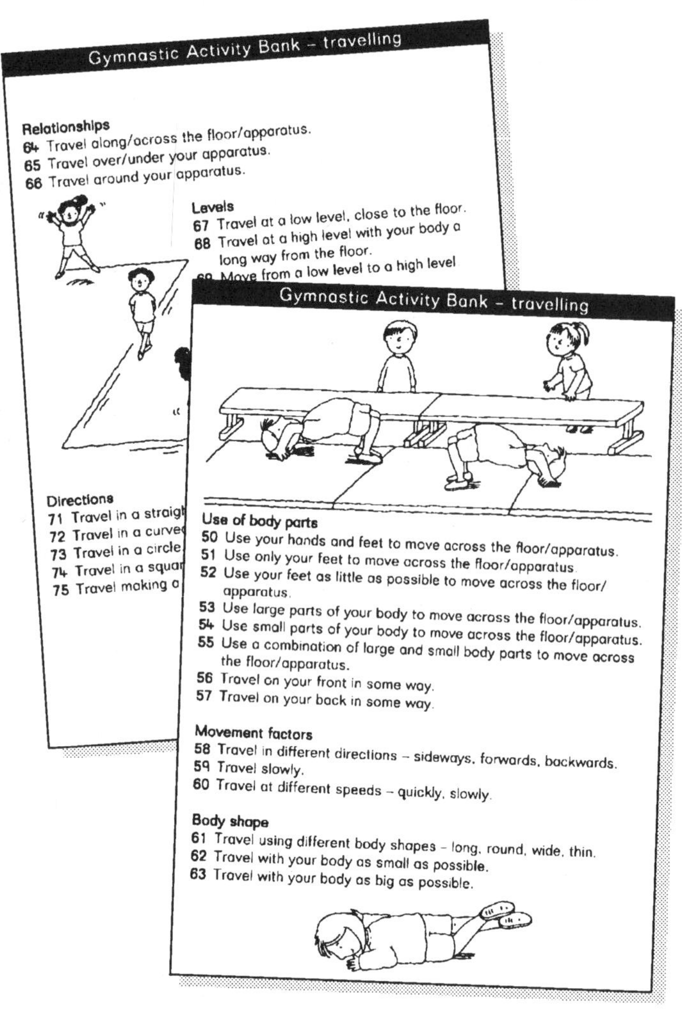

Gymnastic Activity Bank – travelling

Relationships
64 Travel along/across the floor/apparatus.
65 Travel over/under your apparatus.
66 Travel around your apparatus.

Levels
67 Travel at a low level, close to the floor.
68 Travel at a high level with your body a long way from the floor.
69 Move from a low level to a high level

Directions
71 Travel in a straig
72 Travel in a curve
73 Travel in a circle
74 Travel in a squa
75 Travel making a

Gymnastic Activity Bank – travelling

Use of body parts
50 Use your hands and feet to move across the floor/apparatus.
51 Use only your feet to move across the floor/apparatus.
52 Use your feet as little as possible to move across the floor/apparatus.
53 Use large parts of your body to move across the floor/apparatus.
54 Use small parts of your body to move across the floor/apparatus.
55 Use a combination of large and small body parts to move across the floor/apparatus.
56 Travel on your front in some way.
57 Travel on your back in some way.

Movement factors
58 Travel in different directions – sideways, forwards, backwards.
59 Travel slowly.
60 Travel at different speeds – quickly, slowly.

Body shape
61 Travel using different body shapes – long, round, wide, thin.
62 Travel with your body as small as possible.
63 Travel with your body as big as possible.

Previous skills/knowledge needed

Ability to use space effectively and adjust own actions and pathways to take account of others.

Key background information

Educational gymnastics provides opportunities for children to work independently and in their own time. It gives children the scope to seek out their own solutions to movement themes and tasks. The ultimate goal is to link a series of actions together into a smooth sequence. In order to maximise the time available for learning, children will need to be guided away from queuing and waiting in line. They will need to work around their apparatus in a much more free-flowing way – devising pathways of their own choosing. Clearly this requires additional skill beyond simply managing one's own body. The children will have to learn how to adjust and modify their own actions in order to accommodate those of others.

Suggestion(s)for support

Less confident children will find rocking on their back an easier task to perform.

Assessment opportunities

Observe how tightly the children curl when rocking on their backs and how stretched they are when rocking on their fronts. Are they able to think of a variety of ways of returning to their starting points when using apparatus?

Reference to photocopiable sheets

Photocopiable pages 113 and 114 suggest a range of ideas based on the theme of travelling which will further support the sample lesson described above.

Preparation

Ensure that the apparatus is readily accessible around the edge of the working area. Make a copy of each of the photocopiable pages 109, 110, 113 and 114 if required, to develop the main activity.

Resources needed

Benches, padded platforms and mats, photocopiable pages 109, 110, 113 and 114 (optional).

What to do

Warm-up activity

Start the lesson with jumping and stretching activities. Ask the children to look for a space and run and jump high into it. They must hold their landing position for a count of three and then move off to jump into another space. Ask the children to make different shapes while they are in the air but to show stillness on landing.

Gymnastic activity

Now invite the children to roll slowly across the floor making sure that they roll into a space and away from each other. Can they think of two different ways of rolling? Be prepared to use demonstration to stimulate ideas.

Set the following task:

▲ begin in a standing position;

▲ decide what kind of roll you wish to perform and move slowly into it;
▲ return to your feet again and immediately jump high;
▲ repeat this activity several times.

Now ask one half of the class to observe while the other half continue to work on this task. Ask the observers to look and make comments about how smoothly the two movements are put together. Reverse roles so that the performers now have an opportunity to observe.

Organise the children into apparatus groups and set out the apparatus in a similar way to that shown on page 60. Each child in the group should be given a starting point, with the children in any one group spaced out as much as possible around their own apparatus.

Set the following task:
▲ You must start and finish in the place where you are sitting now.
▲ Make a journey around your apparatus and try to use each piece of it before returning to your starting place.
▲ Be careful of others and wait, if necessary, for apparatus to become free before you use it.

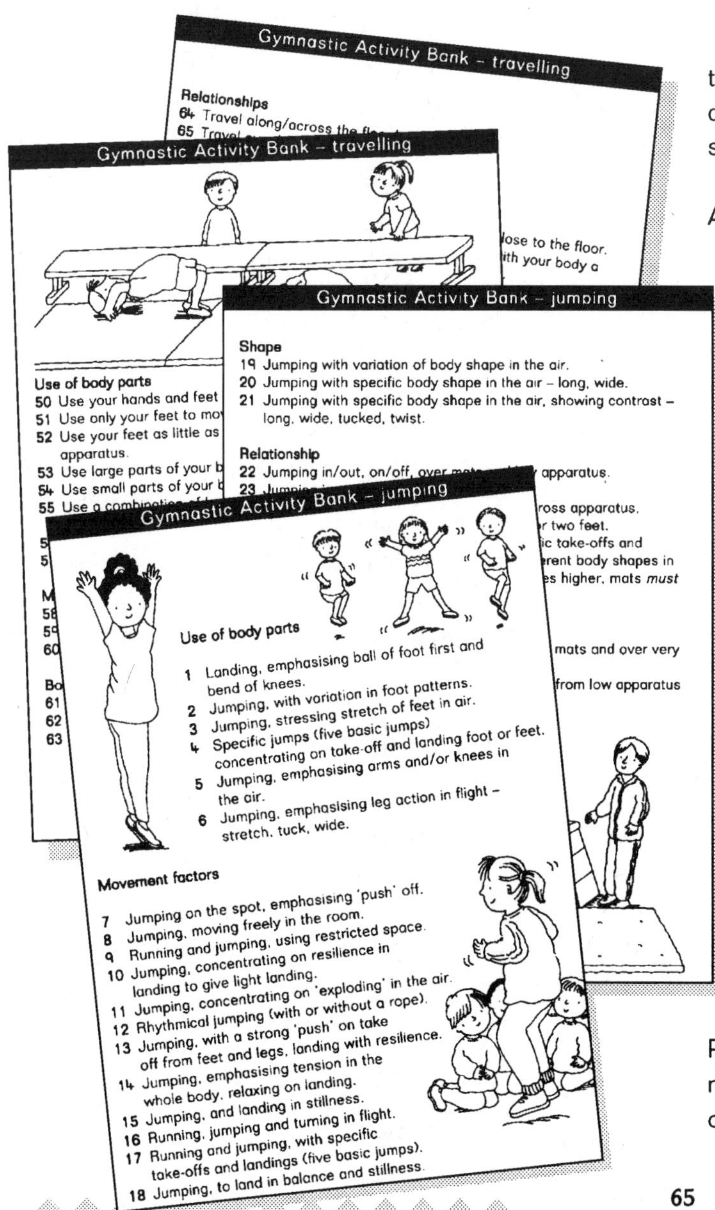

Gymnastic Activity Bank – travelling

Relationships
64 Travel along/across the ...
65 Trave...

...lose to the floor.
...ith your body a...

Gymnastic Activity Bank – travelling

Use of body parts
50 Use your hands and feet ...
51 Use only your feet to mo...
52 Use your feet as little as ... apparatus.
53 Use large parts of your b...
54 Use small parts of your b...
55 Use a combination of ...

Gymnastic Activity Bank – jumping

Shape
19 Jumping with variation of body shape in the air.
20 Jumping with specific body shape in the air – long, wide.
21 Jumping with specific body shape in the air, showing contrast – long, wide, tucked, twist.

Relationship
22 Jumping in/out, on/off, over ... apparatus.
23 ...

...ross apparatus.
...r two feet.
...ic take-offs and ...rent body shapes in ...es higher, mats *must* ...
...mats and over very ...
...from low apparatus

Gymnastic Activity Bank – jumping

Use of body parts
1 Landing, emphasising ball of foot first and bend of knees.
2 Jumping, with variation in foot patterns.
3 Jumping, stressing stretch of feet in air.
4 Specific jumps (five basic jumps) concentrating on take-off and landing foot or feet.
5 Jumping, emphasising arms and/or knees in the air.
6 Jumping, emphasising leg action in flight – stretch, tuck, wide.

Movement factors
7 Jumping on the spot, emphasising 'push' off.
8 Jumping, moving freely in the room.
9 Running and jumping, using restricted space.
10 Jumping, concentrating on resilience in landing to give light landing.
11 Jumping, concentrating on 'exploding' in the air.
12 Rhythmical jumping (with or without a rope).
13 Jumping, with a strong 'push' on take off from feet and legs, landing with resilience.
14 Jumping, emphasising tension in the whole body, relaxing on landing.
15 Jumping, and landing in stillness.
16 Running, jumping and turning in flight.
17 Running and jumping, with specific take-offs and landings (five basic jumps).
18 Jumping, to land in balance and stillness.

After the children have been given sufficient opportunity to explore their apparatus and establish pathways around it, ask them to include at least one rolling movement and one stretched jump in their sequence.

Use demonstration where appropriate to enhance learning. Ask the class to observe, for instance, those groups who are working co-operatively and with good control.

Conclusion

Conclude the lesson by asking the children to put away their apparatus carefully one group at a time. Develop the work in future lessons with selected activities from photocopiable pages 109, 110, 113 and 114.

Suggestion(s) for extension

More confident children should be encouraged to move around their apparatus using feet as little as possible and taking weight on hands as much as they can.

Suggestion(s) for support

Less confident children will find feet-to-feet actions easier in exploring routes around their apparatus.

Assessment opportunities

Observe how well the children link their actions together on the floor and on apparatus. Are they able to modify their movements to accommodate those of others? Do they lift and carry their apparatus safely and responsibly?

Reference to photocopiable sheets

Photocopiable pages 109, 110, 113 and 114 provide a number of ideas that will support and develop the main part of the activity.

GYMNASTICS – YEAR 2/ P3 (LESSON 1)

To explore and refine balancing skills using small and large bases.

Children working individually and with a partner.

30 minutes.

Previous skills/knowledge needed

Ability to work co-operatively with a partner and a movement vocabulary that includes an understanding of stillness.

Key background information

The ability to balance – holding a position of stillness on various body parts – is a fundamental gymnastic skill. It can only be achieved when children are able to demonstrate appropriate body tension. You will need to remind the children of the need to keep their limbs and body 'tight' when holding a balanced position – 'floppy' limbs will not produce a strong balance. It should also be remembered that balancing is hard work but is, by its very nature, static. Consequently, lessons which include balance as a theme or task should include elements of more free-flowing activity.

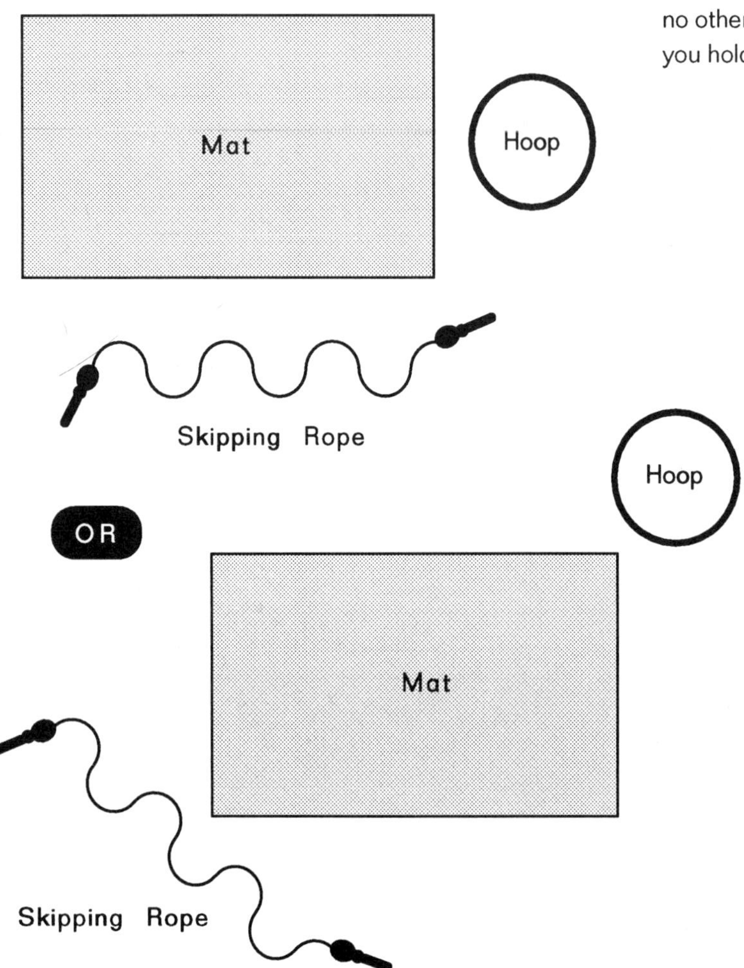

Preparation

Ensure that the apparatus is safely stored around the edge of the hall. Copy each of the photocopiable pages 113, 114, 115 and 116 to develop the activity if required.

Resources needed

Hoops, skipping ropes, mats, photocopiable pages 113, 114, 115 and 116 (optional).

What to do

Warm-up activity

To begin, focus on travelling using feet. Ask the children to move around the hall with different running and skipping actions. Explain to the class that when you clap, the children must jump and show a shape in the air. Then ask the children to show a second shape when jumping, different to their first one. Let the children practise their two different jumps and ask two or three children who hold clear shapes in the air to demonstrate for the rest of the class. Remind the children that stillness on landing is very important.

Gymnastic activity

Ask the children to find a big space. Set them the following task:

▲ Choose a big body part such as side, back or seat and balance on it.

▲ Hold your body still – up to the count of three (remember no other part of your body should be touching the floor while you hold this balance).

▲ Choose a different part to balance on and try to move smoothly from one balance to the other. Start on your feet, move slowly into your first balance, then slowly into your second balance and back to your feet again.

Organise the class into apparatus groups. Ask them to set out the apparatus as shown in the diagram opposite and set them the following task:

▲ Move around your apparatus and find as many places as you can to balance in or over.

▲ Choose a starting and finishing point.

▲ Move around your apparatus showing at least three balances and one jump before returning to your starting point again.

▲ Try to repeat this 'journey' making sure that you hold each of your three balances for the count of three.

Conclusion

Conclude the lesson by asking the class to put away carefully their own apparatus.

Develop the work in future lessons with selected activities from the Gymnastic Activity Bank – 'Travelling' (photocopiable pages 113 and 114), and 'Balancing' (photocopiable pages 115 and 116).

Suggestion(s) for extension

Encourage more confident children to explore balancing on three points, such as two feet and one hand; knees and one hand and so on. Then try balancing on two points.

Suggestion(s) for support

Encourage less confident children to explore balancing on four points.

Assessment opportunities

Observe how steady the children are in balance. Are they able to move into balance smoothly? Can they repeat their actions and balances around their apparatus?

Reference to photocopiable sheets

Photocopiable pages 113, 114, 115 and 116 may be used to develop the main activity or as the basis for a series of follow-up lessons targeting particular skills.

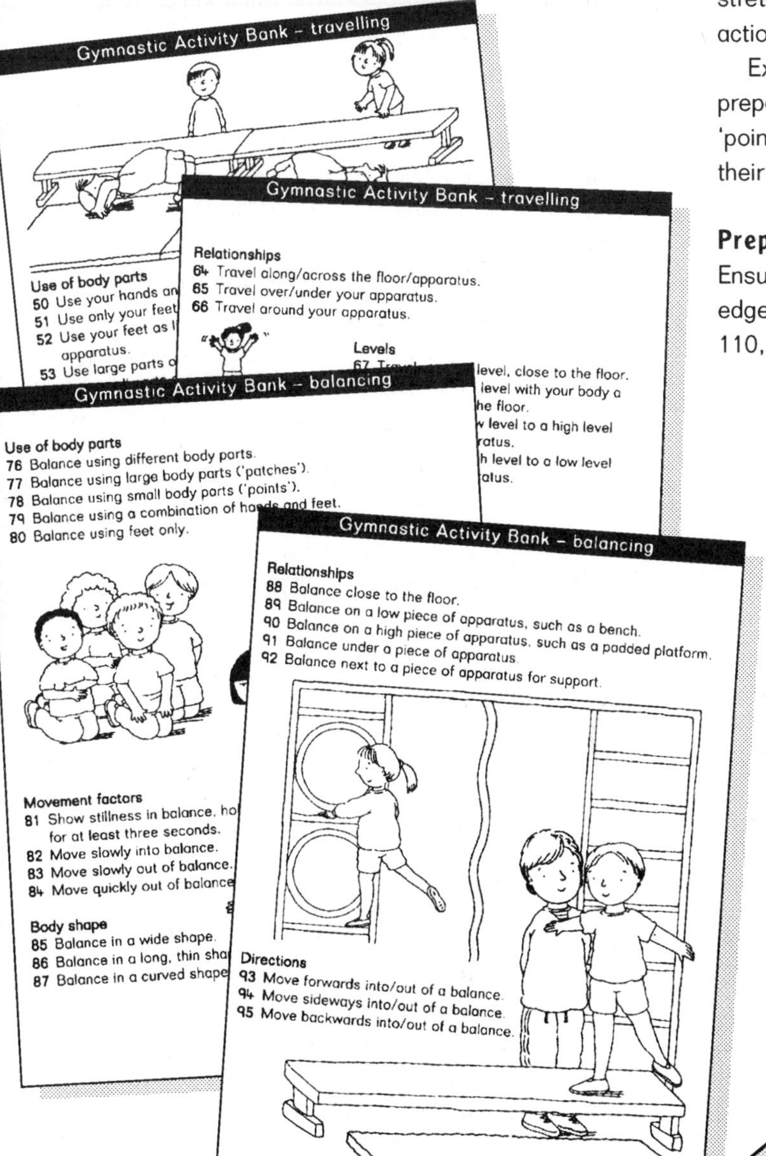

Gymnastic Activity Bank – travelling

Use of body parts
50 Use your hands an
51 Use only your feet
52 Use your feet as l
apparatus.
53 Use large parts o

Gymnastic Activity Bank – travelling

Relationships
64 Travel along/across the floor/apparatus.
65 Travel over/under your apparatus.
66 Travel around your apparatus.

Levels
level, close to the floor.
level with your body a
he floor.
level to a high level
ratus.
h level to a low level
atus.

Gymnastic Activity Bank – balancing

Use of body parts
76 Balance using different body parts.
77 Balance using large body parts ('patches').
78 Balance using small body parts ('points').
79 Balance using a combination of hands and feet.
80 Balance using feet only.

Movement factors
81 Show stillness in balance, ho
for at least three seconds.
82 Move slowly into balance.
83 Move slowly out of balance.
84 Move quickly out of balance

Body shape
85 Balance in a wide shape.
86 Balance in a long, thin sha
87 Balance in a curved shape

Gymnastic Activity Bank – balancing

Relationships
88 Balance close to the floor.
89 Balance on a low piece of apparatus, such as a bench.
90 Balance on a high piece of apparatus, such as a padded platform.
91 Balance under a piece of apparatus.
92 Balance next to a piece of apparatus for support.

Directions
93 Move forwards into/out of a balance.
94 Move sideways into/out of a balance.
95 Move backwards into/out of a balance.

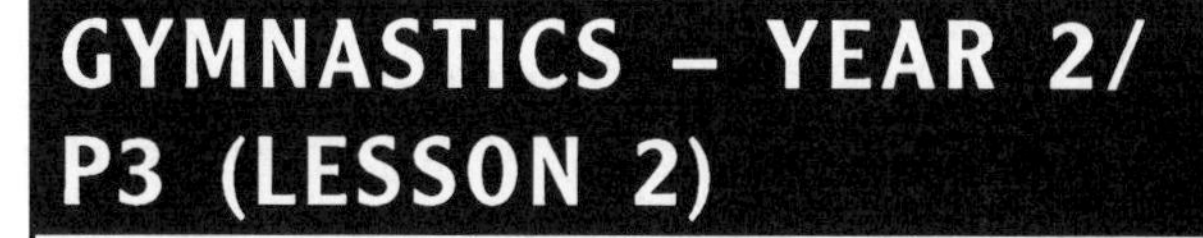

GYMNASTICS – YEAR 2/ P3 (LESSON 2)

To develop movement quality through an understanding of extension in movement.

Children working individually and in groups.

30 minutes.

Previous skills/knowledge needed

Ability to transfer body weight on to different body parts with control and to move about the floor and apparatus in a variety of ways.

Key background information

The ability to extend the body in movement adds an extra dimension to the quality of performance. 'Extension' can be applied to all parts of the body – neck, limbs and trunk. When stretching, the children should be encouraged to make their actions as full as possible.

Extension in movement is primarily related to effort, so be prepared to give constant reminders to the children about 'pointing their toes', 'stretching their fingers', and 'keeping their chins up'.

Preparation

Ensure that the apparatus is positioned safely around the edge of the hall. Copy each of the photocopiable pages 109, 110, 111 and 112, to develop the activity if required.

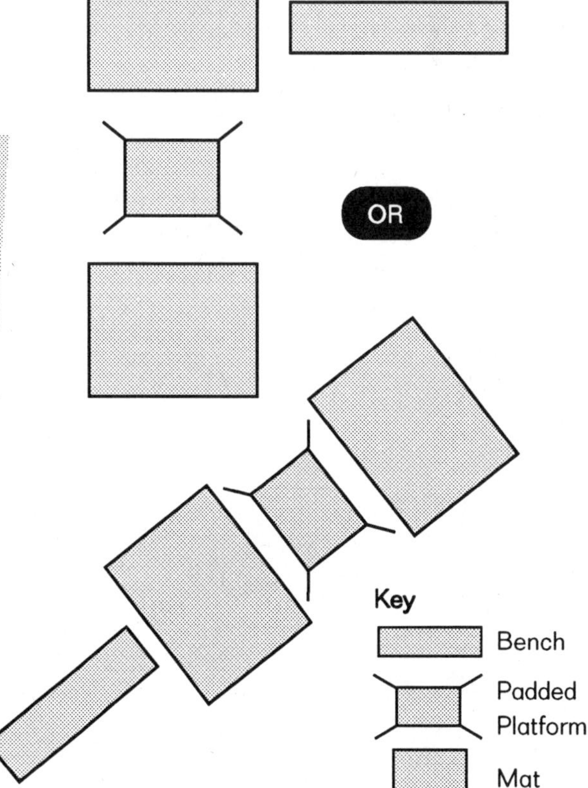

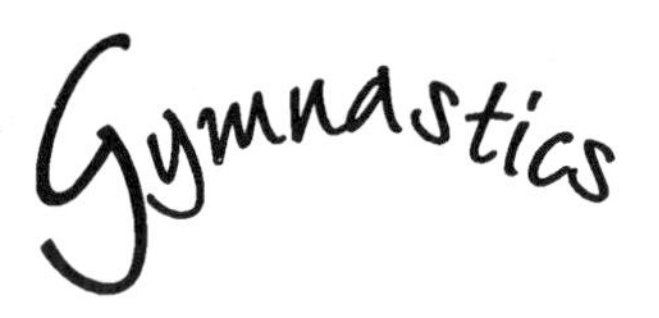

Resources needed

Mats, benches, padded platforms, photocopiable pages 109, 110, 111 and 112 (optional).

What to do

Warm-up activity

Begin the lesson by asking the class to run freely around the hall and jump into spaces showing controlled landings.

Gymnastic activity

Ask the children to find their own space and set the following task:

▲ Stand in a stretched position.

▲ Slowly move to the floor and show a rolling movement across the floor, keeping your body as stretched out as possible.

▲ Return to feet again, moving slowly and smoothly.

▲ Start with a stretched jump, making a long shape in the air. Then move slowly into your stretched roll across the floor, back to feet again and show a second jump – this time try to show a wide shape in the air.

▲ Then practise this sequence – stretched jump (long shape) – stretched roll on the floor – stretched jump (wide shape). Do this several times, trying to link your actions together as smoothly as possible.

▲ Remember to show a good starting and finishing position.

Organise the class into apparatus groups and set out the apparatus as shown in the diagram on page 67. Allow the children to freely explore their own apparatus for a few minutes and then set them the following task:

▲ Choose a place to start. Move around your apparatus but try to include as many stretched jumps and stretched rolls as you can.

▲ Use every piece of apparatus at least once before returning back to your starting point. *Remember to make sure that the mats are free before you jump onto them.* Jump *up* from the platforms looking for as much height as you can.

Conclusion

Develop the work in future lessons with selected activities from the Gymnastic Activity Bank – 'Jumping' (photocopiable pages 109 and 110) and 'Rolling' (photocopiable pages 111 and 112).

Suggestion(s) for extension

Encourage confident children to roll in both directions, and challenge them to get back to their feet without using their hands to assist them after completing their rolling action.

Suggestion(s) for support

You may find it more appropriate to ask less confident children to perform and hold a stretched position on their apparatus, rather than a stretched rolling action.

Assessment opportunities

Observe how extended the children are in movement. Are they able to show a series of stretched jumps and rolls around their apparatus? Do they work effectively as a group in setting out their apparatus and working on it?

Reference to photocopiable sheets

Photocopiable pages 109, 110, 111 and 112 provide a range of ideas that may be used to reinforce or develop the main activity.

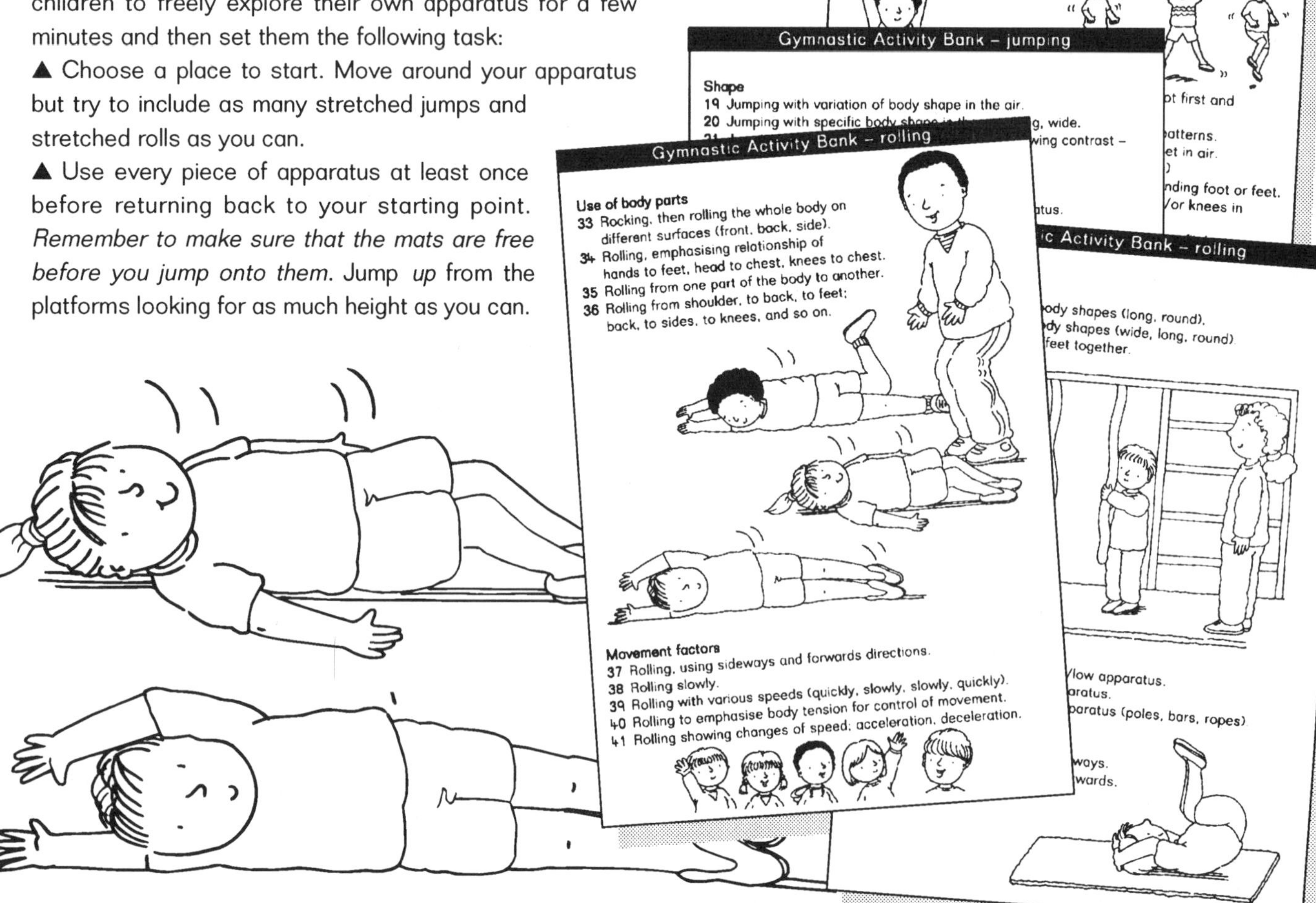
Gymnastic Activity Bank – jumping

Gymnastic Activity Bank – jumping

Shape

19 Jumping with variation of body shape in the air.

Gymnastic Activity Bank – rolling

Use of body parts

33 Rocking, then rolling the whole body on different surfaces (front, back, side).

34 Rolling, emphasising relationship of hands to feet, head to chest, knees to chest.

35 Rolling from one part of the body to another.

36 Rolling from shoulder, to back, to feet; back, to sides, to knees, and so on.

Movement factors

37 Rolling, using sideways and forwards directions.

38 Rolling slowly.

39 Rolling with various speeds (quickly, slowly, slowly, quickly).

40 Rolling to emphasise body tension for control of movement.

41 Rolling showing changes of speed: acceleration, deceleration.

GYMNASTICS – YEAR 2/ P3 (LESSON 3)

To further develop travelling skills linking a variety of actions around large apparatus.

Children working individually and within a group.

35 minutes.

Previous skills/knowledge needed

Children should have experience and confidence in a range of basic movement skills – running; balancing; travelling using other body parts in combination with feet. They should also be able to work within a group, modifying their own movement pathways to take account of others.

Key background information

The excitement and challenge of large apparatus provides young children with enjoyable and meaningful opportunities to explore and refine the adaptability of their bodies in relation to their physical environment.

By the age of seven, the majority of children should feel secure in tackling a range of problems and tasks presented by apparatus set at different heights which requires them to make decisions about appropriate and safe movement pathways. Children at this stage should increasingly be required to combine different actions into *movement sequences* and be challenged to refine these sequences through repetition and practice.

Preparation

Ensure that the apparatus is safely stored around the edge of the hall. Try to place the apparatus near to its layout position, so that setting out takes as little time as possible.

Copy each of the photocopiable pages 109, 110, 111, 112, 113 and 114 to develop the activity if required.

Resources needed

Climbing frame, benches, mats, padded platforms (movement tables), photocopiable pages 109, 110, 111, 112, 113 and 114 (optional).

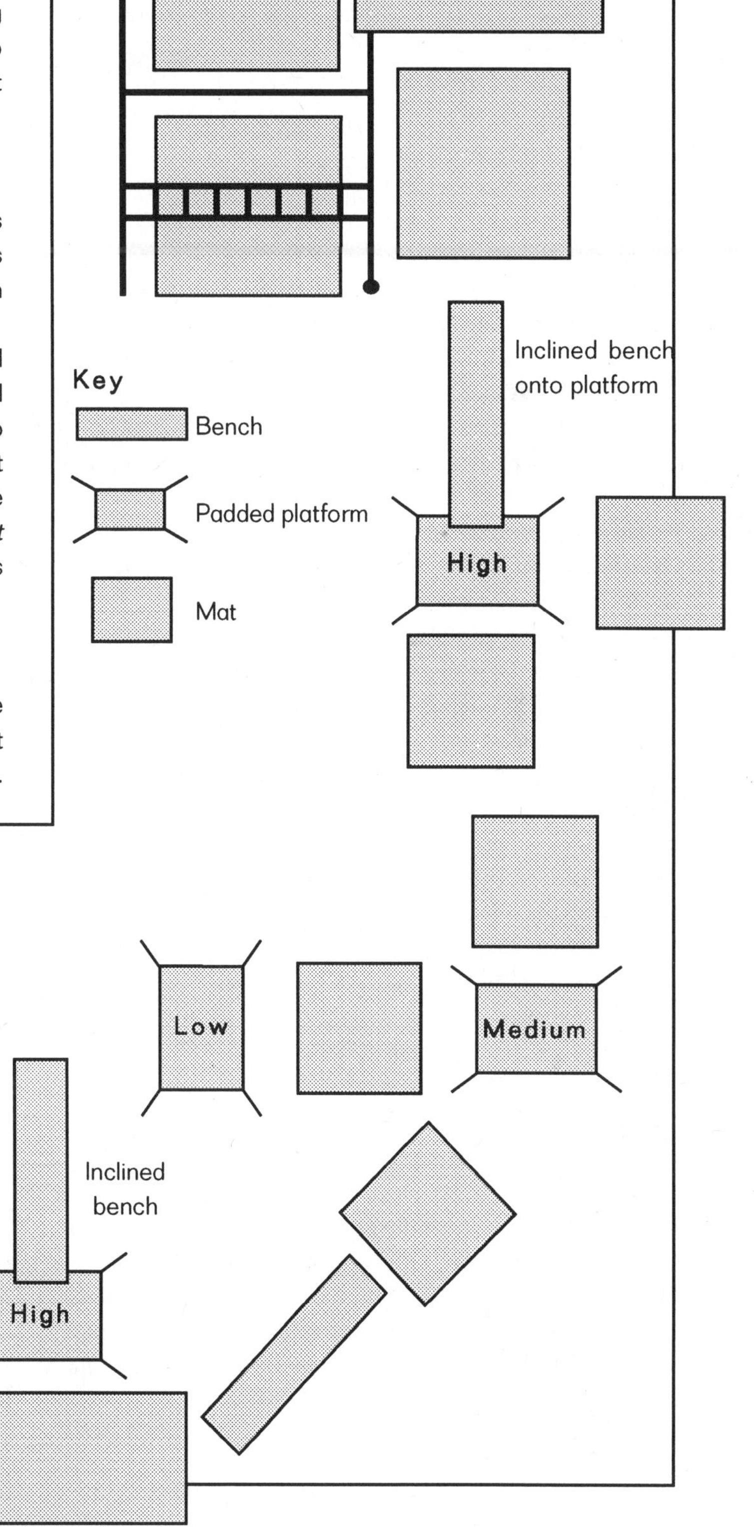

What to do

Warm-up activity

Invite the children to run lightly about the hall. Ask them to show two jumps, each with a different body shape in the air and then a turning jump on the spot.

Gymnastic activity

Now ask the children to explore different ways of travelling across the floor where their bodies are close to the ground. After a few minutes, ask them to choose two ways and link them together. Allow the class to practise this for a few minutes, then select one or two children who are linking their actions smoothly to demonstrate to the rest of the class.

Set the children the following task:

▲ Begin in a standing position.

▲ Move slowly to the floor and travel close to it using one of the actions you have just been practising.

▲ Return smoothly to feet and show a jump with a stretch or wide shape.

▲ Move slowly to the ground again and travel close to it with your second action. Finish with a second jump of your own choice.

▲ Repeat these *same* four, linked actions several times, for example, roll, jump, slide, jump, and try to move as smoothly as you can from one action into the next.

Organise the class into apparatus groups and set out the apparatus as shown in the diagram on page 69. When it is ready, allow the children a few minutes to move freely around their own apparatus and explore actions of their own choosing. Remind the children to be aware of others. Then set the following task:

▲ Choose your own starting point but try not to start too close to anybody else.

▲ Make a journey around your apparatus using every piece of it at least once. As you move from one piece of apparatus to the next, try to travel using your feet as little as possible.

▲ When you move *over* apparatus, try to keep your body as close to it as you can, but leave at least one piece of apparatus with a jump.

▲ Now repeat this journey several times in exactly the same way, trying to link up your different actions as smoothly as you can.

Conclusion

Conclude the lesson by asking each group to demonstrate its work to the rest of the class. Focus the observers' attention upon how smoothly the members of each demonstrating group link their actions together, and upon the imaginative ways they choose to move across the apparatus and travel across the floor. When each group has demonstrated ask the children to carefully put away their own apparatus.

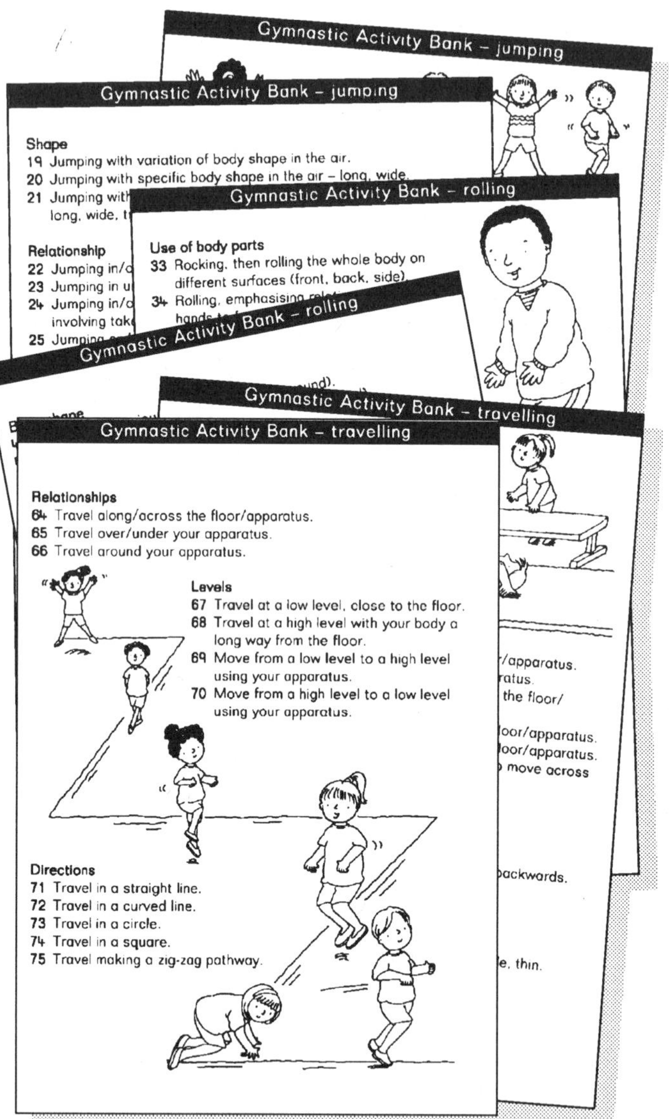
Gymnastic Activity Bank – jumping

Gymnastic Activity Bank – jumping

Shape
19 Jumping with variation of body shape in the air.
20 Jumping with specific body shape in the air – long, wide,
21 Jumping wit[h]
long, wide, t[...]

Relationship
22 Jumping in/[...]
23 Jumping in u[...]
24 Jumping in/[...]
involving tak[...]
25 Jump[...]

Gymnastic Activity Bank – rolling

Use of body parts
33 Rocking, then rolling the whole body on different surfaces (front, back, side).
34 Rolling, emphasising [...]

Gymnastic Activity Bank – rolling

Gymnastic Activity Bank – travelling

Gymnastic Activity Bank – travelling

Relationships
64 Travel along/across the floor/apparatus.
65 Travel over/under your apparatus.
66 Travel around your apparatus.

Levels
67 Travel at a low level, close to the floor.
68 Travel at a high level with your body a long way from the floor.
69 Move from a low level to a high level using your apparatus.
70 Move from a high level to a low level using your apparatus.

Directions
71 Travel in a straight line.
72 Travel in a curved line.
73 Travel in a circle.
74 Travel in a square.
75 Travel making a zig-zag pathway.

Develop the work in future lessons with selected activities from the Gymnastic Activity Bank – 'Jumping' (photocopiable pages 109 and 110), 'Rolling' (photocopiable pages 111 and 112) and 'Travelling' (photocopiable pages 113 and 114).

Suggestion(s) for extension

When the more confident children are moving around their apparatus encourage them to take their weight on hands as much as possible.

Suggestion(s) for support

Less confident children will answer the task with less difficult and less demanding actions. Ensure that they try to perform them as well as possible with good control and poise.

Assessment opportunities

Observe how well the children organise their movement around apparatus. Do they answer the task by using their feet as little as they can as they move around it? Are they able to remember and replicate their individual journeys around apparatus?

Reference to photocopiable sheet(s)

Photocopiable pages 109, 110, 111, 112, 113 and 114 suggest a range of ideas which will be useful to reinforce and develop the activity.

Dance

Typical five-year-olds are active and energetic. They enjoy all physical activities and delight in the joy of moving. Most are physically confident and eager to accept new challenges, master new skills and explore creative ideas. In Key Stage 1 (P1 to P3 in Scotland) the emphasis should be on helping children to develop control and co-ordination when performing simple actions such as travelling, jumping, turning and gesturing with different parts of the body. Pupils should be given the opportunity to explore contrasts of rhythm, speed, shape, direction and level and encouraged to express moods and feeling through movement. Give plenty of encouragement and praise to children who show variety in interpretation of a task. Invite them to share their different ideas with the rest of the class.

It is important for children to be introduced to basic dance steps, such as skipping, galloping, walking and so on, that will, in Key Stage 2, enable them to participate in set dances from the British Isles and abroad. Initially, the children's work will be mainly individual, as they experiment with simple movements and react to a variety of stimuli, including words and music. Gradually they will begin to link movements until short sequences are formed and they will begin to be able to talk about what they are doing. Some children will be able to make simple judgements about what they observe. Towards the end of the key stage children should be able to plan and practise short dances with a beginning, middle and end. With help they should be able to suggest ways to improve their own performance and that of others. By the end of the key stage a number of children should also be able to work constructively with a partner to answer simple tasks.

Dance

The sample dance lessons

The nine sample lessons that follow have been split into groups of three lessons for each age group covered in this book. Each group of three lessons follows a different theme and covers progression in dance activity suitable for the intended age group.

The themes covered in this book are 'Teddy bears' (Reception/P1); 'Caterpillars and butterflies' (Year 1/P2); and 'Washday' (Year 2/P3).

A unit of work comprising three lessons indicates a suitable progression for each theme, but this is, of course, left to the individual teacher's own judgement. Some children or classes may need longer to explore a theme and the material provided for three sample lessons may be stretched and expanded to cover a half term's work. Progress will depend upon the creativity and movement quality of the children involved.

In addition to the lesson material there are a number of photocopiable pages provided for the teachers' use, which are found on pages 127–135.

Photocopiable pages 127, 128 and 129 act as reminder sheets that outline the progression of the three dances (one for each year group).

Photocopiable pages 130 to 135 provide a bank of Dance Activity Poems; a number of action rhymes that can be used as an introduction or conclusion to the main activity, or may even stand alone to be developed in further dance lessons. These rhymes help children to familiarise body parts, and increase their co-ordination skills through simple verse. Although it is not necessary to link them to the main theme of the lesson, they have been divided into themes, such as 'Animals', 'Shapes' and 'High and low' to help make the links easier. For example, the rhyme about the caterpillar on photocopiable page 132 would be an appropriate link to make with the work suggested for Year 1.

Dance lesson structure

Every dance lesson needs to embrace an idea or have a central theme, which will, in turn, require an appropriate stimulus such as a story, a picture or a piece of music. Effective dance lessons also need an overall structure, such as the one suggested below.

1. *Warm-up activity*

Warm-up activities should be related, where practical, to the rest of the lesson and may be used to recap previous related lessons. Action poems or rhymes are often useful in this respect (see photocopiable pages 130 to 135). Alternatively, refer to books such as *This Little Puffin* (ed. Elizabeth Matterson, Puffin) for traditional rhymes such as 'I'm a little teapot' or 'Wind the bobbin up'.

This phase of the lesson should not be prolonged. Four to five minutes is generally sufficient to raise the body temperature, mobilise the joints and sensitise the children to the new working environment – the hall.

2. *The development and exploration of the main theme*

In this phase of the lesson the children will have the opportunity to increase their movement vocabulary (see page 73 for an outline of the basic movement vocabulary) and improve the quality of their actions, while exploring a range of movement responses to the stimuli.

3. *The task*

This phase of the lesson requires the pupils to adopt a more focused approach in beginning to select and refine those previously explored movements and actions which they think are appropriate to the theme and assemble them to make their dance.

4. *Concluding activity*

This usually involves bringing the whole class together for some gentle stretching activity and may also include engaging the pupils in discussion, where appropriate, about further development of their work.

Dance

Movement vocabulary

The following list outlines the basic movement vocabulary that the teacher at Key Stage 1 (P1 to P3 in Scotland) will be concerned with, in planning effective dance lessons.

Intention
What (action)
Where (space)
How (dynamics)
Who (relationships)

▲ **Intention** – this provides the starting point. Give the class some time to consider what their dance is about and the effects they are hoping to create.

▲ **What** (action) – this refers to what the body does. There are five basic actions – travelling, jumping, balancing, turning and gesture. There are three 'body' actions – bending, twisting and stretching. All these actions can be performed using a variety of body parts, shapes and body surfaces.

▲ **Where** (space) – locates the dance, for example, levels, directions, pathways, zones (in front and behind), personal (on the spot) and general space.

▲ **How** (dynamics) – describes the effort put into a particular phrase or action. For example, is it sustained or sudden? Is it fast or slow? Strong or light?

▲ **Who** (relationships) – establishes the context of the dance in terms of interaction with others or objects. For example, alone; with a partner; with a group and so on.

Using stimuli

Children should be given the opportunity to experience working with a range and variety of contrasting stimuli and, in particular, with music.

Ideas for stimuli that may be used are as follows:

Music:

▲ can help set mood;

▲ can give structure, helping children to recognise beginnings, middles and endings of dances.

Percussion:

▲ can develop rhythm or suggest movement quality (for example, drum beat suggesting strong, marching action; shaker suggesting lighter, faster steps).

Action words, stories, and poems:

▲ can provide a source of movement ideas or a rhythm for a dance.

Photographs, objects and props:

▲ can be used as stimuli for a dance, or be included within a dance.

Suitable dance themes

As suggested, good dance lessons require a central theme or topic, with its associated stimulus, such as a story or piece of music. Most of the themes that are used by teachers at Key Stage 1 (P1 to P3 in Scotland) are suitable for exploring in dance lessons. The lists on the following page are some suggestions that are considered suitable for the different age groups specified.

Dance

Themes for Reception/Year 1 (P1 to P2):

▲ seasons or weather;
▲ growth;
▲ rain or water;
▲ animals.

Themes for Year 1/Year 2 (P2 to P3):

▲ earth, air, fire, water;
▲ space and stars;
▲ circus or fairground;
▲ moods;
▲ skeletons;
▲ patterns and pathways;
▲ machines or working actions;
▲ occupations.

Features of a good dance lesson

This has certain key features that should be observed when planning, implementing and assessing a dance activity. The features described below are broken down into three distinct areas: the lesson, the teacher, and the children. They are as follows.

The lesson:

▲ is thoroughly planned with specific learning outcomes;
▲ has a high level of physical activity.

The teacher:

▲ is enthusiastic and motivating;
▲ shares the learning outcomes with the pupils before the lesson;
▲ prepares an introductory activity reviewing aspects of the previous weeks' work;
▲ follows this with an extension activity which develops previous work or introduces new material;
▲ selects a closing activity appropriate to the learning outcome for the lesson;
▲ reviews the lesson with the pupils in simple terms and identifies targets for the next lesson.

The children:

▲ are enthusiastic and eager to participate;
▲ respond well to the tasks;
▲ show progress during the lesson;
▲ are sorry when the lesson is over.

Key stage progression

Over the key stage, children will develop and progress and will need to be given structured guidance and encouragement in order to do this. The summary below gives guidelines for the content appropriate to each specific year group.

Reception (P1)

Pupils should explore and experience the following.

What the body can do:

▲ travelling – walking, hopping, skipping, marching, rolling, moving on hands and feet;
▲ turning – turning the whole body around;
▲ jumping – two feet, one foot, one foot to another;
▲ gesture – telling simple stories with hands, expressing ideas with different parts of the body, for example, angry feet, floating fingers and so on;
▲ stillness – standing still, 'freezing' part way through a movement.

Where the body can move:

▲ on the spot – growing/shrinking;
▲ in the room – finding a space, changing level, changing direction, different pathways, for example, circles, zigzag and so on.

How the body can move:

▲ changing the weight of a movement – light/heavy;
▲ changing tension – gripping, pulling, smoothing, shaking, pushing and so on.

Differences in the time it takes for movement:

▲ changing time of movement from slow to quick. Responding to different rhythms, for example, skipping, walking, galloping and so on.

The children should be able to describe, in simple terms, what they are moving, how they are moving and where.

Year 1 (P2)

Previous work should be developed and in addition pupils should review, explore and experience the following.

What the body can do:

▲ travelling – by walking, running, skipping, hopping and galloping; without feet; using hands and feet;

▲ turning – whole body turns, half turns, circling with different parts of the body, combining turning jumps and travelling;

▲ jumping – combining jumping with travel and jumping in different shapes, landing softly and with control;

▲ gesture – further opportunities to express ideas and moods with different parts of the body or the whole body, for example, grumpy, happy, sad;

▲ stillness – stopping with control.

Where the body can move:

▲ on the spot – movements near to or far away from the body;

▲ in the room – combining pathways with different ways of travelling, changing direction;

▲ combining two directions to move diagonally (linked with work on the compass).

How the body can move:

▲ changing the weight of a movement – light/heavy;

▲ different qualities of movement, using 'action' words, such as, slide, pounce, wave, press, dash and drag;

▲ changing tension – gripping, pulling, smoothing, shaking, pushing and so on.

Differences in the time it takes for movement:

▲ combining changes in speed;

▲ practice in moving to different rhythms and at responding to changes in music.

Children should begin to respond to a partner in simple tasks, for example doing the same, following movement, taking turns. They should begin to plan short dances which have starting and finishing positions and be able to make observations describing the actions, speed and direction of their own and others' work.

Year 2 (P3)

Previous work should be developed and in addition pupils should review, explore and experience the following.

What the body can do:

▲ leading movements with different parts of the body into different areas of space, for example at different levels, in different directions/pathways;

▲ jumping and turning in different shapes.

Where the body can move:

▲ filling the space available, piercing space;

▲ responding to the concepts of over, under, around, towards, away.

How the body can move:

▲ responding to an increasing number of 'action' words;

▲ combining different qualities of movement, for example, quickly and lightly, slowly and forcefully, quickly with force, slowly with lightness.

Differences in the time it takes for movement:

▲ combining changes in speed;

▲ moving in different rhythms and responding to changes in music;

▲ moving to more complex clapping and stepping rhythms.

By the end of Year 2, children should be able to plan and execute dances with a beginning, a middle and an end, with increasing independence. Working with a partner should be more interactive, with the most able children sharing their ideas and making joint decisions with their partner about what to do. Children should be encouraged to make positive and constructive comments about their work and make judgements related to the interpretation of the task.

DANCE – RECEPTION/P1 (LESSON 1)

To develop a dance based upon the movements of a teddy bear. To develop spatial awareness skills and to appreciate how the body can move with an emphasis on tension.

Children working individually.

25 minutes.

Previous skills/knowledge needed

Ability to find space and to move safely about the working area.

Key background information

To maximise the potential of a dance activity, children need to be able to relate to a familiar situation and object. The majority of children will be familiar with a teddy bear and the way it is able to move and this will provide a good starting point for the dance activity.

Dance

The activity requires some basic counting skills and the ability to sequence movement and action. Be aware that many young children will find this difficult and will require some support and guidance in this area. For example, you may find that you will need frequently to remind the children about the next stage of the story or dance.

Preparation

Make a copy of photocopiable page 127. Ensure that you are familiar with the overall structure of the dance.

Resources needed

A teddy bear, a rag doll, photocopiable page 127, a tambourine, a Swanee whistle (available from most music shops).

What to do

Warm-up activity

Choose a suitable action rhyme or poem from the Dance Activity Poem Bank (photocopiable pages 130 to 135).

Dance activity

Gather the children together and show them the rag doll. Focus their attention on its floppiness.

Ask the children to find their own space and make themselves into a long, thin, stretched shape. Invite them to loosen their bodies to resemble the movement of the rag doll. Use the Swanee whistle to further stimulate this action from high to low to high. (The Swanee whistle makes a continuous sliding change of pitch from high to low.) Ask the children to touch the floor and then straighten up again. Repeat this activity several times.

Then encourage the children to make a wide shape by extending their arms and legs as much as possible. Can they walk keeping their arms and legs fully extended?

Gather the children back around you and show them the teddy bear. Focus their attention upon its rigid arms and legs. Show the children how the teddy bear cannot bend its knees or elbows.

Ask the children to find their own space and show their wide shape. Remind them that this shape is similar to the teddy bear's. Can they walk like a teddy bear? Remind them to keep their arms and legs stiff.

Use the tambourine to develop a rhythm of eight beats. Repeat several times. Now ask the children to stand in a space and move an arm like a teddy bear. Repeat using the other arm. Introduce a rhythm to the count of four (a count of four for each arm) by using the tambourine.

Try to combine the 'teddy bear walk' with the 'teddy bear arm action'.

Perform the dance using the tambourine.

Conclusion

To conclude the lesson ask the children to stand in a circle and remind them of the contrasting quality of movement in the rag doll. Focus their attention upon floppiness. Ask them to stretch high and then touch the floor like a rag doll. Use the Swanee whistle as a stimulus.

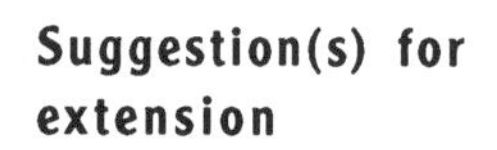

Suggestion(s) for extension

The nature of dance is such that children have the opportunity to work at their own level and capability. Clearly, individual needs will differ and some children will need the benefit of additional explanation and teacher support. Differentiation in dance, however, will be primarily achieved through outcome.

For this activity, more able children could try to walk and move like a floppy rag doll in contrast to their 'teddy' movements.

Suggestion(s) for support

Less confident children will require additional support when asked to combine the two actions they have learned. They will also need help with keeping a rhythm and counting the number of beats.

Dance

Assessment opportunities

Observe how well the children are able to show contrast between floppiness when representing the rag doll and tension in the teddy bear dance. How effectively do the children find their own space?

Reference to photocopiable sheet

Photocopiable page 127 provides a handy reference, outlining the main points of the 'Teddy bear dance'.

Teddy bear dance
▲ Starting position – teddy bear on his back.
▲ Teddy bear rocks slowly from side to side.
▲ He sits up.
▲ He stands up.
▲ He walks for eight counts.
▲ He moves one arm up and down for four counts.

DANCE – RECEPTION/P1 (LESSON 2)

To further develop the 'Teddy bear dance' and to gain experience of where the body can move – changing levels.

Children working individually and with a partner.

25 minutes.

Previous skills/knowledge needed

Ability to use space safely. Basic counting skills.

Key background information

Few children will be skilful enough to move from a sitting to a standing position with straight legs. Allow them time to explore and plan their own way of fulfilling this task. For example, by turning over on to their fronts and walking hands towards their feet.

Preparation

Make a copy of photocopiable page 127 to remind yourself of the overall structure of the dance. Have a teddy bear available.

Resources needed

A teddy bear, a rag doll, photocopiable page 127, a tambourine, a Swanee whistle.

What to do

Warm-up activity

Use the same action poem from the Dance Activity Poem Bank, as used in the previous lesson.

Dance activity

Ask the children to stand in a circle. Remind them of the movement quality of the rag doll. Ask them to show this floppiness as they touch the floor and reach for the sky. Repeat several times.

Now remind them of the 'Teddy bear dance' from their last lesson. Ask them to perform the dance. Use the tambourine to help the rhythm.

Gather the children together and show them how the teddy bear looks when he is sitting or lying down. Focus their attention upon the way that its arms and legs stay out in front of the body.

Encourage the children to find a space and lie on their backs just as a teddy would. Ask them to rock slowly from side to side keeping their teddy bear shape. Remind them to keep their arms and legs stiff!

Ask the children to sit on the floor with feet and legs wide apart and arms in front of the body. Can they rock from side to side? Challenge them to find a way of moving from their sitting position to standing, keeping their arms and legs as straight as possible.

Try now to combine the previous lesson's work with this new sequence, so that the dance becomes:

▲ starting position – teddy bear on his back;
▲ teddy bear rocks slowly from side to side;
▲ he sits up;
▲ he stands up;
▲ he walks for eight counts;
▲ he moves one arm up and down for four counts;
▲ he moves the other arm in a similar way for four counts.

Allow the children sufficient time to practise this and use the tambourine to assist rhythm.

Conclusion

Conclude the lesson by asking the children to move about the hall like a teddy bear. On the count of eight they should greet another teddy bear with a 'teddy bear' handshake – four counts on each arm. Repeat this several times.

Suggestion(s) for extension

Encourage more able children to find more than one way of moving from a sitting to a standing position.

Suggestion(s) for support
Less confident children will need help to remember the sequence of their actions.

Assessment opportunities
Observe how well the children move from sitting to standing. On the count of eight, are they able to find a partner to shake hands with?

Reference to photocopiable sheet
Photocopiable page 127 acts as a handy reference sheet outlining the main structure of the 'Teddy bear dance'.

DANCE – RECEPTION/P1 (LESSON 3)

To conclude and perform the 'Teddy bear dance' accompanied by music.
Children working individually and with a partner.
25 minutes.

Previous skills/knowledge needed
Ability to use space safely and to sequence a series of simple 'teddy bear' actions.

Key background information
The movement memory of young children is limited. In this third lesson, additional actions and musical accompaniment are added. You may feel that the children would not successfully cope with additional actions being added to the existing dance. If this is the case it would be appropriate to simply add the musical accompaniment.

Preparation
Make a copy of photocopiable page 127 to remind you of the overall structure of the dance.

Acquire a recording of the song 'Teddy Bears' Picnic'.

Resources needed
Cassette/CD of 'Teddy Bears' Picnic', cassette/CD player, photocopiable page 127.

What to do
Warm-up activity
Practise the same action rhyme or poem as used in the previous two lessons.
Dance activity
Begin the lesson by asking the children to walk around the hall like a teddy bear. Play the music and encourage the children to move in rhythm.

Remind the children about the previous lesson's concluding activity:
▲ walk for a count of eight, turn to a partner;
▲ shake hands (four on one side, four on the other);
▲ walk, shake hands and so on.

Allow suitable time for practice and then add the music. Tell the children that the teddy bears are very thirsty. Let the children explore the manner in which a teddy bear might pick up a drink from the floor. Ask them to repeat this bending action four times. Add this new section to their existing dance, using the music.

Conclusion
The dance is completed by asking the children to walk away from their partner then turn to give a 'teddy bear' wave.

Suggestion(s) for extension
More able children will find it easier to work with a partner and should be encouraged to develop their interpretation of the task, such as, by adding gesture and expression.

Suggestion(s) for support
Less confident children will need help to remember the sequence and may have difficulties working with a partner.

Assessment opportunities
Observe how well the children remember the order of the different parts of the dance.

Reference to photocopiable sheet
Photocopiable page 127 acts as a handy reference sheet outlining the basic structure of the dance.

DANCE – YEAR 1/P2 (LESSON 1)

To develop travelling skills at a low level.
Children working individually.
25 minutes.

Previous skills/knowledge needed
Ability to share space. Knowledge and understanding about the appearance of caterpillars and their movement characteristics.

Key background information
This particular theme provides excellent opportunities for linking with other areas of the curriculum, particularly science.

Preparation
Find some suitable music to stimulate the slow, curling and stretching movement of the caterpillar. For example, Bach's, *Suite No 3 in D Major,* 'Air on the G String'. Make a copy of photocopiable page 128 for reference. Copy photocopiable page 132 if required for the 'Warm-up activity'.

Resources needed
Cassette or CD player, recording of Bach's, *Suite No. 3 in D Major,* tambourine, photocopiable page 128, photocopiable page 132 (optional).

What to do
Warm-up activity
Choose an action poem from the Dance Activity Poem Bank (photocopiable pages 130 to 135). A suitable poem for this activity might be 'Caterpillar walk' on photocopiable page 132.
Dance activity
Begin the lesson by inviting the children to skip and step lightly around the hall showing changes in direction and using the space well. Next, encourage them to show simple stretching and curling in a standing position. Can the children lie down on their tummies and show a long, thin, stretched shape in this position? Can they show a curled shape by bringing their knees up towards their chest?

The task now is to travel across the floor alternating their stretched and curled shapes like a caterpillar. Play the music

as the children explore these ideas.

Explain to the children that birds can be a danger to caterpillars and that when a caterpillar senses danger, it curls up. Adopt the role of a predatory bird, explaining that when the children hear the noise of the shaking tambourine approaching they must curl tightly into a round shape. When the 'bird' moves away they can begin to stretch out again.

Conclusion

To conclude the lesson ask the children to stand up in a space and then travel around the room gently on their toes like a bird.

Caterpillar and butterfly dance

▲ The children crawl across the floor like a caterpillar to music.

▲ When the music stops they make a long, stretched shape.

▲ A bird approaches – to the accompaniment of a tambourine – and the caterpillars curl up.

▲ The children stand up and collect their cocoons (crêpe paper strips). They hold one end of the strip against their chest and slowly turn on the spot gradually wrapping the paper around their bodies.

▲ The children then emerge from their cocoons by turning in the opposite direction and proceed to fly away as newly formed butterflies holding their paper strips above their heads with both hands.

▲ The children now re-form their pairs for the pursuit and touch phase.

Dance Activity Poem Bank – animals

Now walk like a dog
Slither like a snake
Stand up and shake!

Caterpillar walk
Close to the floor
First with both hands
1, 2, 3, 4
Then with your feet
1, 2, 3, 4
Now with your hands
Just like before.

Suggestion(s) for extension

Encourage more confident children to be imaginative with their choice of bird at the end. For example, is it a tiny sparrow or a sweeping seagull?

Suggestion(s) for support

Children who find difficulty in responding to the noise of the tambourine may have to be lightly touched by the teacher to prompt their curling action.

Assessment opportunities

Observe whether the children can travel with a combination of curls and stretches like a caterpillar. Are they able to respond appropriately to the presence of the 'bird'?

Reference to photocopiable sheets

Photocopiable page 128 acts as a handy reference sheet, outlining the progression of the 'Caterpillar and butterfly dance'. Photocopiable page 132 is a selection of action poems on the theme of animals. It includes a rhyme about a caterpillar which may be particularly appropriate here.

DANCE – YEAR 1/P2 (LESSON 2)

To further develop travelling skills showing contrasts in speed and levels of movement.

Children working individually.

25 minutes.

Previous skills/knowledge needed

An ability to share space. An ability to move like a caterpillar using a series of stretching and curling movements.

Key background information

The use of props in dance activities can be extremely useful and stimulating for the children. In this particular lesson crêpe paper can be used effectively to simulate cocoon building.

Preparation

Cut up two rolls of crêpe paper into 4cm strips (approximately 1m long) – one strip for each child. Obtain a copy of Brittain's 'Lark Arising'. Make a copy of photocopiable page 128 for your reference.

Resources needed

Crêpe paper, cassette or CD player, recording of Vaughan Williams's 'The Lark Ascending' and music from the previous lesson, photocopiable page 128.

What to do

Warm-up activity

Warm up with the action poem used in the previous lesson.

Dance activity

Remind the children of the two dance phrases they developed in the previous lesson. Play the music and allow time for the children to further develop their methods of travelling showing curls and stretches like a caterpillar. When the music is switched off, the children should become stationary, showing a long, stretched shape. As the 'bird' approaches, the caterpillars make a tight, round shape. Use the tambourine to help the children identify when the bird is close to them.

Call the children together and briefly remind them how the caterpillar builds its cocoon. Explain that they are going to make their own cocoon by turning very slowly.

Ask the children to stand in their own space. Give each child one of the strips of crêpe paper and show them how to hold one end close to their chest. They must turn slowly so that the strip of paper begins to wrap around them so enclosing them in their own cocoon.

The caterpillar is then transformed into a butterfly. Ask the children to carefully *unwrap* their cocoon and hold the strip of paper with both hands above their head. The butterfly then flies away. Encourage the children to make light, fluttering movements.

Conclusion

Conclude the lesson by collecting the paper strips and asking the children to demonstrate a stretch and a curl in their own space.

Suggestion(s) for extension

Encourage more confident children to use their imagination to add their own extra touches to the dance.

Suggestion(s) for support

Some children may need help and support in wrapping their paper around their body as they turn. Alternatively, supply shorter lengths of paper to those children you anticipate will have difficulty.

Assessment opportunities

Observe how well the children are able to demonstrate light fluttering movements. How responsible were they when creating their own cocoon?

Reference to photocopiable sheet

Photocopiable page 128 acts as a handy reference material which outlines the main features of the 'Caterpillar and butterfly dance'.

Caterpillar and butterfly dance

- ▲ The children crawl across the floor like a caterpillar to music.
- ▲ When the music stops they make a long, stretched shape.
- ▲ A bird approaches – to the accompaniment of a tambourine – and the caterpillars curl up.
- ▲ The children stand up and collect their cocoons (crêpe paper strips). They hold one end of the strip against their chest and slowly turn on the spot gradually wrapping the paper around their bodies.
- ▲ The children then emerge from their cocoons by turning in the opposite direction and proceed to fly away as newly formed butterflies holding their paper strips above their heads with both hands.
- ▲ The children now re-form their pairs for the pursuit and touch phase.

DANCE – YEAR 1/P2 (LESSON 3)

To develop and consolidate travelling skills around the theme of caterpillars and butterflies, to work with a partner and to appreciate the work of others.

Children working individually and with a partner.

25 minutes.

Previous skills/knowledge needed

Ability to demonstrate lightness in movement and to move using a series of stretches and curls close to the ground. Ability to work effectively with a partner.

Key background information

This lesson completes the unit of work and the children will be performing the complete dance. In this activity the children will be given the opportunity to work closely with a partner and will be able to develop the important skills of evaluation and appreciation of others. This will be achieved by allowing the children to perform for each other.

Preparation

Ensure that the paper strips are easily accessible. Make a copy of photocopiable page 128 for your reference.

Resources needed

Recordings of music from the previous two lessons, tambourine, crêpe paper, photocopiable page 128.

What to do

Warm-up activity

Use the action poem used in the previous two lessons to begin the warm-up. Continue by asking the class to move around the hall like butterflies with light and springy actions.

Dance activity

Invite the children to sit in groups of two. One partner should adopt the role of a child who wants to touch the butterfly whilst the other continues to move like a butterfly. The butterfly then 'flies away'. When you give a signal it comes to rest again. The child skips after the butterfly in pursuit and touches the resting butterfly. When you give a signal, the butterfly sets off again and the sequence of pursuit and touch continues.

Then help the class to put the complete dance together, as shown on photocopiable page 128.

When the children have rehearsed their dance several times, split the class into two halves. Ask one half to observe while the other half performs the dance and then change over. Focus the observation upon how well the children think the performers travel. Can they travel lightly like a butterfly? Do they travel using small steps? Do they travel lightly on their toes?

Suggestion(s) for extension

Encourage more confident children to use their imagination to develop their skills of gesture and interpretation.

Suggestion(s) for support

It may be helpful to pair a confident child with a less confident one in the partner phase of the dance.

Assessment opportunities

Observe how well the children are able to construct the complete dance. Are they able to remember the sequence? How effectively do they combine their actions with their partner? Are they able to communicate their observations when acting as an audience?

Reference to photocopiable sheet

Photocopiable page 128 is a handy reference sheet outlining the main features of the 'Caterpillar and butterfly dance'.

DANCE – YEAR 2/P3 (LESSON 1)

To develop an appreciation of level and shape in dance form. To develop a sense of rhythm in dance.
Children working individually and as part of a larger group.
30 minutes.

Previous skills/knowledge needed
Ability to match movement and action to a sound stimulus (story and percussion).

Key background information
Young children are not able to bring an abstract dimension to dance. They are most comfortable, in terms of their own understanding, with the daily, practical things that surround their lives. The following three lessons focus upon a series of activities that will be found in most homes and to which the children will be able to relate and give meaning through dance. Although this unit of work should provide three lessons it is possible to be flexible and extend the time available if necessary to accommodate the progress of the class.

Preparation
Ensure that a range of percussion instruments is available.

Resources needed
Drum or tambourine, the story *Tidy Titch* by Pat Hutchins (Red Fox).

What to do
Warm-up activity
Choose an action poem from the Dance Action Poem Bank (photocopiable pages 130 to 135).
Dance activity
Gather the children together and tell them the story *Tidy Titch*. Discuss the story and talk about how the children had left their clothes and toys all over the place:
▲ on the floor;
▲ under the bed;
▲ down the sides of cupboards;
▲ behind furniture.

Now ask the children to find a space. Ask them to move lightly around the hall – skipping, walking or running – as they might imagine a young child to do when playing in a garden or park.

When the children are warm, change the scene to the child's bedroom. Encourage the children to pretend they are gathering up clothes and toys. They will need to do some bending, reaching and stretching. Use the drum or tambourine to beat out an eight beat rhythm with an emphasis upon the first beat. Ask the children to change their actions after eight beats.

Gather the children into a big circle. Organise them into pairs and label them A and B. Ask the 'A's to enter the circle. The 'B's – with your help, will then clap out the eight beat rhythm whilst the 'A's perform their stretching, reaching and bending shapes, holding each shape for a count of eight. Repeat the sequence of shapes several times. Now ask the children to change over roles.
Conclusion
Conclude this lesson with marching around the room. Invite the children to pretend that they are an angry parent on his or her way to see if the room has been tidied. Reinforce this action with strong beats on the drum or tambourine.

Suggestion(s) for extension
More confident children should be encouraged to perform a greater range of shapes.

Suggestion(s) for support
Less confident children might be paired with another child in order to shadow or copy the work.

Assessment opportunities
Observe how well the children sustain and hold their shapes to the eight beat count. Are they able to clap out the eight beat rhythm?

DANCE – YEAR 2/P3 (LESSON 2)

To learn circles, turns and twists in a simple dance form and to develop movement patterns to sound.

Children working individually.

30 minutes.

Previous skills/knowledge needed

Good listening skills. Knowledge of a basic movement vocabulary, including turning and twisting.

Key background information

Ensure that you are clear about the difference between a turning action and a twisting action so that you can explain it to the children. A turning action usually involves the whole body – or body part – rotating around a particular axis, for example, spinning or circling movements. Twisting usually implies that one part of the body turns in one direction whilst another part turns at the same time in an opposing direction.

Preparation

Gather together the visual resources required (see 'Resources needed' below). Make a recording of a washing machine.

Resources needed

A picture/photograph of a washing machine, a towel, a picture/photograph of a washing line with somebody hanging out washing and a tape-recording of a washing machine, cassette recorder, tambourine.

What to do

Warm-up activity

Warm up by using the same action poem as used in the previous lesson.

Dance activity

Invite the children to sit in a circle. Play the recording of a washing machine in action and ask the children if they recognise the sound being made. Ask them to listen in particular to the steady rhythm that the machine is making. Use the picture/photograph of a washing machine to reinforce what will be the focus of the activity to follow.

Encourage the children to spread out around the hall and remind them of the last lesson and the children who had to tidy their rooms. Use a skipping activity as a further warm-up activity. This will also bring balance to the lesson since much of the activity will involve the children working in their own space.

Now ask the children to find their own space again. Ask them to copy the action of a washing machine as it spins around, by turning various body parts:

- hands;
- feet;
- a shoulder;
- elbows.

Use a tambourine to count out eight beats and then change the body part. Now extend this turning action to involve large body parts. Ask the children to make big circles with:

- their hands together and feet slightly spaced out (trunk rotation). Ask the childen to imagine they are windmills. (See (A) in the diagram below);
- their hips;
- their legs by laying flat on their back;
- their arms stretched out wide and turning on the spot. Ask the children to imagine they are roundabouts. (See (B) in the diagram below).

After a little practice, use the tambourine again to count out an eight beat rhythm, while the children choose one of the turning actions to try. After eight beats they should change to a different turning action.

Encourage the children to imagine the clothes in the washing machine being churned around and use the towel to demonstrate a twisting action. Ask them to show a twisting action with their bodies – first one way and then the other. Use the tambourine again to determine the speed of the action to an eight beat count – alternating between fast and slow twisting but only changing on the count of eight.

Now tell the children that the machine has stopped. Ask them to 'take out the clothes' and to give them a good shake.

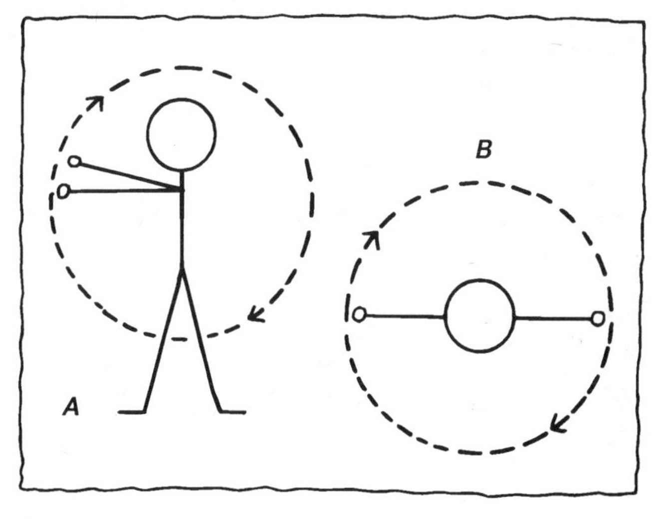

Conclusion

To conclude the activity ask the children to stretch and hang out the clothes, and to hold this hanging body shape very still – for at least four strong beats of the tambourine. Repeat this several times as the conclusion to the lesson.

Suggestion(s) for extension

More confident children should be encouraged to devise their own circling actions in addition to those suggested by the teacher.

Suggestion(s) for support
Less confident children should be paired with a more able partner and asked to copy their actions, if needed.

Assessment opportunities
Observe the quality of turning and twisting. Are the children able to discriminate between the two? Are they able to work confidently to a count of eight?

DANCE – YEAR 2/P3 (LESSON 3)

To combine previous work into a composite dance around the theme of washday and to work as a group and develop combination skills.

Children working individually and in small groups.

30 minutes.

Previous skills/knowledge needed
Ability to sequence actions around a simple theme.

Key background information
This lesson represents the culmination of previous work and challenges the children to remember and perform the overall sequence associated with their dance. Some new elements are added, however, in order to bring better continuity to the dance, seeking to build upon the existing actions/body shapes of the children and combining these with the actions of others.

Preparation
Gather together the visual resources required (see 'Resources needed' below). Make a recording of a washing machine. Make a copy of photocopiable page 129 for your reference.

Resources needed
A picture/photograph of a washing machine, a towel, a picture/photograph of a washing line with somebody hanging out washing and a tape-recording of a washing machine, cassette recorder, tambourine, photocopiable page 129.

What to do
Warm-up activity

Warm up using the action poem used in the previous lessons.

Dance activity

Organise the children into pairs. Ask them to imagine themselves as a pile of clothes. One partner lays flat on the ground and the other makes a shape over them. Allow the children plenty of time to practise. Now remind the class about the overall sequence of the dance they are about to perform, using photocopiable page 129 as a prompt.

Guide the actions of the children through the complete dance. It may help to display large pictures/photographs of the various phases of the dance at the side of the working area to help the children remember the full sequence.

After the dance has been rehearsed several times, ask the children to respond to the tambourine alone, changing their actions to the count of eight.

Conclusion

Conclude the lesson by asking half the class to observe while the other half performs and then changes over. The observers should be asked to comment on how well the performers are able to link their actions to the sound of the tambourine.

Suggestion(s) for extension
Ask more confident children to perform to suitable music or the steady rhythms of machine sounds.

Suggestion(s) for support
Less confident children will need guidance about when to change their actions.

Assessment opportunities
Observe how well the children bring a sense of rhythm to their dance. Are they able to reproduce the sequence of actions? Do they make positive comments about the performance of others when in the role of observers?

Reference to photocopiable sheet
Photocopiable page 129 acts as a handy reference material, outlining the main features and progression of the 'Washing machine dance'.

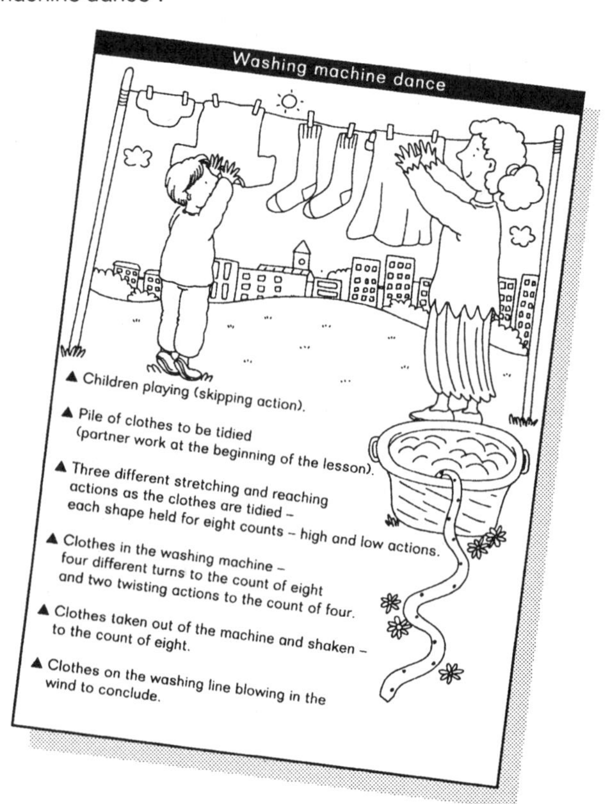

Washing machine dance
▲ Children playing (skipping action).
▲ Pile of clothes to be tidied (partner work at the beginning of the lesson).
▲ Three different stretching and reaching actions as the clothes are tidied – each shape held for eight counts – high and low actions.
▲ Clothes in the washing machine – four different turns to the count of eight and two twisting actions to the count of four.
▲ Clothes taken out of the machine and shaken – to the count of eight.
▲ Clothes on the washing line blowing in the wind to conclude.

Assessment and record keeping

Assessment in physical education is concerned with:

▲ informing the teacher about the individual strengths and weaknesses of children relating to their physical development;

▲ informing the children themselves about how well they are doing;

▲ providing the teacher with information about the overall progress of children as a means of evaluating the planning and the teaching of physical education.

Physical education is an active, practical subject. As a result of this and other factors, assessment is dealt with in a slightly different way from usual.

Physical education takes place in an environment in which children are more widely dispersed than in the usual classroom. Learning outcomes are usually expressed through the actions of children rather than in a written form. Health and safety obligations require the teacher to be aware of the whole class at all times. These rather unique features which surround physical education require assessment procedures that are straightforward and manageable, yet achieve the objectives outlined above.

Much knowledge about the progress of individual children and that of the class in general will not necessarily need to be written down. Many of the observations included in the 'Assessment opportunities' sections of the sample lessons throughout this book are of this nature. Provided the school has a well-established whole-school scheme of work for physical education with clearly defined learning outcomes and all staff have had a meaningful involvement in its planning and development, then teachers can be confident that progression will usually take place.

Assessment and record keeping

There does come a time, however, when teachers need to make a permanent record of pupil achievement – a *summative* assessment. It is also necessary for teachers to record the work that they have covered with their class, to avoid any unnecessary duplication of skills and themes. Some skills, of course, will be covered to a greater or lesser depth across the whole of the key stage. To help ensure that every teacher has an awareness of where their next class of children is coming from, in terms of physical development, it helps to use a whole-school documentation system. Photocopiable page 136 is an example of a way in which teachers can keep track of the work they have done with their respective classes.

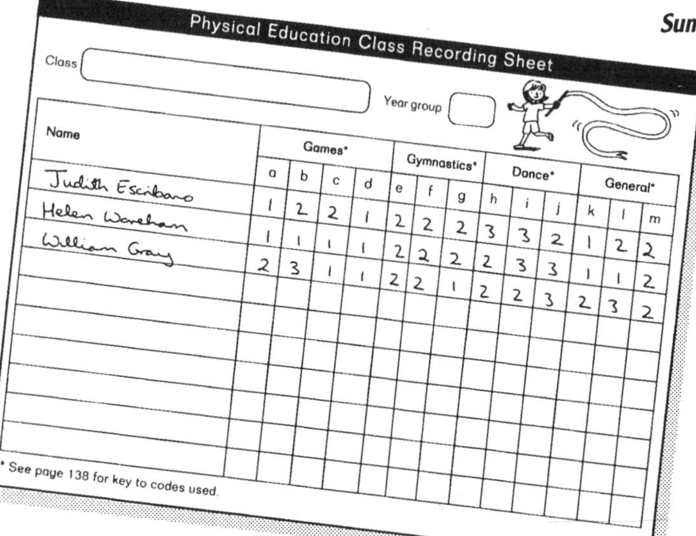

Physical Education Class Recording Sheet

Class ______ Year group ______

Name	Games*				Gymnastics*			Dance*			General*		
	a	b	c	d	e	f	g	h	i	j	k	l	m
Judith Escribano	1	2	2	1	2	2	2	3	3	2	1	2	2
Helen Wareham	1	1	1	1	2	2	2	2	3	3	1	1	2
William Gray	2	3	1	1	2	2	1	2	2	3	2	3	2

* See page 138 for key to codes used.

Summative assessment at Key Stage 1

The 'Class Recording Sheet' – photocopiable page 137, supplemented by photocopiable pages 138 and 139, will help the teacher to maintain a meaningful record of the progress and achievement of young children in physical education, while providing written evidence to inform assessment against the 'End of Key Stage Description' in the National Curriculum. The 'Class Recording Sheet' should be reviewed and, if necessary, updated twice a year by the teacher to allow for the rapid progress that some children display in the course of their physical development.

Formative and summative assessment

Assessment in physical education is achieved by the careful observations of the class teacher. It is a necessary process for establishing and communicating the achievement of pupils. This chapter considers ways of making this assessment process manageable.

It would naturally be too difficult for a teacher to record in fine detail every aspect of a child's progress through the physical education curriculum. In general, the teacher will constantly be evaluating how individual children and groups of children cope with the work presented to them. The 'Assessment opportunities' sections in the lesson plans suggest some observations for teachers to make. These types of observations help to inform the teacher of each pupil's progress and development. They can also help the teacher to plan future work in an informed and effective way, keeping pace with the development of the children in their class. Some teachers prefer to make some regular written records of pupil progress through a particular unit of work in order to sustain their teaching. Others prefer to keep this information in their heads, remembering their observations and using this knowledge to inform the next stage of their teaching. This type of assessment is referred to as *formative* assessment.

Assessment and record keeping

It is recommended that a three-tier system of assessment, indicating three levels of achievement, is used for each activity and area of development:

▲ working below expectations (denoted by 1);
▲ working in line with expectations (denoted by 2);
▲ working beyond expectations (denoted by 3).

This system enables the teacher to see at a glance the profile of class and individual pupil achievement across the three activities. Examples of the way in which these sheets may be filled in are shown on page 88.

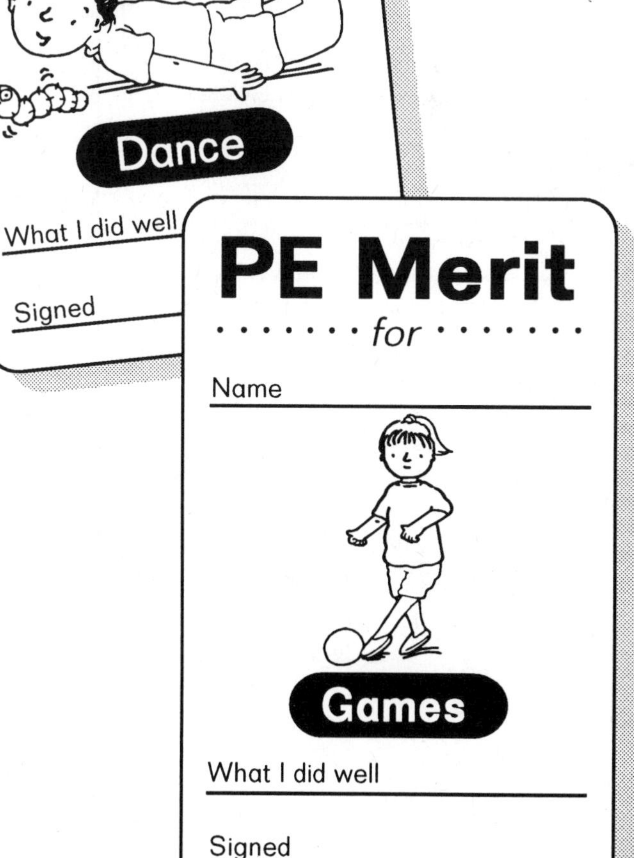

Merit cards in PE

The 'Class Recording Sheet' can be usefully complemented by awarding 'merits' to those children who produce good work in physical education or who simply try hard and practise conscientiously. This serves to provide the children with direct acknowledgement of their efforts. Some examples of merit cards are offered on photocopiable pages 140 and 141.

The 'merit cards' may be awarded for a variety of reasons. Some should be skill-based covering the three areas of physical education at this age range. Others should be based on personal effort and could include the categories:

▲ working with others;
▲ perseverance;
▲ outstanding effort;
▲ careful handling of apparatus;
▲ awareness of safety/working sensibly.

The 'merit cards' may be used in a variety of ways, depending on school policy/teacher preference. Some examples of ways to use them are listed below. Many teachers may find that a combination of these procedures works well.

▲ They may be collected in a box which is periodically emptied by the teacher who then 'celebrates' the children's achievements at a group gathering (possibly a school/class assembly).

▲ They may be sent home with the child, to share their success with their family.

▲ You may use them to inform your own recording of the children's achievements, adding them to individual children's records.

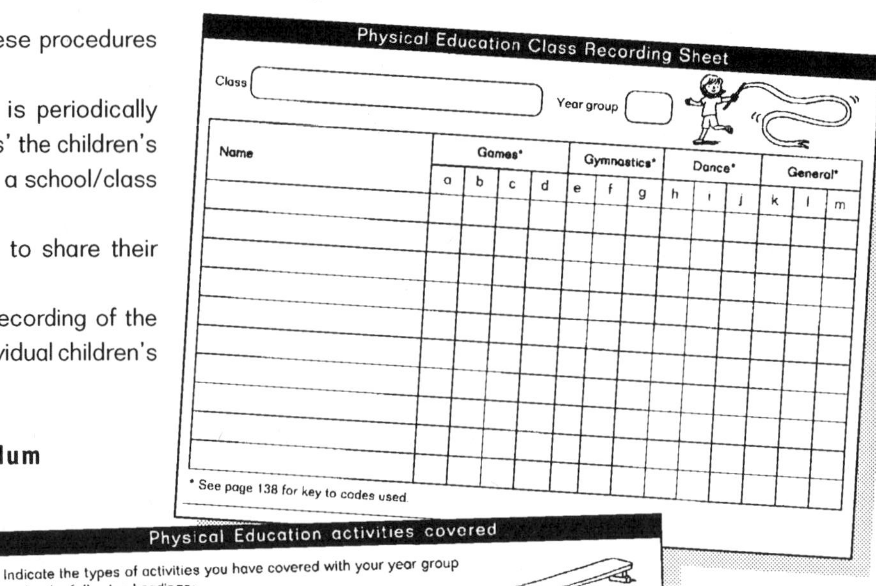

Physical Education Class Recording Sheet

Class ____ Year group ____

Name	Games*				Gymnastics*			Dance*			General*		
	a	b	c	d	e	f	g	h	i	j	k	l	m

* See page 138 for key to codes used.

Evaluating delivery of the PE curriculum

It is important that teachers themselves carry out some form of evaluation of the success of their own teaching. The photocopiable page 107, which is used in conjunction with the 'Games' activity chapter provides a good starting point for conducting reflection of this kind.

Physical Education activities covered

Indicate the types of activities you have covered with your year group under the following headings:

Class ____ Year group ____

Games	
Gymnastics	
Dance	

Games Lesson Evaluation – Are my games lessons effective?

Teacher – Did I give helpful guidance?

Pupils – Did the children become more skilful?

Teacher – Did I plan effectively?

Pupils – Did the activities match the abilities of the children?

Teacher – Was my organisation sound and the equipment accessible?

Pupils – Did the children have sufficient time to practise?

Teacher – Did I maintain a good working atmosphere?

Pupils – Did the children practise conscientiously and with concentration?

Teacher – Was the lesson vigorous enough with high activity levels?

Pupils – Were the children pleasantly tired and out of breath?

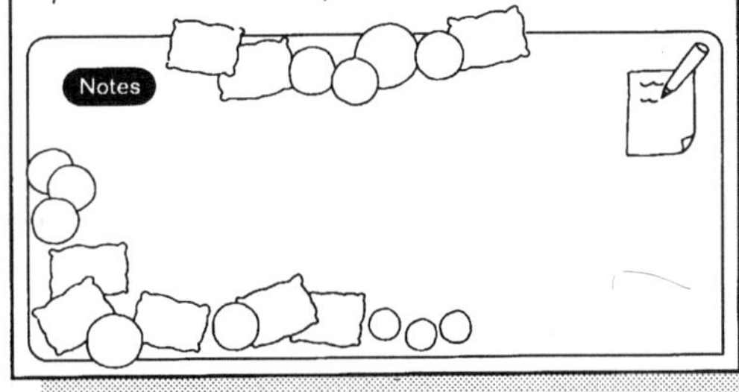

Photocopiables

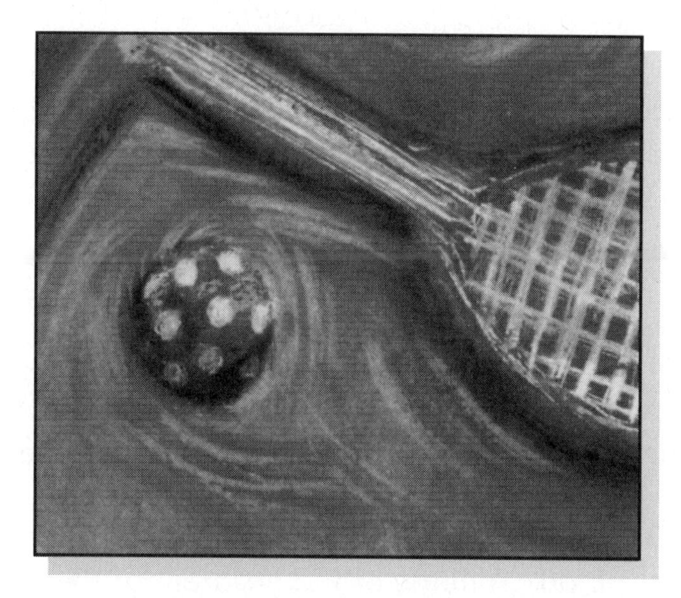

The pages in this section can be photocopied for use in the classroom or school which has purchased this book, and do not need to be declared in any return in respect of any photocopying licence.

They comprise a varied selection of both pupil and teacher resources, including pupil worksheets, resource material and record sheets to be completed by the teacher or children. Most of the photocopiable pages are related to individual activities in the book; the name of the activity is indicated at the top of the sheet, together with a page reference indicating where the lesson plan for that activity can be found.

Individual pages are discussed in detail within each lesson plan, accompanied by ideas for adaptation where appropriate – of course, each sheet can be adapted to suit your own needs and those of your class. Sheets can also be coloured, laminated, mounted on to card, enlarged and so on where appropriate.

Pupil worksheets and record sheets have spaces provided for children's names and for noting the date on which each sheet was used. This means that, if so required, they can be included easily within any pupil assessment portfolio.

Photocopiable sheets 136 to 141 are to be used for the purposes of summative assessment and accompany the activities in the Assessment chapter.

The essentials of physical education, see page 17

Guidelines for producing a Key Stage 1 PE policy document

Rationale

Why do we include PE in the curriculum?

Statement of aims of the PE policy

▲ as related to the aims of the school;

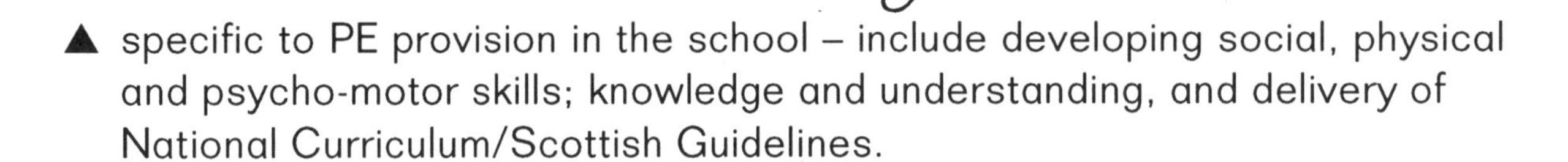

▲ specific to PE provision in the school – include developing social, physical and psycho-motor skills; knowledge and understanding, and delivery of National Curriculum/Scottish Guidelines.

Planning the policy

▲ Content – a balanced programme of activities including games, gymnastics and dance.

▲ Continuity and progression – using the National Curriculum Programmes of Study/Scottish Guidelines, curriculum plan, schemes and units of work.

▲ Assessment – of PE programme, of the children, of the lessons – who, when, and how will this be done?

▲ Staff development – LEA courses, college courses, support/input by adviser/advisory teacher/consultant/co-ordinator.

▲ Resources – facilities and availability (books, videos, curriculum units, activity areas, teaching packs, schemes, equipment) – who uses which resources and when?

▲ PE development (within school development plan) – plan, proposed time scale and priorities.

▲ Raising awareness of PE within the school – displays, assemblies, parental involvement, videos, open evenings, extra-curricular/clubs.

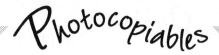

The essentials of physical education, see page 17

General Issues

Could include:

- ▲ a statement regarding who delivers PE, addressing the class teacher/co-ordinator support;
- ▲ the school's commitment and response to equal opportunities issues – mixed-class activities, curriculum access and differentiation;
- ▲ acknowledgement of SEN provision, including current policy, records available and addressing the issue of updating and reviewing;
- ▲ safety statement, for example, as a staff you may choose to follow the guidelines as set out in *Safe Practice in the Teaching of Physical Education*, (BAALPE), highlighting any areas that you are particularly concerned with;
- ▲ dress statement, including: recommended kit, no jewellery policy, changing clothes, changing facilities and privacy, staff changing and suitable footwear;
- ▲ participation for all and a recommendation for 'non-participants' (what the criteria are for non-participation and mention the benefits for all of PE);
- ▲ equipment – responsibility for maintenance, storage and re-ordering;
- ▲ extra-curricular activities – clubs and activities, staff, voluntary helpers and transport;
- ▲ first aid – emergency procedures, qualified first aiders, location of first aid equipment.

Appendices

May include:

- ▲ whole school programme
- ▲ schemes of work
- ▲ curriculum units
- ▲ assessment structure
- ▲ arrangements for swimming (if appropriate)
- ▲ certificates or merits
- ▲ arrangements for 'sports day'

My exercise diary, see page 20

My exercise diary

Name ______________________ **Date** ______________

▲ Draw or stick down a picture next to each day to show what kind of exercise you did then.

Monday

Tuesday

Wednesday

Thursday

Friday

Saturday

Which activity did you enjoy the most? ______________________

My exercise diary, see page 20

How does exercise keep me fit?

My body and exercise, see page 21

How does exercise keep me fit?

Name ______________________________ Date ________________

Something happens to your heart when you exercise.

▲ Show where your heart is on the picture.

Can you feel your heart beating? __________

▲ Now do some exercise.

What does your heart feel like now? __________________________

____

Games chapter, see pages 25–52

Games Activity Bank – sending and receiving

Individually:

1 Put the ball close to your feet. Roll the ball *slowly* in front of you. Can you walk alongside your ball?

2 Roll a ball or quoit forwards. Chase it and capture it.

3 Roll the ball against the wall. Collect the ball when it rebounds.

4 Roll a ball towards a skittle, collect it and repeat. Each time you hit the skittle take a step further away.

5 Bounce the ball gently in front of you. Catch it and repeat.

6 Bounce the ball hard on the ground. Catch it and repeat.

7 Bounce the ball hard on the ground. Can you jump and catch it?

8 Bounce a ball continuously in front of you. Can you bounce it under a leg?

9 Throw the ball in the air. Let it bounce then catch it.

10 Throw a bean bag up in the air. Catch it and repeat.

Games chapter, see pages 25–52

Games Activity Bank – sending and receiving

Individually:

11 Throw the ball high in the air.
Let it bounce, catch it and repeat.

12 Throw a ball in the air.
Catch it and repeat.

13 Throw a ball in the air. Clap and catch it.

14 Put the ball by your feet. Push the ball gently with your foot, follow it, collect it and repeat.

15 Push the ball with your foot against the wall. Collect it using your hands then repeat.

16 Strike the ball against the wall using your foot.
Collect it using your hands then repeat.

17 Push the ball against the wall using your foot and stop it with your foot.

18 Place a large ball in front of you.
Strike the ball with your hand, chase it, pick it up. Look for another space and repeat.

19 Using a bat and ball, push the ball slowly along the ground.

20 Using a bat and ball, bounce the ball on the ground with your bat.

Games chapter, see pages 25–52

Games Activity Bank – sending and receiving

With a partner:

21 From a kneeling position, roll the ball slowly to your partner. Stop the ball with your hands and repeat.

22 Roll the ball to your partner. Stop the ball with your hands.

23 Roll the ball to your partner. Stop the ball with your feet.

24 Roll the ball to your partner. Stop the ball with your stick.

25 Roll the ball to your partner. Stop the ball with your body.

26 Roll the ball slowly to the side of your partner. Move to stop the ball with your hands.

27 Roll the ball between two markers. Your partner fields the ball and returns it to the starting position. Take five turns each.

28 Roll the ball into a space. Your partner fields the ball and brings it back to you.

29 One partner has a ball. They point to the space where they are going to send it. Their partner chases and collects the ball and returns to the starting position. Take turns in sending the ball.

Games chapter, see pages 25–52

Games Activity Bank – sending and receiving

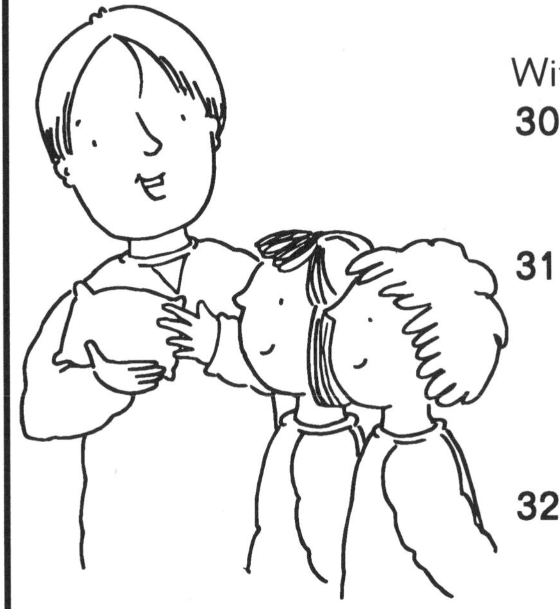

With a partner:

30 Throw a bean bag underarm for your partner to catch. Repeat.

31 Throw a bean bag to your partner. Run into a space and stop. Your partner then throws the bean bag to you and runs into a different space.

32 Bounce the ball on the ground for your partner to catch.

33 Bounce the ball into the hoop for your partner to catch.

34 Throw a ball underarm (two-handed) to your partner. He or she catches and returns it by rolling it along the floor.

35 Throw a ball (chest pass) to your partner. He or she catches it and returns it by rolling it along the ground.

36 Throw a bean bag or ball underarm to your partner. He or she catches and returns it by throwing underarm. Now throw the ball to your partner. Run into a space and stop. Your partner catches the ball and then throws it back to you and runs into a space. Repeat.

37 Throw a ball overarm to your partner. He or she catches and returns the ball overarm.

Games chapter, see pages 25–52

Games Activity Bank – sending and receiving

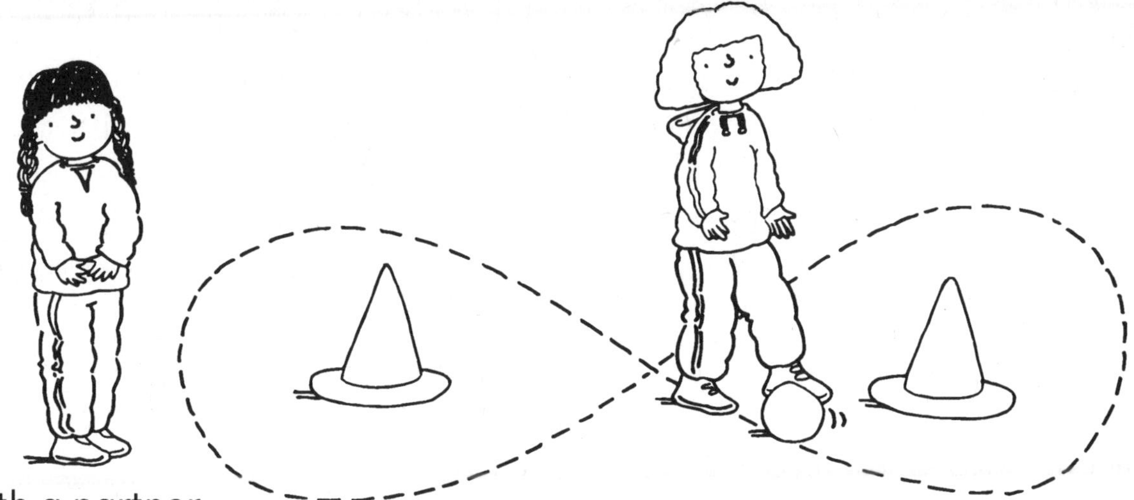

With a partner:

38 Dribble the ball, using your feet, between two cones in a figure of '8'. Have two turns, then your partner has two turns.

39 Dribble the ball using a hockey stick between the two cones in a figure of '8'. Have two turns, then your partner takes two turns.

40 Roll a ball to your partner's hockey stick. Your partner stops the ball with the stick and pushes the ball, using the stick, to return it to you.

41 Each partner has a hockey stick. Push the ball to each other. Stop the ball with the stick before sending it back.

42 Each partner has a hockey stick. Push the ball to your partner, run into a space and stop. Your partner must push the ball back to you and then run into a space.

43 Place a large ball in front of you. Strike the ball with your hand along the ground to your partner. Repeat.

Games Activity Bank – sending and receiving

With a partner:

44 Place a large ball in front of you. Strike the ball using the inside part of your foot. Your partner stops the ball and returns it.

45 Kick the ball to your partner. Run into a space and stop. Your partner must kick the ball back to you and then run into a space.

46 Using two cones as a target, strike the ball between the cones with your hand. Your partner then rolls the ball back to you. Have five turns each.

47 Using two cones as a target, push the ball between the two cones with your foot. Your partner collects the ball and rolls it back to you. Have five turns each.

48 Using a bat and ball, push the ball along the floor to your partner. Your partner stops the ball with his or her hands and brings it back to you. Repeat five times then change over.

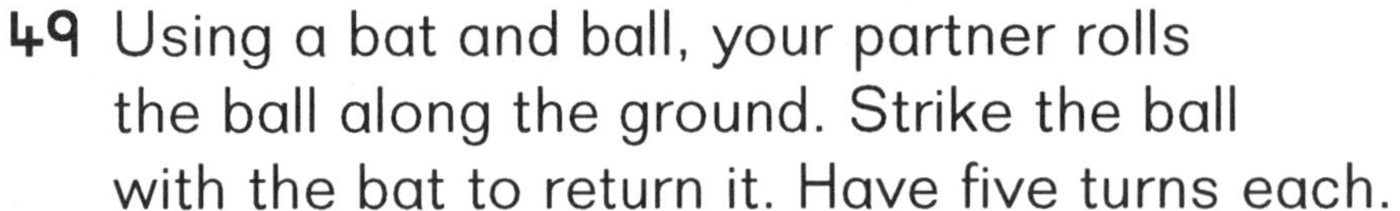

49 Using a bat and ball, your partner rolls the ball along the ground. Strike the ball with the bat to return it. Have five turns each.

Games chapter, see pages 25–52

Games Activity Bank – sending and receiving

With a partner:

50 Using a bat and ball, drop the ball in front of you. Hit the ball into a space. Your partner fields the ball and brings it back to you. Have five turns each.

51 Using a bat and ball drop the ball in front of you. Hit the ball between two cones. Your partner fields the ball and brings it backto you. Have five turns each.

52 Place a hoop between you and your partner. Throw the ball gently into the hoop. Your partner gently hits the ball back with a bat for you to catch.

53 Place a rope between you and your partner. Bounce the ball over the rope. Your partner catches it after one bounce then bounces the ball back to you over the rope.

54 Each partner has a bat. Bounce the ball (self-feed) to hit it to your partner. Your partner hits it to return it to you. Can you each hit the ball after just one bounce?

55 In threes, using a large ball, play 'piggy in the middle'.

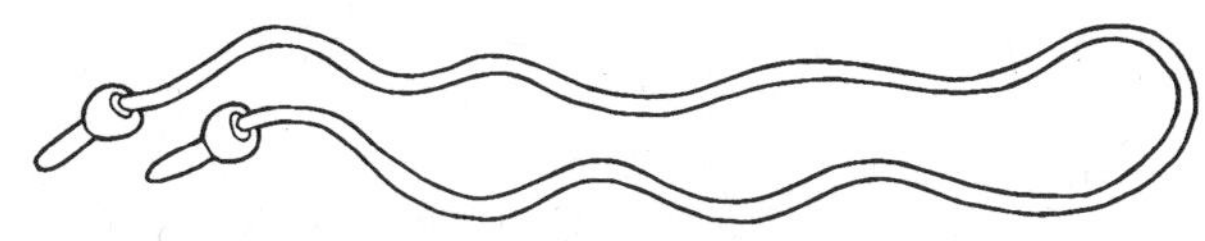

Games chapter, see pages 25–52

Games Activity Bank – travelling and co-ordination skills

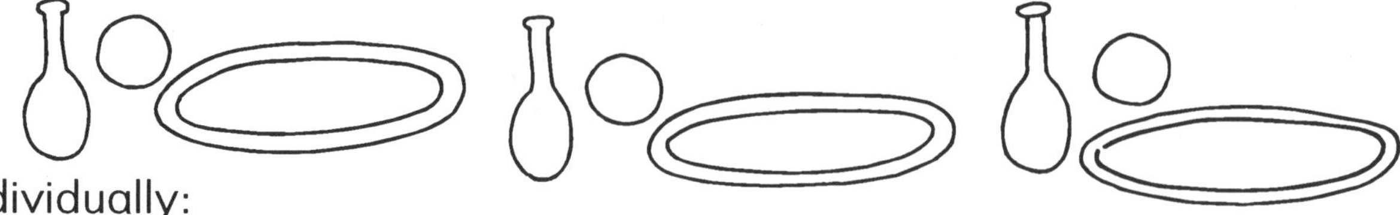

Individually:

56 Without making a sound, travel around the space like a motor car. When you hear 'stop', show how good your brakes are!

57 Place your hoop on the floor. Jump in, out and around it.

58 *Place skittles and hoops in the working area and give each child a ball.* Travel with your ball in different directions. Bounce your ball in the hoops and roll it towards the skittles.

59 Place a rope on the floor, jump over it with two feet together.

60 Stand on a line. Can you jump from two feet to two feet, backwards and forwards over the line?

61 Hold a ball against your tummy. Roll the ball around your waist.

62 Hold a ball against your tummy. Roll the ball around other body parts.

63 Using a rope, skip on the spot. Can you travel forwards while skipping?

64 Put the ball close to your feet. Using your feet, take your ball for a slow walk. Keep it close to you.

Games chapter, see pages 25–52

Games Activity Bank – travelling and co-ordination skills

Individually:

65 Find a line on the playground.
Dribble the ball along the line using your feet.

66 Using your feet, dribble the ball between two cones in a figure of '8'.

67 Using a hockey stick, dribble the ball between the two cones in a figure of '8'.

68 Using a bat, push the ball across the playground.
Stop the ball with the bat.

69 Using a hockey stick and ball, take your ball for a slow walk. Keep the ball close to the stick (slightly in front of your body).

70 Find a line on the playground. Using a stick and ball, dribble the ball along the line.

71 Balance a ball on your bat. Let the ball move around.
Can you go for a slow walk?

72 Balance a ball on your bat. Let it fall off and bounce.
Can you collect it on your bat again?

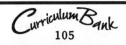

Games Activity Bank – travelling and co-ordination skills

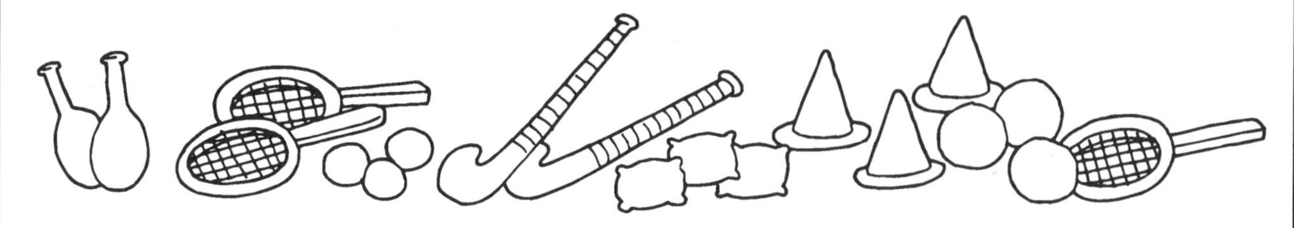

73 *Each child in the class travels with a ball. Choose three children to be taggers who try to tag class members.* Hold your ball with two hands and use it to tag. When tagged, you must stand with your feet apart. If you're still free then try to roll the ball between the feet of the children who are trapped. This will free them.

74 Travel showing changes in direction. When you hear a number, get into groups of that number and sit down.

75 *Have a box of bean bags/balls to hand and space the children out in front. Throw the balls to the children.* You must catch/intercept/retrieve them and return them to the box.

76 Take a ball, travel with it and try to touch the ball of the other children. When you lose your ball you must stand still and bounce it five times before you can move on.

77 Choose a piece of equipment. Think about the activities we have done in PE. Make up a game on your own using your equipment.

78 Choose a piece of equipment. Think about the activities we have done in PE. Make up a game with your partner using your equipment.

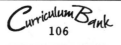

Games chapter, see pages 25–52

Games Lesson Evaluation – Are my games lessons effective?

Teacher – Did I give helpful guidance?

Pupils – Did the children become more skilful?

Teacher – Did I plan effectively?

Pupils – Did the activities match the abilities of the children?

Teacher – Was my organisation sound and the equipment accessible?

Pupils – Did the children have sufficient time to practise?

Teacher – Did I maintain a good working atmosphere?

Pupils – Did the children practise conscientiously and with concentration?

Teacher – Was the lesson vigorous enough with high activity levels?

Pupils – Were the children pleasantly tired and out of breath?

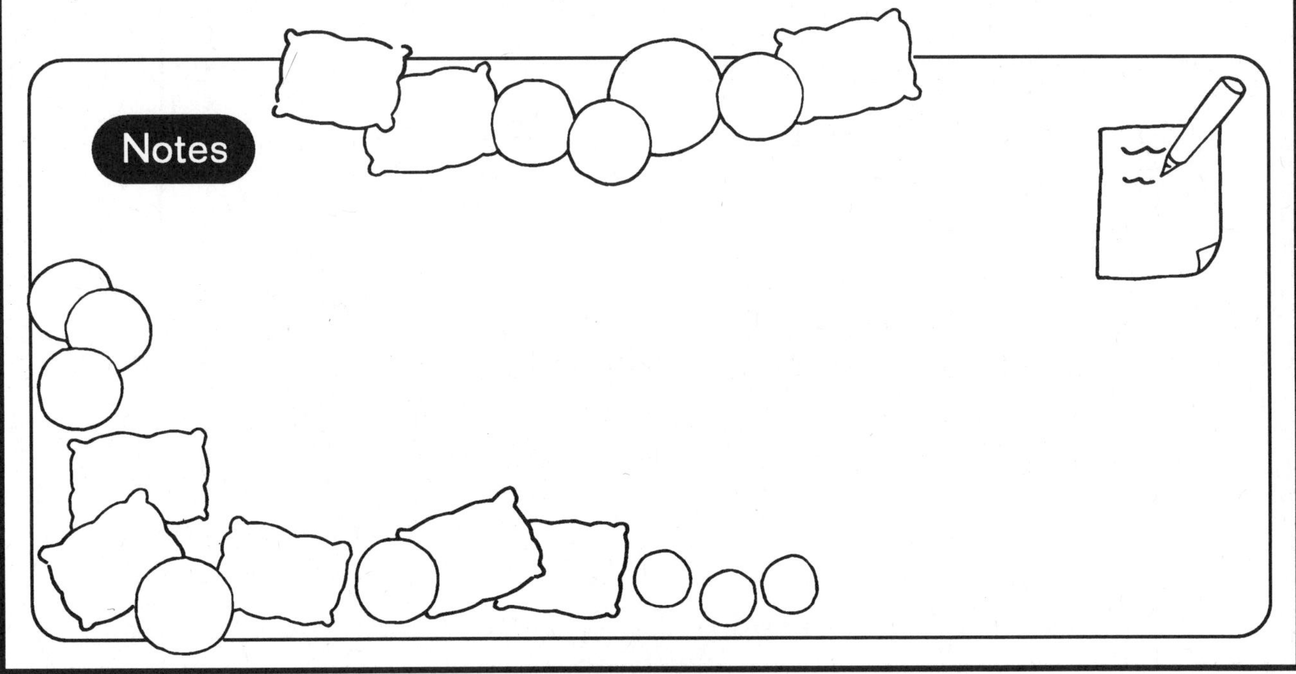

Gymnastics chapter, see pages 53–70

Gymnastic Activity Bank – defining basic actions

Travelling involves moving from one place to another.

Jumping involves movement of the whole body from feet to feet.

Rolling involves movement of the whole body on the floor.

Balancing involves stillness with control of the whole body.

Turning involves movement while standing up.

Hanging involves suspending the whole body from a fixed point.

Climbing involves changing levels while maintaining contact with the apparatus.

Gymnastics chapter, see pages 53–70

Gymnastic Activity Bank – jumping

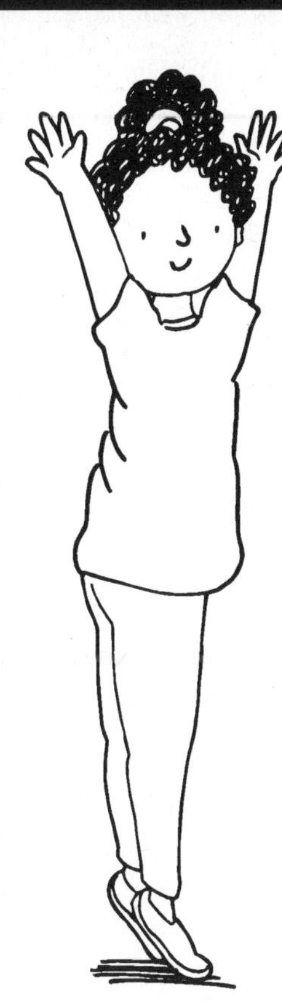

Use of body parts

1 Landing, emphasising ball of foot first and bend of knees.
2 Jumping, with variation in foot patterns.
3 Jumping, stressing stretch of feet in air.
4 Specific jumps (five basic jumps) concentrating on take-off and landing foot or feet.
5 Jumping, emphasising arms and/or knees in the air.
6 Jumping, emphasising leg action in flight – stretch, tuck, wide.

Movement factors

7 Jumping on the spot, emphasising 'push' off.
8 Jumping, moving freely in the room.
9 Running and jumping, using restricted space.
10 Jumping, concentrating on resilience in landing to give light landing.
11 Jumping, concentrating on 'exploding' in the air.
12 Rhythmical jumping (with or without a rope).
13 Jumping, with a strong 'push' on take off from feet and legs, landing with resilience.
14 Jumping, emphasising tension in the whole body, relaxing on landing.
15 Jumping, and landing in stillness.
16 Running, jumping and turning in flight.
17 Running and jumping, with specific take-offs and landings (five basic jumps).
18 Jumping, to land in balance and stillness.

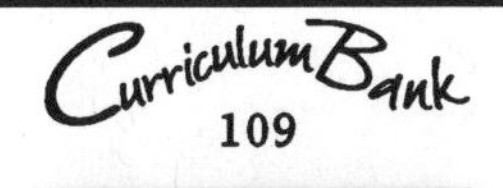

Gymnastics chapter, see pages 53–70

Gymnastic Activity Bank – jumping

Shape

19 Jumping with variation of body shape in the air.
20 Jumping with specific body shape in the air – long, wide.
21 Jumping with specific body shape in the air, showing contrast – long, wide, tucked, twist.

Relationship

22 Jumping in/out, on/off, over mats and low apparatus.
23 Jumping in unison with a partner.
24 Jumping in/out, on/off, over, along and across apparatus, involving take-offs and landings from one or two feet.
25 Jumping on/off large apparatus with specific take-offs and landings, with a turn in the air and with different body shapes in the air. (Note that as the apparatus becomes higher, mats *must* be used to land on.)

Levels

26 Jumping at a low level – on the floor, across mats and over very low apparatus.
27 Jumping from the floor to low apparatus and from low apparatus to the floor.
28 Fast run and jump for distance.
29 Slow springy run and jump for height.
30 Jumping from higher apparatus.

Directions

31 From standing – jumping forwards, backwards and sideways.
32 Making a sequence of jumps to show changes of direction.

Gymnastics chapter, see pages 53–70

Gymnastic Activity Bank – rolling

Use of body parts

33 Rocking, then rolling the whole body on different surfaces (front, back, side).

34 Rolling, emphasising relationship of hands to feet, head to chest, knees to chest.

35 Rolling from one part of the body to another.

36 Rolling from shoulder, to back, to feet; back, to sides, to knees, and so on.

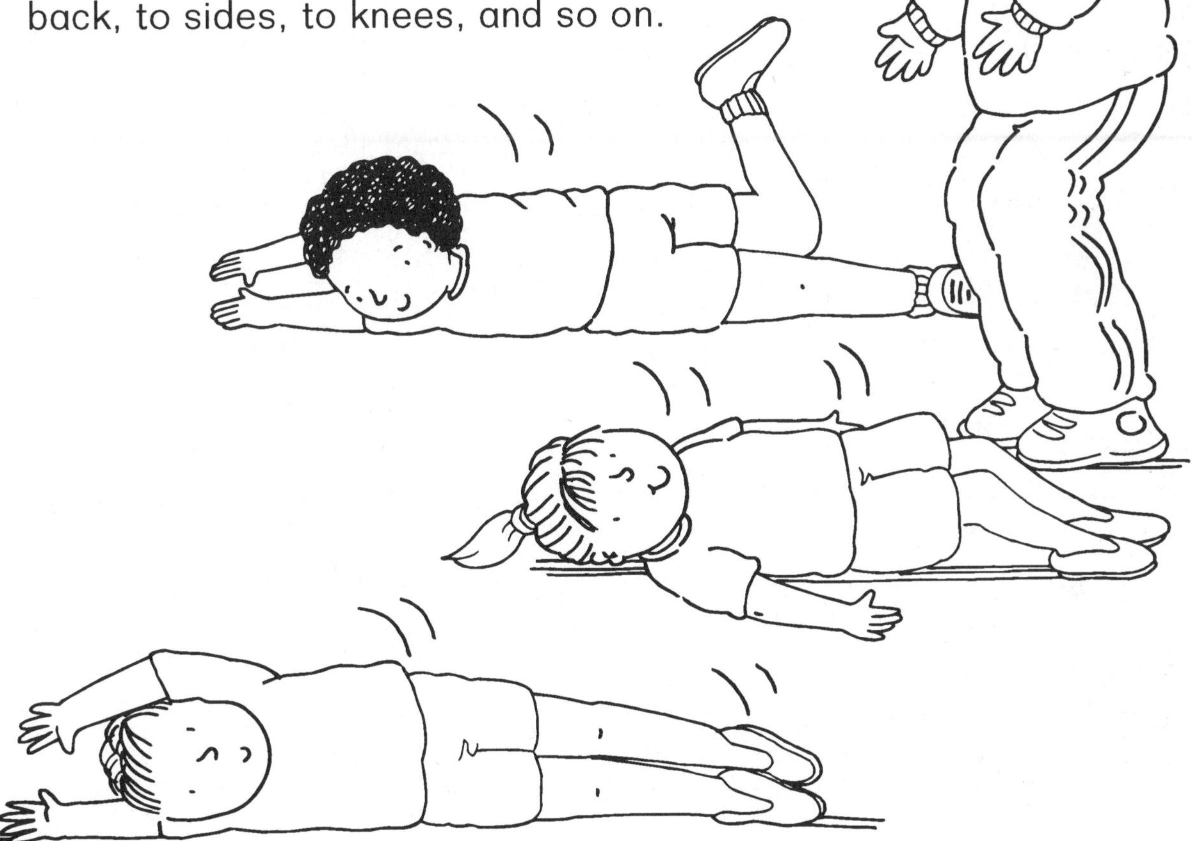

Movement factors

37 Rolling, using sideways and forwards directions.

38 Rolling slowly.

39 Rolling with various speeds (quickly, slowly, slowly, quickly).

40 Rolling to emphasise body tension for control of movement.

41 Rolling showing changes of speed; acceleration, deceleration.

Gymnastic Activity Bank – rolling

Body shape

42 Rolling using various body shapes (long, round).
43 Rolling with specific body shapes (wide, long, round).
44 Rolling with feet apart/feet together.

Relationships

45 Rolling across and along mats/low apparatus.
46 Rolling on, over/under, off apparatus.
47 Circling/rolling around large apparatus (poles, bars, ropes).

Directions

48 Rolling sideways, forwards, sideways.
49 Rolling sideways, forwards, backwards.

Gymnastics chapter, see pages 53–70

Gymnastic Activity Bank – travelling

Use of body parts

50 Use your hands and feet to move across the floor/apparatus.
51 Use only your feet to move across the floor/apparatus.
52 Use your feet as little as possible to move across the floor/apparatus.
53 Use large parts of your body to move across the floor/apparatus.
54 Use small parts of your body to move across the floor/apparatus.
55 Use a combination of large and small body parts to move across the floor/apparatus.
56 Travel on your front in some way.
57 Travel on your back in some way.

Movement factors

58 Travel in different directions – sideways, forwards, backwards.
59 Travel slowly.
60 Travel at different speeds – quickly, slowly.

Body shape

61 Travel using different body shapes – long, round, wide, thin.
62 Travel with your body as small as possible.
63 Travel with your body as big as possible.

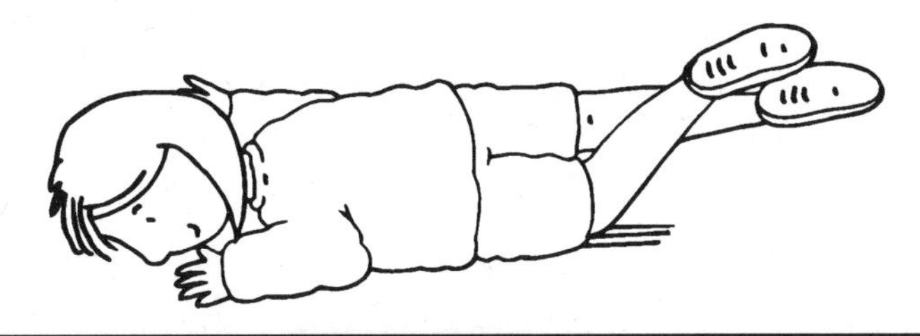

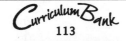

Gymnastics chapter, see pages 53–70

Gymnastic Activity Bank – travelling

Relationships

64 Travel along/across the floor/apparatus.
65 Travel over/under your apparatus.
66 Travel around your apparatus.

Levels

67 Travel at a low level, close to the floor.
68 Travel at a high level with your body a long way from the floor.
69 Move from a low level to a high level using your apparatus.
70 Move from a high level to a low level using your apparatus.

Directions

71 Travel in a straight line.
72 Travel in a curved line.
73 Travel in a circle.
74 Travel in a square.
75 Travel making a zig-zag pathway.

Gymnastics chapter, see pages 53–70

Gymnastic Activity Bank – balancing

Use of body parts

76 Balance using different body parts.
77 Balance using large body parts ('patches').
78 Balance using small body parts ('points').
79 Balance using a combination of hands and feet.
80 Balance using feet only.

Movement factors

81 Show stillness in balance, holding each balance for at least three seconds.
82 Move slowly into balance.
83 Move slowly out of balance.
84 Move quickly out of balance.

Body shape

85 Balance in a wide shape.
86 Balance in a long, thin shape.
87 Balance in a curved shape.

Gymnastics chapter, see pages 53–70

Gymnastic Activity Bank – balancing

Relationships

88 Balance close to the floor.
89 Balance on a low piece of apparatus, such as a bench.
90 Balance on a high piece of apparatus, such as a padded platform.
91 Balance under a piece of apparatus.
92 Balance next to a piece of apparatus for support.

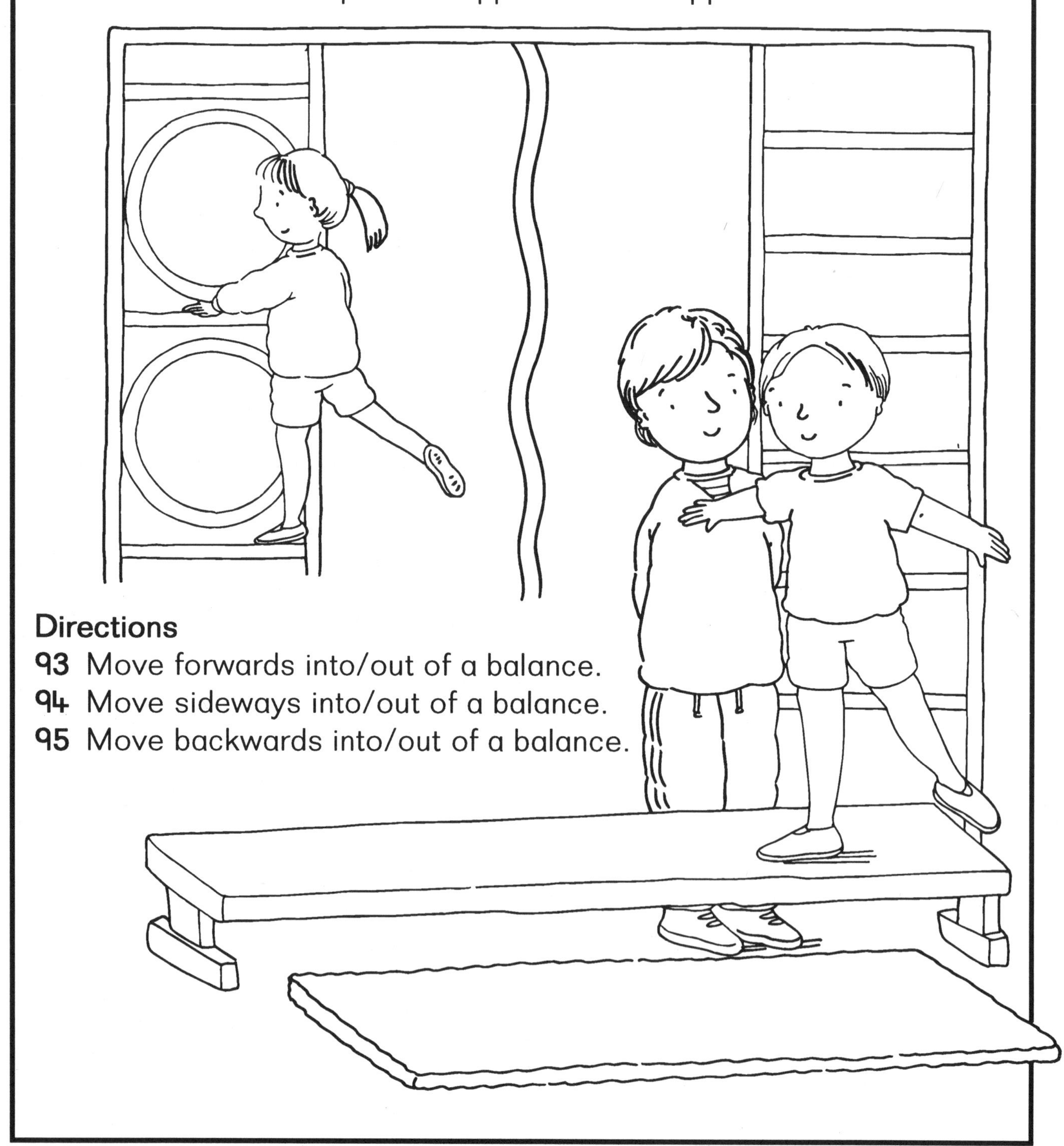

Directions

93 Move forwards into/out of a balance.
94 Move sideways into/out of a balance.
95 Move backwards into/out of a balance.

Gymnastics chapter, see pages 53–70

Content of gymnastics

Setting

floor
apparatus

Variants

pathways

directions

levels

Type of activity

travelling
turning
rolling
jumping
balancing
hanging
climbing
weight on hands

Variants

speed

shape

body parts

Who with?

self
partner

Gymnastics chapter, see pages 53–70

Levels

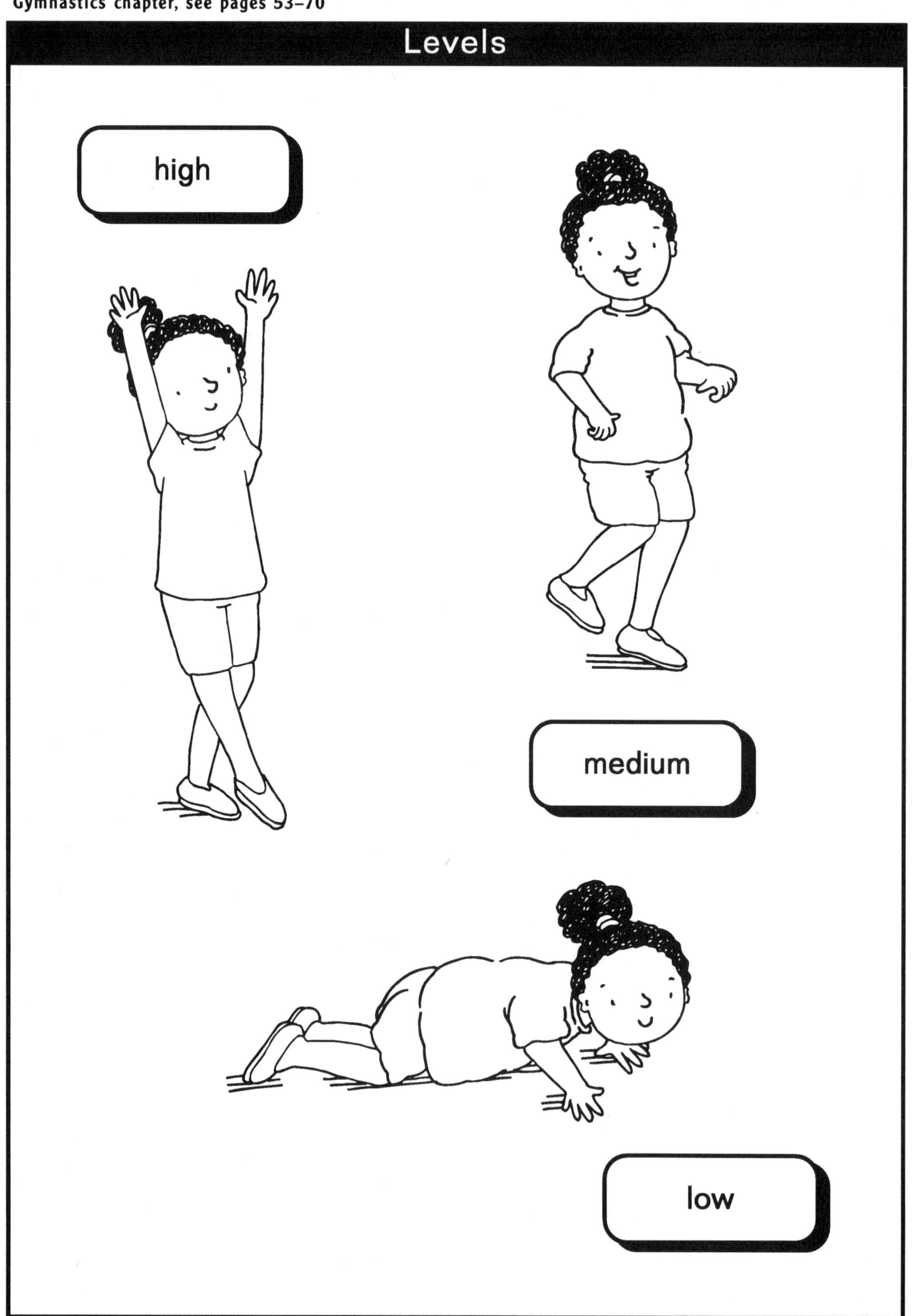

Gymnastics chapter, see pages 53–70

Shape

round

wide

twisted

feet together

asymmetrical

symmetrical

long

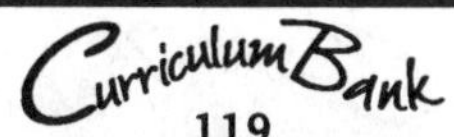

Gymnastics chapter, see pages 53–70

Body parts

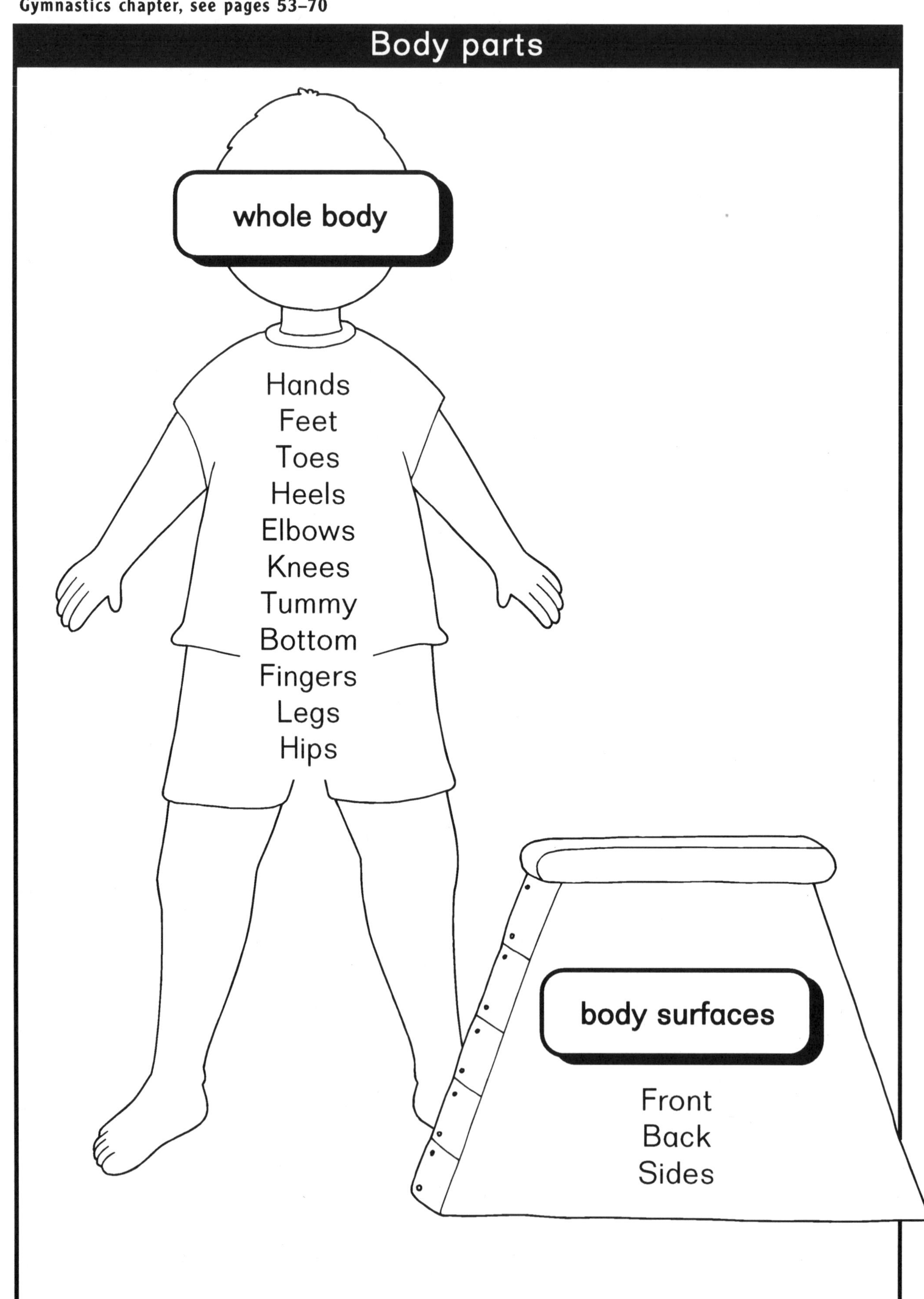

Gymnastics chapter, see pages 53–70

Pathways

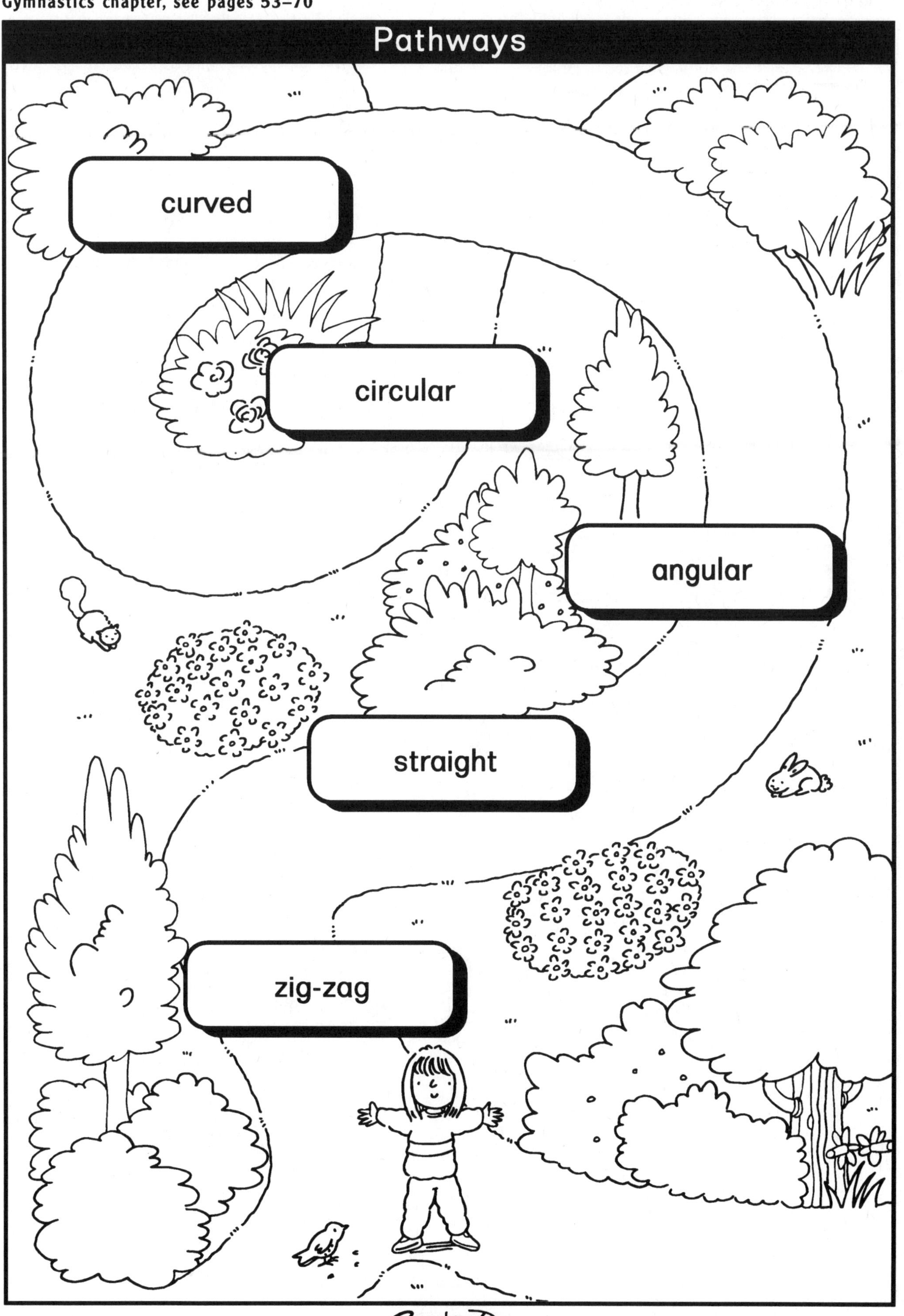

Gymnastics chapter, see pages 53–70

Directions

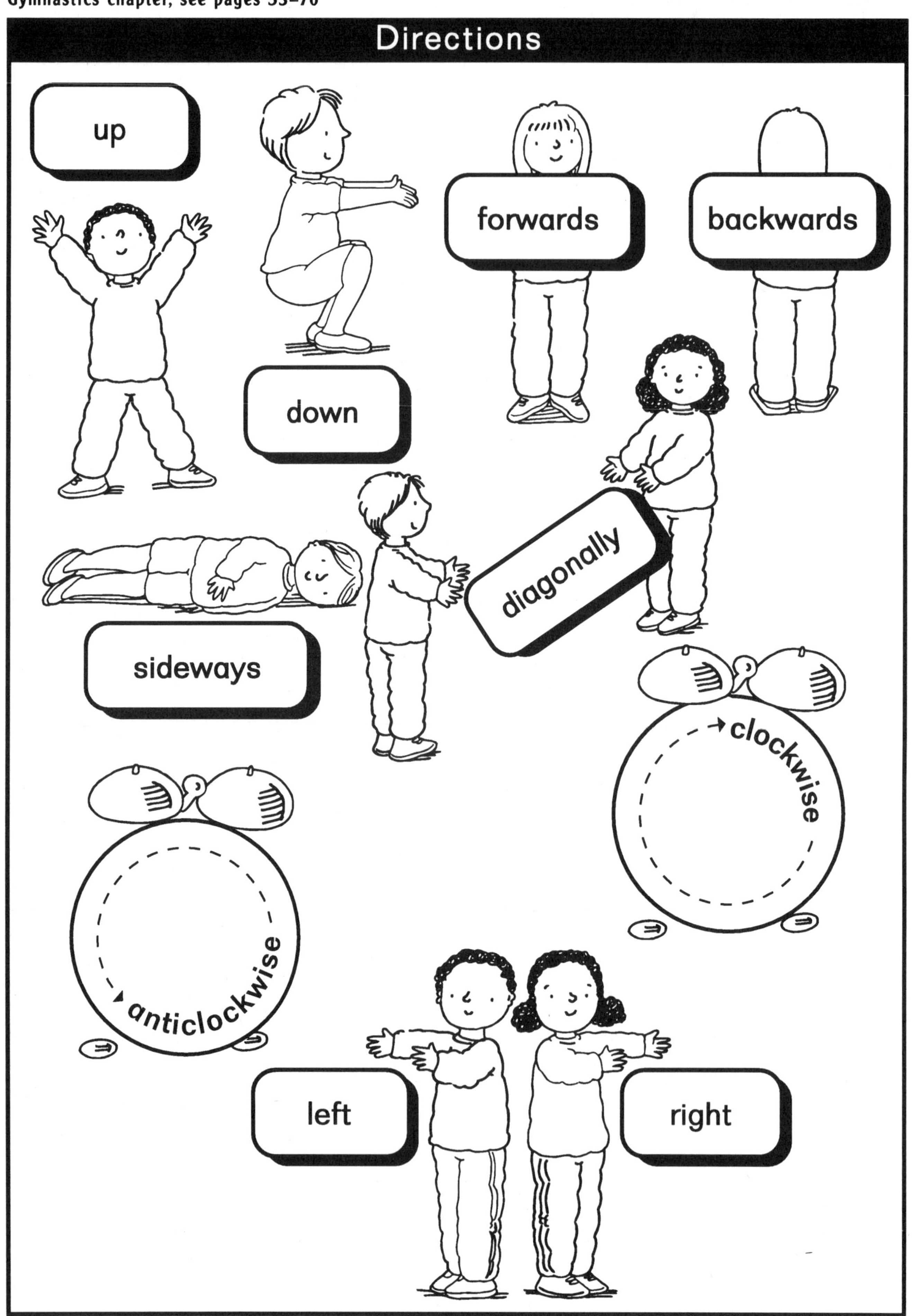

Gymnastics chapter, see pages 53–70

Movement factors

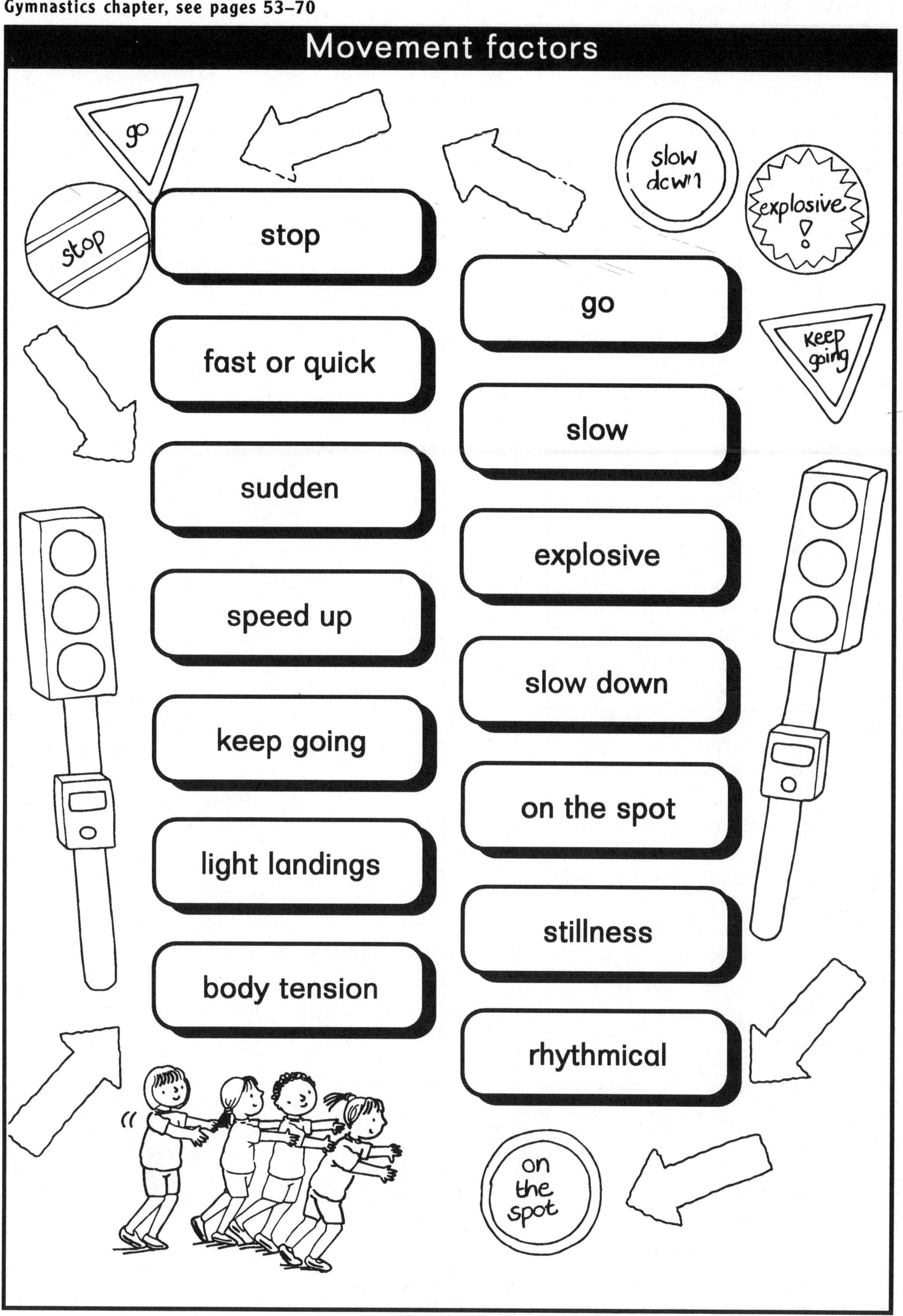

Gymnastics chapter, see pages 53–70

Relationships

- on
- off
- over
- under
- through
- across
- along
- around
- away
- towards
- near
- far
- in
- out
- in front
- behind
- above
- below
- matched
- mirrored

May be in relation to: apparatus

May be in relation to: class members

May be in relation to: a partner

May be in relation to: the floor

Gymnastics chapter, see pages 53–70

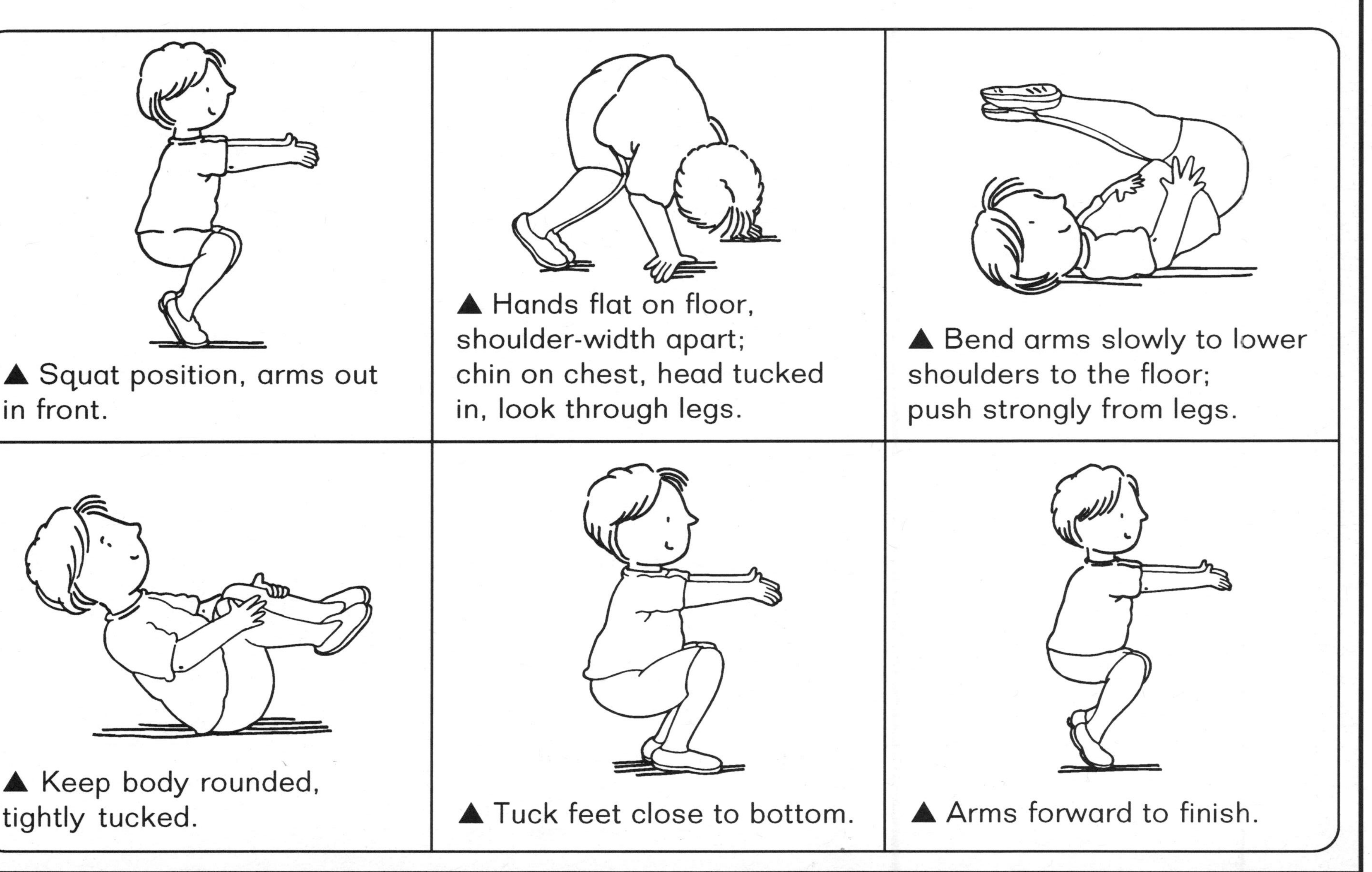

Forward roll
Before rolling, practise tucked rocking.
▲ Squat position, arms out in front.
▲ Hands flat on floor, shoulder-width apart; chin on chest, head tucked in, look through legs.
▲ Bend arms slowly to lower shoulders to the floor; push strongly from legs.
▲ Keep body rounded, tightly tucked.
▲ Tuck feet close to bottom.
▲ Arms forward to finish.

Gymnastics chapter, see pages 53–70

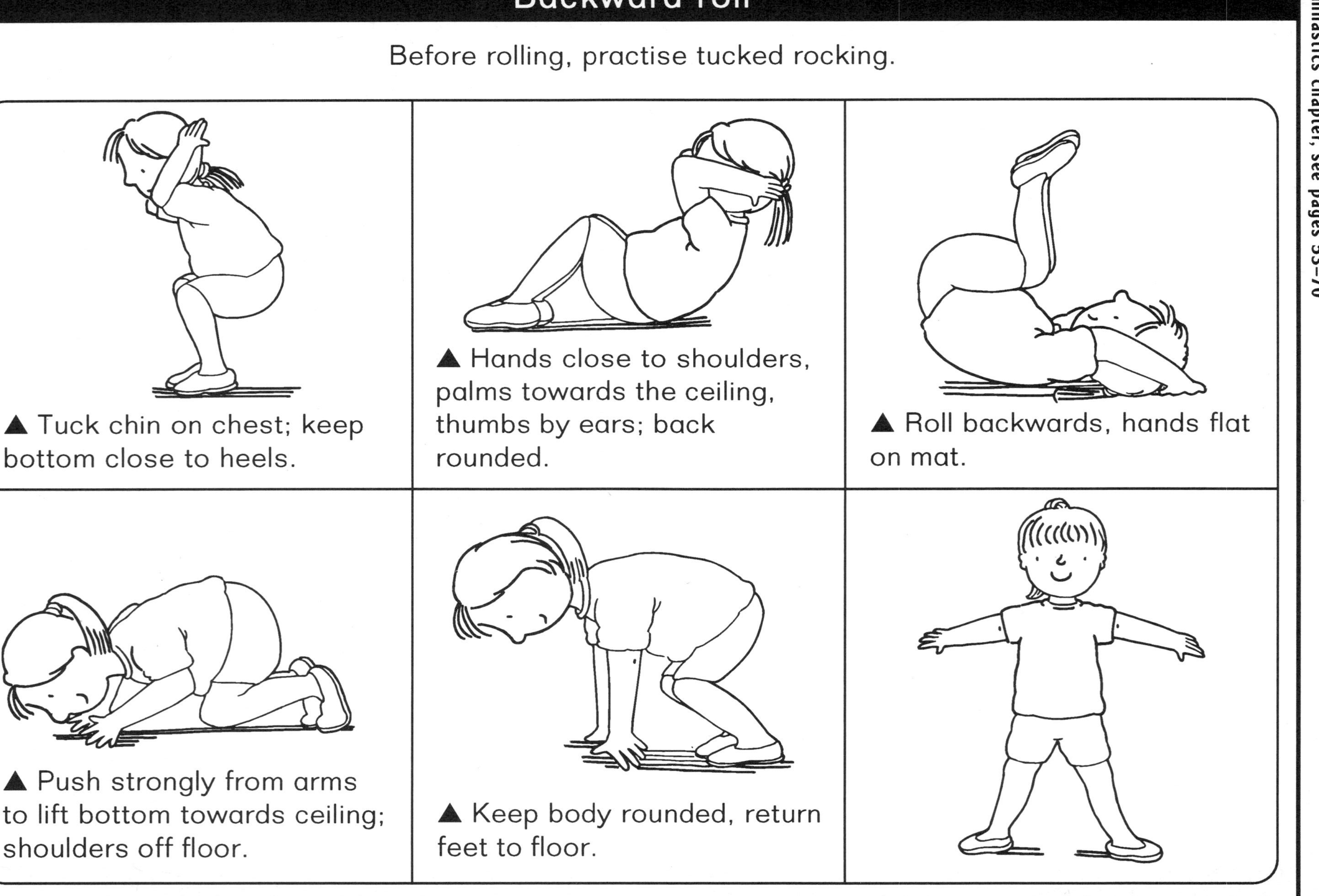

Backward roll
Before rolling, practise tucked rocking.
▲ Tuck chin on chest; keep bottom close to heels.
▲ Hands close to shoulders, palms towards the ceiling, thumbs by ears; back rounded.
▲ Roll backwards, hands flat on mat.
▲ Push strongly from arms to lift bottom towards ceiling; shoulders off floor.
▲ Keep body rounded, return feet to floor.

Dance chapter, see pages 71–86

Teddy bear dance

▲ Starting position – teddy bear on his back.
▲ Teddy bear rocks slowly from side to side.
▲ He sits up.
▲ He stands up.
▲ He walks for eight counts.
▲ He moves one arm up and down for four counts.
▲ He moves the other arm in a similar way for four counts.
▲ He turns to bend and pick up a drink from the floor four times.

Dance chapter, see pages 71–86

Caterpillar and butterfly dance

- ▲ The children crawl across the floor like a caterpillar to music.
- ▲ When the music stops they make a long, stretched shape.
- ▲ A bird approaches – to the accompaniment of a tambourine – and the caterpillars curl up.
- ▲ The children stand up and collect their cocoons (crêpe paper strips). They hold one end of the strip against their chest and slowly turn on the spot gradually wrapping the paper around their bodies.
- ▲ The children then emerge from their cocoons by turning in the opposite direction and proceed to fly away as newly formed butterflies holding their paper strips above their heads with both hands.
- ▲ The children now re-form their pairs for the pursuit and touch phase.

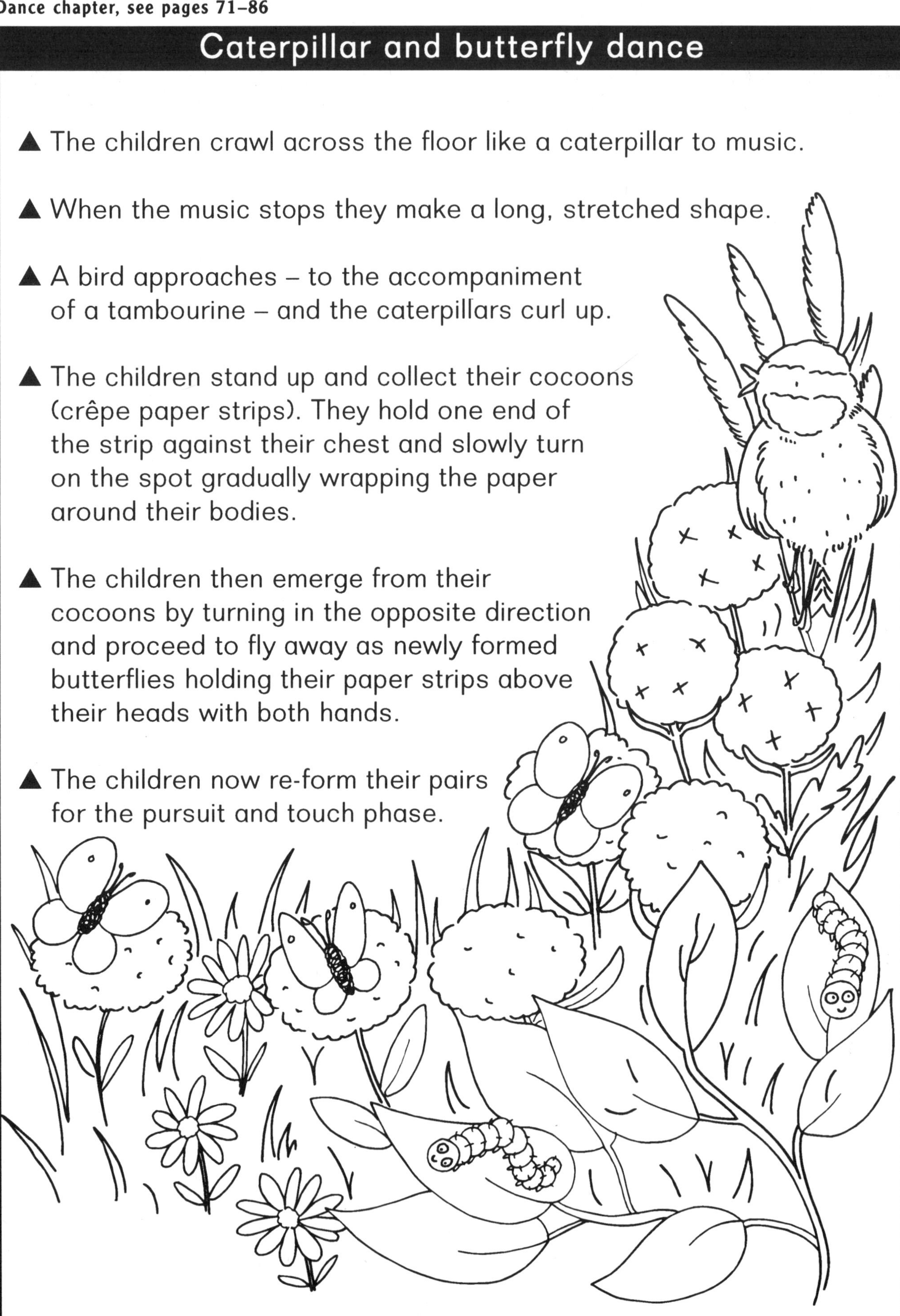

Dance chapter, see pages 71–86

Washing machine dance

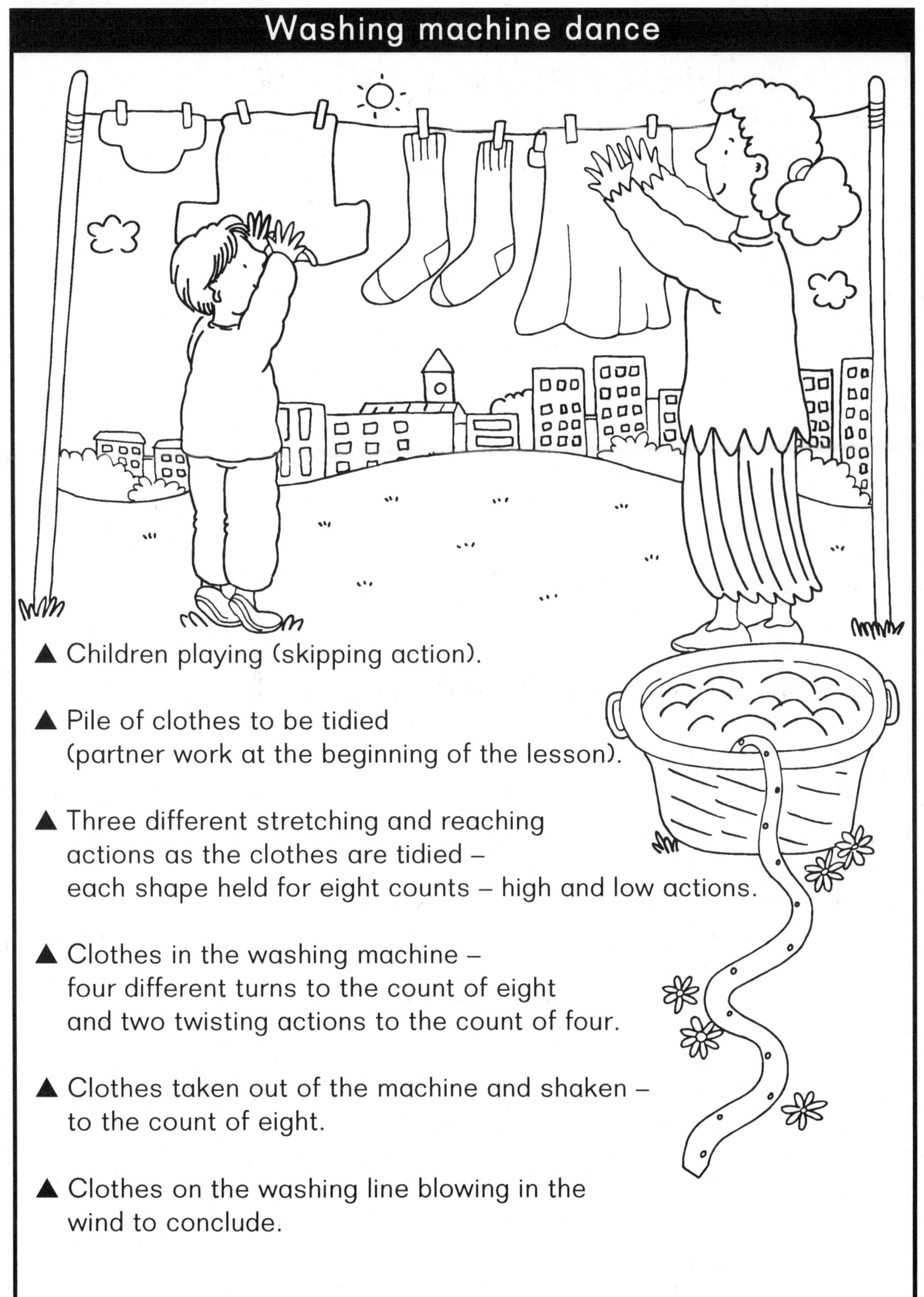

▲ Children playing (skipping action).

▲ Pile of clothes to be tidied
(partner work at the beginning of the lesson).

▲ Three different stretching and reaching
actions as the clothes are tidied –
each shape held for eight counts – high and low actions.

▲ Clothes in the washing machine –
four different turns to the count of eight
and two twisting actions to the count of four.

▲ Clothes taken out of the machine and shaken –
to the count of eight.

▲ Clothes on the washing line blowing in the
wind to conclude.

Dance chapter, see pages 71–86

Dance Activity Poem Bank – high and low

Crouch down low
Reach up high
Touch the floor
Reach for the sky.

Reach up high
Curl down low
Now back to your feet
Nice and slow!

I make myself high
I make myself low
I spin like a top
And round I go.

Dance chapter, see pages 71–86

Dance Activity Poem Bank – big and small

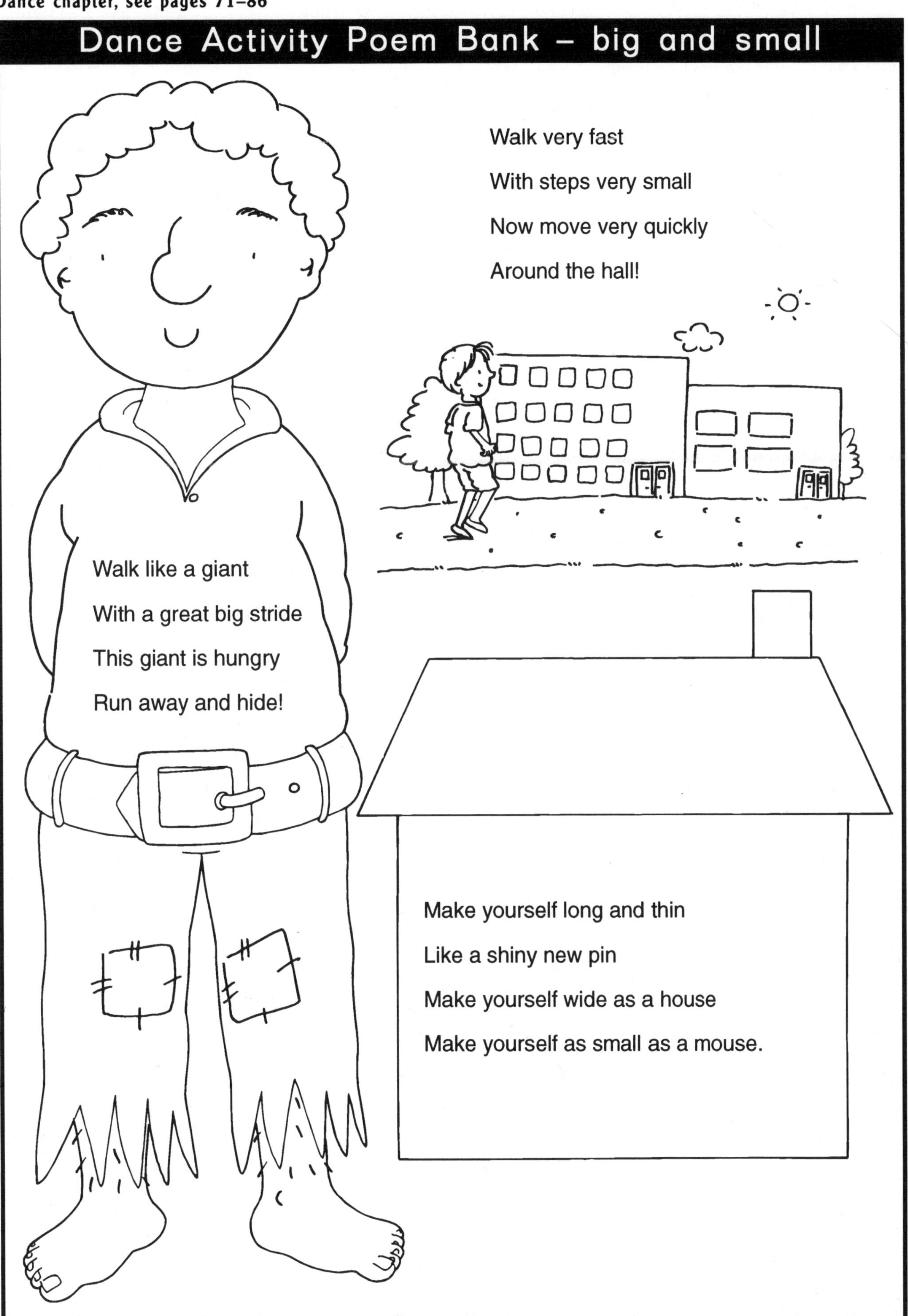

Walk very fast
With steps very small
Now move very quickly
Around the hall!
Walk like a giant
With a great big stride
This giant is hungry
Run away and hide!
Make yourself long and thin
Like a shiny new pin
Make yourself wide as a house
Make yourself as small as a mouse.

Dance chapter, see pages 71–86

Dance Activity Poem Bank – animals

Now walk like a dog
Slither like a snake
Stand up and shake!
Caterpillar walk
Close to the floor
First with both hands
1, 2, 3, 4
Then with your feet
1, 2, 3, 4
Now with your hands
Just like before.

Dance chapter, see pages 71-86

Dance Activity Poem Bank – animals

Jumping this way, jumping that
Springing like a farm cat
Jumping low, jumping tall
Jumping high like a bouncing ball!

Furry and round
Beneath the ground
Sleeps a rabbit
Without a sound

He slowly wakes
Big breaths he takes
He stretches his paws
Then peers outdoors

He scampers out
And looks about
Better not stay
He jumps away!

Dance chapter, see pages 71–86

Dance Activity Poem Bank – shapes

I run in a circle

I run in a square

I run to a space

And jump in the air!

Clap, clap, clap

Above your head

Clap, clap, clap

Behind your knees

Clap, clap, clap

In front and back

Stand up straight

As tall dark trees

Lift your arms up

Let your arms down

Making them circle

Like a merry-go-round!

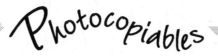

Dance chapter, see pages 71–86

Dance Activity Poem Bank – movement

Stand up straight
Now lie on the floor
Now back on your feet
Just like before!

First we skip
Then we hop
Then we run
And now we stop!

Giants' feet go
Stamp, stamp, stamp!
Soldiers' feet go
Tramp, tramp, tramp!

Donkeys' feet go
Clip, clop, clip
And my little feet go
Skip, skip, skip!

Touch your head
Touch your toes
Touch your knees
Now your nose.

Assessment and record keeping, see page 88

Physical Education activities covered

Indicate the types of activities you have covered with your year group under the following headings:

Class ______________ Year group ______

Games	
Gymnastics	
Dance	

Assessment and record keeping, see page 88

Physical Education Class Recording Sheet

Class ______________________ Year group ______

Name	Games*				Gymnastics*			Dance*			General*		
	a	b	c	d	e	f	g	h	i	j	k	l	m

* See page 138 for key to codes used.

Assessment and record keeping, see page 88

Class Recording Sheet – key

Games

a Sending a ball or object, such as a bean bag.
b Receiving a ball or object.
c Travelling with a ball or object.
d Games play.

Gymnastics

e Individual skills (control, poise, technique).
f Use of space.
g Linking movements together.

Dance

h Control.
i Expression.
j Remembering dance patterns and movements.

General

k Awareness of bodily response to exercise.
l Safe and responsible participation.
m Attitude and social skills.

Assessment and record keeping, see page 88

Recording, planning and evalutaing skills

Class

Year group

Name	Planning Skills		Evaluation Skills		
	Explore tasks set	Select movements actions / responses	Recognise actions	Describe actions	Compare and contrast actions

Assessment and record keeping, see page 89

PE Merit Cards

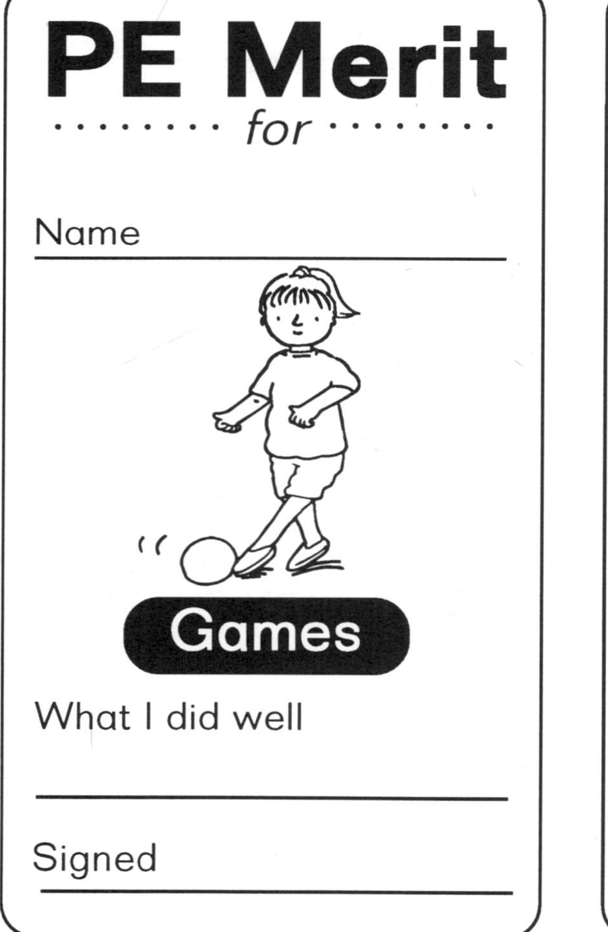

PE Merit

.... for ....

Name

Games

What I did well

Signed

PE Merit

.... for ....

Name

Gymnastics

What I did well

Signed

PE Merit

.... for ....

Name

Dance

What I did well

Signed

Assessment and record keeping, see page 89

PE Merit Cards

PE Merit

.... *for* ....

Name ____________________

Trying hard

Signed ____________________

PE Merit

.... *for* ....

Name ____________________

Being sensible and careful

Signed ____________________

PE Merit

.... *for* ....

Name ____________________

Working well with others

Signed ____________________

INFORMATION TECHNOLOGY WITHIN PE AT KEY STAGE 1

There are many opportunities to link Information Technology work with the children's work in physical education. Below are some suggestions for activities linked to each chapter of the book.

Chapter 1 – Essentials of Physical Education

Use the data in the children's exercise diary in pictogram or simple graphing software to present the information they have collected. In order to get some consistency in the results, it is a good idea to discuss with the children a set of exercise categories to be used. This may mean grouping different types of the same exercise together so, for example, that the playing of any ball game comes under a single category.

If pictogram software is used encourage the children to select or create a picture for each type of exercise and then show these against each day of the week.

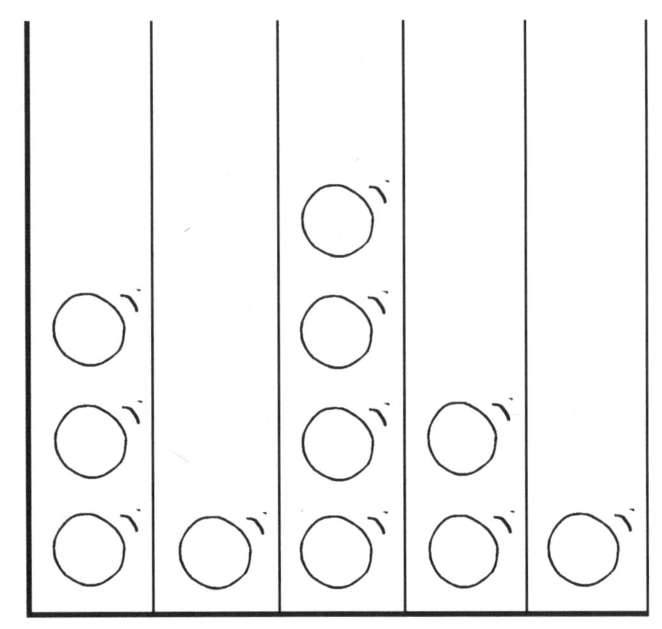

Invite older children to use the same data to create block graphs instead of pictograms. Suggest that they record the actual exercise time in ten-minute blocks, and then record this on their graphs against the different forms of exercise.

To link with the activities in Chapter 1, the children could use an art or drawing package to create a poster about the importance of exercise for a healthy body. Simple framework software like *My World 2* with appropriate files could also be used to label parts of the human body.

Introduce the children to the idea of computer monitoring using a pulse meter. This could be a simple pulse meter, like those on exercise bikes, which clip onto the ear lobe or fit over the finger and give a digital readout of the pulse rate. It is also possible to connect sensors to the computer and a digital readout of the pulse rate is displayed on the screen. Older children might also be interested to see the pulse rate plotted as a graph on the computer and discuss how the rate changes with exercise.

Where children are involved in research about their bodies, information can be obtained from CD-ROMs. These can be simple encyclopaedia CD-ROMs or more interactive titles such as Dorling Kindersley's *Ultimate Human Body*.

Chapter 2 – Games

Most of the activities in this chapter involve children in developing games' skills or in simple games which use the new skills. This can provide a good context for developing children's IT capability in creating, organising and presenting information.

After the introduction of each of the new skills, such as sending or receiving a ball using feet, invite some of the children to use a word processor to write simple captions for a wall display about this particular skill. Alternatively, a class book of skills could be produced with a page for each new skill.

Encourage the children to make the writing brief but informative and focus on different elements of the new skills such as:

- ▲ use the inside of your foot;
- ▲ follow through with your foot;
- ▲ don't kick the ball too hard.

Once these have been written, invite the children to experiment with the presentation of them. They could try using a different font and change the font size or colour so the captions can be read from a distance. The captions can be printed out, cut into sections and used for a wall display. Older children might want to include a border with each caption.

Invite the children to create some pictures using an art or drawing package to include as a central part of the display. They could be representational, using stick people and give enough information so that the new skills are evident from the picture. This would involve the children in simple line drawings and they will need to know how to draw lines for the body parts, a circle for the head and also how to alter the thickness of the different lines.

An alternative approach to adding pictures would be to take photographs of the children during the lesson. Mount these in the middle of the work and add captions around the outside. If the school has a scanner the photographs could be scanned into digital images and used within the word processed work. A digital camera could also be used to produce electronic images that can be added to word processed work. It is also possible to use digitised images from a video camera so that a number of different images can be selected from the video clip of the activity.

Where children have been involved in playing or making up simple games encourage them to work in a small group to word process the rules for the games. Show them how to use the *cut and paste* or *drag and drop* facilities to move blocks of text around. This will help them to get the rules in the right sequence. If the games are played over a series of lessons the rules can saved and then retrieved for further editing or development as the games evolve. The rules for the Mr Wolf game developed in this way, with children adding their own variations of the rules.

Once the rules have been completed the group will need to decide how they are going to present them. They should be able to select suitable fonts and font sizes to present their rules. The rules could be printed out and bound to make a simple book of rules.

Chapter 3 – Gymnastics

The children could use the computer to present and develop some of the ideas introduced during gymnastic lessons.

Invite the children to work individually or in pairs using an art or drawing package to make simple body shapes to illustrate some of their body positions and shapes created during the lesson. If children create stick people they can be drawn to represent some of the different shapes made:

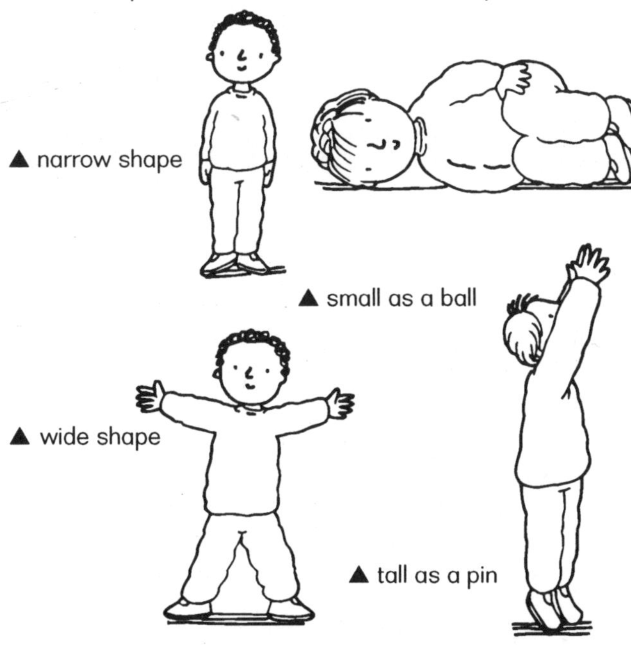

Their pictures would be representational, showing the basic body parts and shapes. The children will need help to learn how to draw lines for the body parts, how to create a filled circle for the head, and also how to alter the thickness of the different lines. They will also need to know how to move the parts together to join them up and how to draw a curved line for a back in a crouched position.

Encourage older children to use this technique to record the different shapes in a sequence of movements. When doing this, children should be shown how to make copies of their shapes so that they do not have to start from the beginning each time, but can alter a copy of the previous shape. They could also add apparatus, again drawn as a two dimensional object.

Use the journeys theme of some of the lessons as a way in to using a floor turtle or robot, such as a ROAMER or PIPP. Set up a course in advance and ask the children to plan and program a route around it. Where a hoop is used the children will need to work out how to make a circular shape with the ROAMER by using lots of small turns and forward movements.

Many of the activities in this chapter require the children to use hoops. Link the children's use of hoops to their work on the computer, by using hoops as a stimulus for creative art work using an art package. Suggest that the children draw multiple circles of the same or different sizes and position them on the screen to make a 'circles' pattern, adding different colours to the circles. They could also explore the idea of symmetry of shape, pattern and colour. Encourage the children to explore the range of tones available from the art package by selecting appropriate ones from the palette. This will add a colour theme to the activity.

Chapter 4 – Dance

Although there is little direct use of information technology in this chapter, some of the ideas used as a theme for the dances could be extended using a computer.

Invite the children to use a word processor to make their own record of the dance movements. Encourage younger children to use a concept keyboard with an overlay which has each of the instructions for the dance already on it. These could be in pictures or words, or both. By pressing the relevant instruction or picture the instructions for the dance can be built up on screen. Similar work could be undertaken using framework software like *My World 2* with a file created by the teacher in advance.

Older children should be encouraged to type in the instructions for each part of the dance and arrange them in the right order. Alternatively, you could prepare a file in advance with the instructions in a jumbled order and then invite the children to re-arrange them on the screen. The children will need to be shown how the use the *cut and paste* or *drag and drop* commands for arranging their text on the screen. Invite older or more able children to extend the original sequence, or make up their own. Print out the final sequence for display in the classroom.

Ask the children to use an art or drawing package to create their own pictures to accompany the dances or the instructions for them. They could experiment with the caterpillar theme to draw pictures showing the movement of a caterpillar. Suggest that they draw butterflies and make them symmetrical by drawing one half, copying it, and then flipping it so that it is turned over. This can then be joined to the other half. Extend the idea of the washing day theme by asking the children to draw their own washing line of clothes.

GRID 1

AREA OF IT	SOFTWARE	CHAPTER 1	CHAPTER 2	CHAPTER 3	CHAPTER 4
Communicating Information	Word Processor		✓		✓
Communicating Information	Art Package	✓	✓	✓	✓
Communicating Information	Drawing Software	✓	✓	✓	✓
Communicating Information	CD-ROM	✓			
Handling Information	Graphing Software	✓			
Monitoring	Data Logging	✓			
Control	ROAMER			✓	✓

GRID 2

SOFTWARE TYPE	BBC/MASTER	RISCOS	NIMBUS/186	WINDOWS	MACINTOSH
Word Processor	*Stylus* *Folio* *Prompt/Writer*	*Phases* *Pendown* *Desk Top Folio* *Text Ease*	*All Write* *Write On*	*My Word* *Kid Works 2* *Creative Writer* *Word for Windows*	*Kid Works 2* *EasyWorks* *Creative Writer* *Word for Windows*
Framework		*My World 2*		*My World 2*	
Art Package		*1st Paint* *Kid Pix* *Splash*		*Colour Magic* *Kid Pix 2* *Paint Box*	*Kid Pix 2* *PaintBox*
Drawing Package	*Picture Builder*	*Draw* *Picture IT*	*Picture Builder*	*Claris Works*	*Claris Works*
CD-ROM		*Children's* *Macropaedia* *Hutchinson's* *Oxford Junior*		*Encarta 96* *Children's* *Macropaedia* *Grolier*	*Encarta 96* *Grolier*
Graphing Software	*Datashow*	*Pictogram* *Picture Point* *DataSweet*	*Datagraph*	*Datagraph* *Easy Works*	*Easy Works*